MORE THAN SHEEPHERDERS

The Basque Series

Thanks to Robert Laxalt and William A. Douglass, the University of Nevada Press launched its Basque Series in 1970 with the re-publication of Rodney Gallop's *A Book of the Basques*. As director of the Press, Laxalt made the series a priority for the Basque Studies Program, which Douglass had helped to create a few years earlier. From the start the goal was to bring the Basques to the attention of readers in the English-speaking world—a goal which continues to this day.

More Than Sheepherders

The American Basques of Elko County, Nevada

Joxe K. Mallea-Olaetxe
With the Assistance of Jess Lopategui

And Contributions by Anita Anacabe Franzoia
and Mercedes Mendive

UNIVERSITY OF NEVADA PRESS | *Reno & Las Vegas*

University of Nevada Press | Reno, Nevada 89557 USA
www.unpress.nevada.edu
Copyright © 2025 by University of Nevada Press
All photos © 2025 by Joxe K. Mallea-Olaetxe unless otherwise noted
All rights reserved
Manufactured in the United States of America

FIRST PRINTING

Cover design by Caroline Dickens
Cover photographs © by Sebas Velasco

Library of Congress Cataloging-in-Publication Data
Names: Mallea-Olaetxe, J. (Joxe), 1941- author. | Lopategui, Jess, 1938- author.
Title: More than sheepherders : the American Basques of Elko County, Nevada
    / Joxe K. Mallea-Olaetxe and Jess Lopategui.
Other titles: Basque series.
Description: Reno, Nevada : University of Nevada Press, [2025] | Series:
    The Basque series | "And contributions by Anita Anacabe Franzoia and
    Mercedes Mendive." | Includes bibliographical references and index. |
    Summary: "In the remote community of Elko, Nevada, the Altube brothers
    and the Garats started fabled ranches in the early 1870s. These hardy
    citizens created the foundation of a community that still exists today,
    rooted in the traditions and cultures of American Basque families. Joxe K.
    Mallea-Olaetxe presents a modern study focused on the post-1970s, when
    the retired Basque sheepherders and their families became the dominant
    Americanized minority in the area."—Provided by publisher.
Identifiers: LCCN 2024038706 | ISBN 9781647791919 (paperback) | ISBN
    9781647791926 (ebook)
Subjects: LCSH: Basque Americans—Nevada—Elko County. | Shepherds—
    Nevada—Elko County. | Basques—Nevada—Elko County—History. | Elko
    County (Nev.)—History.
Classification: LCC E184.B15 M35 2025 | DDC 979.3/16—dc23/eng/20250122
    LC record available at https://lccn.loc.gov/2024038706

ISBN 978-1-64779-191-9 (paper)
ISBN 978-1-64779-192-6 (ebook)
LCCN: 2024038706

The paper used in this book meets the requirements of American
National Standard for Information Sciences—Permanence of Paper
for Printed Library Materials, ANSI/NISO Z39.48-1992 (R2002).

To the people of Elko County, Nevada

Contents

Illustrations

Preface

It was circa 1880, and Old Man Winter was showing his nasty temper in the Basque Country on the Bay of Biscay in Europe. Cold rain combined with a fierce wind from the Atlantic lashed at the flimsy window encased in the thick stone walls of the *baserri* (farmstead). While the mother was busy in the kitchen, Patxi, the father, was carving figures of birds and stars on his new hazelnut *makila* (walking stick). Sitting across the table was his youngest son, Mattin. Both are sitting at the long walnut table in the cozy kitchen, warmed by the fireplace where stumps of oak are crackling.

"Ze ein biok ba?" Patxi asks. "Have you thought about what you want to do? Your brother Peru is staying at the farm, and next year when he gets married there will be less room here. You remember your uncle Manu? He is in Galipornia or someplace they call Elko, Nevada. He wrote that running sheep is good business over there. In fact, he asked about you, after all, he is your godfather. He says he will send money for the passage too. So, what do you say?"

The son looked down, waited a little, and responded by singing an old verse:

Amerikara nua, nere borondatez	I am going to America by my own free will
Emen baino obeto izateko ustez	Hoping to be better off than here
Aspertua bainago emengo bizitzez	Because I am bored with my life here

> *Adio aita ta ama, ondo*   Goodbye, father and mother,
> *bizi bitez.*   take care of yourselves.

For many Basque herders who ended up in Elko, their immigration to the US may have started something like this.

~

Whoever said that "all history is local" is deserving of a citation, especially when dealing with this corner of the American West, which runs south from Boise, Idaho, to Jordan Valley, Oregon, to McDermitt and Winnemucca in Nevada, and then turns east to Battle Mountain and Elko. You could easily add the towns of Eureka and Ely, Nevada, and a few others as well. There was a time when Basque immigrants with their sheep concentrated their pastoral activities in this huge and mostly desert expanse. They clustered into other places, such as Bakersfield and San Francisco, California, but proportionately, one can argue that they did not number as high as in this Idaho-Oregon-Nevada triangle, nor was their social and economic impact elsewhere as great as here.

In 1966, I happened to be in Jordan Valley visiting family members and friends, when I saw, coming down the street, a burly guy with two huge pistols hanging from his belt. At the time, I was living in the East Coast, and to me he was the mirror image of an actor in a Hollywood Western. My imagination transported me instantly into a Wild West–movie scene. Pointing at him, the Bizkaian next to me says: "Au ba'kik nor dan?" (Do you know who this guy is?) Before I could answer "no," the two started talking in Basque. "Auxe dok txerife" (This is the sheriff), my companion said, and soon I was shaking hands with a real lawman of the West, whose parents happened to be from Bizkaia, where I came from. Interestingly, in 1988 another American Basque, Ron Mallea (not related to me) of Jordan Valley, was elected sheriff, and later in the narrative we will meet the sheriff of Elko County, Nevada, a man of Basque descent.

This immense tristate area comprises 55,457 square miles (over

143,632 square kilometers) of desert, canyons, forested areas, rugged-mountain ranges higher than 11,000 feet, few roads, and even fewer towns. The area in question is larger than the state of New York, which has about 20 million people, while the total population of this western triangle may be home to only about 100,000 people today (not counting Boise). Even by western standards, this section of the West is thinly populated. A little over a century ago a sizable number of the people roaming here were Paiutes, Western Shoshones, and Basque sheepherders.

I often thought that if Wilber, Nebraska, can label itself "The Czech Capital of America," this territorial slice of the West is "The Basque Country of the United States." Particularly, the 175-mile-long corridor from Jordan Valley to Winnemucca, where Paiutes and Basques were in the majority. This is one place in the world where the Indigenous population and the Indigenous people of western Europe comingled for decades. The Basques have a strong claim to being the oldest human population of Atlantic Europe, thus deserving the designation of Indigenous people, like the Paiutes and the Shoshones.

Soon after I began my research, I called Anamari Garijo Smith in Winnemucca to ask what the population of the Basques in town and the county might be. She said, "thousands, if you are talking about Basques and part-Basques." I was not expecting such an emphatic answer, but it determined the scope of my investigation: I would have to write only about Elko County, where I was a resident in the 1960s.

Contributors to the Research

Elko County is unquestionably at the heart of mainstream western history. It has a rich museum and a courthouse with records going back to the 1860s, when Elko was established as a town. Scattered bands of Te-Moak, Western Shoshones, were here before that, and they are still here. All history being local, to conduct the present research I have gone first to local sources, including members of families that descend from pioneer sheepmen and herders. They have not only memories of their parents and grand-parents but also photos and old papers. In some cases, they still own the ranches their grandparents established.

Jess Lopategui came to Elko to herd sheep in 1958, and he still resides there today. He married Denise Arregui, and they raised two children: Mikel and Amaya. Lopategui had family here before he came. More important, he took an active part in the Basque community and has been saving documents and looking at archives because of his interest in history. He plays a major role as a source of information in the current narrative.

Anita Anacabe Franzoia too has deep roots in Elko, where her father arrived in 1936 to set up a business that in 2025 is still run by Anita herself. Many people in Elko seem to know her, and in turn, she knows a lot of them. She has been active in the Basque community inside and outside Elko, and she is the author of chapter 20.

Mercedes Mendive and Janet Iribarne, both of Elkoan origin, come from musical families; thus, no wonder they turned out to be musicians themselves. Moreover, they are promoters and leaders of the Basque-dancing groups, along with Anamarie Sarratea Lopategui, an accordion player. Mercedes, in chapter 14, tells us about music and dancing. Jan Petersen, a local historian who knows a thing or two about the Basques, will be our sounding board.

A good deal of information on the Basques is curated at the Northeastern Nevada Museum (NNM), Elko, under Family Archives in drawers in alphabetical order. The twenty-something valuable interviews by Prof. Gretchen Skivington are in the same museum, and the interviews on women conducted by Begoña Pecharroman can be found in the Family Archives as well. In addition, I had the availability of the two local newspapers, the photo archives, and the Births and Deaths/Obituaries collections.

The American Basques of Elko—and all Elkoans when perti-nent—are front and center of this story. I conducted numerous oral interviews and conversations, impromptu and otherwise,

Jess Lopategui and wife, Denise Arregui Lopategui.

with members of the community who provided a firm baseline, and that began with notes I started keeping in the 1960s.

A note to the reader: Whenever a name is followed by two last names, the first is often the Basque family name and the second the married surname.

MORE THAN SHEEPHERDERS

Introduction

The Eye of the Study

Elko County comprises an area of 17,203 square miles, fourth-largest county in the nation. This land mass is twice as large as Euskal Herria's, the Homeland of the Basques between France and Spain. But while the county may have 60,000 people within its boundaries (48,818 according to the 2010 Census), the Basque Country has over 3 million.

While the meaning of Elko is debated, the town itself was born with the Central Pacific Railroad in 1869. Bands of Te-Moak, Western Shoshones were the Indigenous population in this part of Nevada, where they and the Paiutes share a reservation of almost 193 acres by the City of Elko. Elko is considered high desert, very different from the Basque Country, which is mostly green and humid. Comparing the two is difficult, but that didn't deter the Basques, who, as soon as they saw the empty miles of land, had an idea of what to do.

Incidentally, the Basques are very attached to land, to a place. When two of them meet, usually their first question is not "Who are you?" or "What is your name?" but rather "Nungo haiz?" (Where are you from?). This instinct to affix a person to a place on the map stems from the fact that most Basque surnames are toponyms that describe a place somewhere in the Basque Country. Surnames often derive from the name of the farmsteads where the original family members lived. Even Americans seem to have picked up on this because, when addressing a Basque, they often ask: "French Basque or Spanish Basque?" In 2023 most Basques

Map of Nevada and its sixteen counties, with Elko in the northeast corner, roughly measuring 100 by 100 miles in all directions. Cartography by Bill Nelson.

in the US have given up on Old Country markers, and they are happy to be just Basques, or Basque Americans, and thousands of them call Elko, Nevada, home.

When a century ago (1922) Angela Odriozola arrived in Elko, she found two rickety wooden sidewalks and cows in the street.

A fellow female traveling companion from Los Angeles tried to dissuade her from getting off the train. "Come to LA with me," she told her, but Elko was Angela's destination. If she had not stepped down from the train, the history of the Elko Basques would not have been the same. We will find her later in this narrative (chapter 4) as Angela Aguirre, Amuma (grandmother) to many.

Looking back, Elko has two historical phases, and the early Basques are part of "Old Elko." In 1969 traveler Lowell Thomas passed through, and he wrote that Elko was "The only real Cow Country left in the West," that is, Old Elko. True enough, but he obviously missed the 100,000-plus sheep. Elko was as much a sheep town then as a cow town, but the cows and the cowboys had an uncle in Hollywood, and the sheepherders did not.

The *History of Nevada* textbook (first edition by Russell R. Elliott), taught in many Nevada schools, didn't mention sheep or sheepherders—a huge historical gap but one that was repeated in many other parts of the West. The sheepherders were everywhere yet nowhere to be seen, like a historical secret. Incidentally, they created another secret of their own: the tens of thousands of arborglyphs they left on the aspens of the high country, which for decades remained the biggest little secret in the West. As immigrants, the herders wandered away from towns, and that is a good recipe to be ignored by historians. The present historical narrative seeks to remedy that, with the emphasis on the last fifty years of Elko.

The county has undergone a drastic change in the last forty years. By 1970, a new type of gold mining was all the rage in Northern Nevada, which would become the fifth-largest producer of gold in the world. The big push came with a technology called "microscopic mining," and one of its early practitioners was the Newmont Mine in Carlin, Nevada. In the early 1960s, Newmont started digging twenty miles west of Elko and soon lured away from the ranches cowboys and sheepherders by offering higher wages. One such individual was a relative of mine who at the time worked on a ranch fifty miles north of Elko. The ranch owner said,

"He will be back soon when they close the mine." The rancher was going by the history of mining in Nevada, often short-lived. Well, thirty-five years later, my cousin retired from Newmont, which is still going strong. In 2016, Newmont produced 1.6 million ounces of gold and 42 million pounds of copper; it employed about 5,000 employees and contractors, though not all of them in Elko.

There is Newmont, and then there is Barrick Goldstrike. After long talks, the two finally merged in 2019—but only in Nevada—as Nevada Gold Mines. The two companies were neighbors. Barrick was a Johnny-come-lately and started digging where Newmont had abandoned explorations in Carlin. Domingo Calzacorta Jr., son of an immigrant Basque and the head of mining engineers for Newmont, decided (according to one source) that the test holes were too expensive and allowed Barrick to buy the claims. Barrick spent the money digging deeper and hit pay dirt. Today, Elko still has cows and sheep, but its mushrooming population is driven by mining and the high wages it pays. Almost a century after the Basques started arriving in Elko, we could say that another group, miners, are the new migrants in town. There are roughly 12,500 miners in the state, earning close to $100,000 a year by some accounts, and an additional 65,000 people work in support services of mining. About twenty-one mines were active in Northern Nevada in 2018, many of them in Elko County. According to thediggins.com, Elko has 833 producers of minerals.

In the 1960s, an ounce of gold was worth $35 and in October of 2021, $1,784. "In 2018 Nevada produced 5,581,160 troy ounces (173.6 tons), representing 78% of US gold and 5% of the world's production." Output is down to 4.63 million ounces in 2021, but value is up to $8.2 billion.

Contrast this to agricultural output in Nevada. In 2015 there were 4,200 farms and ranches in the whole state, and their total production was valued at $831 million. Despite the disparity, for two centuries ranching has been, unlike mining, the stable foundation of livelihood and the economy in Northern Nevada. Basque ranchers and herders played an important part in that history, though the present narrative takes place mostly during the new economy of Elko: the mining period.

In 2018 I asked Alfonso Ygoa, who had spent many years in the sheep business, which Elko he prefers, the old one of the cowboy-sheepherder town or the newer, more affluent one of today of a miners' town. His answer was unequivocal—the Old Elko. He is not alone. Many others miss the Old Elko and decry the current rise in crime, drug problems, and child abuse, among other maladies brought by the booming gold economy.

~

The present study looks at the Basque community of the new Elko from the 1970s to the present. Basque businesspeople reacted to the new economic situation by adjusting, joining in, and supporting the new economy but not exactly by becoming miners, though there were a few of them as well. Among them can be counted the entrepreneurs who opened restaurants and the general contractors who built homes and commercial buildings. Our story here examines the Basques in town and their activities, especially their festivals.

It's not my intention to revisit fully the heyday period of sheepherding that in this study can be loosely "fenced in" between 1880s and the 1970s. William A. Douglass and Jon Bilbao's *Amerikanuak* (1975) generally covers that subject, but there is much more to tell, so the narrative does revisit some of the pioneers and the ranches they built.

One persistent characteristic of historical accounts is that they too often focus on the contributions of a few prominent people at the expense of everyone else. Here we will not repeat that approach. Accounting for as many individuals as possible is part of this work's focus, and this can only happen by using local sources. Here we would like to at least mention the names of as many Basques as we can find, those who for a time lived or worked in the county, but logistics do not allow us to print all their names. Therefore, a deal was reached with the Elko Euzkaldunak Basque

Club, which gladly agreed to include the whole list of their compatriots in their website.

Sol Silen, for example, mentions only twenty-six Basques in
Elko, all of them men: Pedro (later Pete) Jauregui, John Saval, Joe
Saval, Pedro Corta, Balbino Achabal, Juan Quintana, Pedro Orbe,
Vicente Juaristi, Pedro Olabarria, Feliz Plaza, Andres Inchausti,
Domingo Calzacorta (Sr.), Celso Madarieta, Miguel Lostra, L. P.
Arena, Domingo Recatume, Pedro Itcaina, Martin Amestoy, Juan
Madarieta, Manuel Oscoz, Florencio Corta, Domingo Sabala, Fran-
cisco Odiaga, Miguel Arregui, Andreu Fourreuill, Pedro Altube,
Bernardo Altube (he spells it *Altuve*), and Pedro Goicoechea.

Having Smith as a last name is not very helpful in locating
the origin of the person, but Basque surnames are different. A
herder named Barainca is very probably from Bizkaia; one named
Etcheverry is from Iparralde, the French area; while Echeverria
could be from Gipuzkoa or Navarre. Chances are that their origin
reflects the origin of the ranch owner who hired them. That was
the general pattern observed. The Goicoecheas came from Bizkaia, and most of their herders did too. The Heguys were from
the northern part of the Basque Country, Iparralde, as most of
their herders were.

In addition, I chose to call the people in Elko American Basques,
rather than Basque Americans, because their grandparents arrived
in Elko County almost 150 years ago. By now they are more American than Basque. However, if during several days a year when
they celebrate their heritage at festivals, they want to be called
Basque Americans or simply Basques, who has a problem with
that? I was a resident of Old Elko, and emotionally I will always
remain attached to it, but even today Elko's culture there is still
firmly anchored in the Old West. People chose to work and live
there, attracted by its overwhelming open spaces and the freedom that came with it, which gave birth to a culture of friendly
people who still inhabit the county.

CHAPTER 1

Better Representatives
of Western Tradition

The perennial question is, *Who are the Basques*? I cannot remember how many people told me, "So, you are Basque? So, that's like Portuguese, right?" Others, who know more, will ask you right away, "French Basque or Spanish Basque?" If I answer, "Just Basque," they seem a little annoyed. My answer would be that the Basques are much older than either of those two nations. It is like asking a Paiute if he is of Irish or Italian descent.

Recently, thanks to DNA research, there are some answers that we did not have before, even though experts are still struggling to understand this distinctive population. They do agree that the Basques are an ancient human group of the Pyrenees facing the Bay of Biscay. Prehistorians such as Jose Miguel Barandiaran, Telesforo Aranzadi, and Jesus Altuna, among others, have shown that we can be sure the Basques were in their present homeland at least 5,000 years ago and very probably for double that, 10,000 years.

If you exclude the Basques from the map of Europe, we will have such questions as, Who painted all those cave murals in the region where they live? How do you explain so many toponyms with Basque roots all over the Pyrenees reaching the Mediterranean, the Iberian Peninsula, in the Midi, and beyond according to Theo Vennemann? Most linguists, schooled in traditional learning centers, however, have serious reservations about Vennemann's theories. He postulated that the names of rivers and mountains in Europe have Basque roots.

Basque history is mostly unknown, and much of what we think we know was written by others, who often were at odds with the Basques politically, and always culturally and linguistically. The written word, true or false, sticks. If you keep repeating something, you perpetuate it, and eventually you may even glorify it. It can be religion, it can be history, it can be culture, or it can be a lie. You can canonize a lie if you repeat it long enough.

To a Basque, there is nothing as puzzling as why history books, especially those of Spain and France, always begin by going far away from home. It could be the Greeks, the Romans, or somewhere in the Mediterranean. At some Nevada colleges, historians may even begin their classes with the older civilizations of the Middle East and Egypt, which are not considered the source of Western traditions. Most Europeans fundamentally, if not exclusively, base the origins of their civilization on the Greeks and the Romans. Never mind that the languages the Greeks and Romans spoke are considered long dead, though a few educated people might understand classical Greek or Latin. Nobody today speaks the Egyptian of the pharaohs or the Sumerian language.

By constantly talking about the Greeks and Romans, historians have downplayed or displaced other cultures that may have contributed to our current Western culture, such as the Phoenicians, Carthaginians, Iberians, Etruscans, Celts, and Basques. An absolute difference with these populations is that in the case of the Basques, they are still in their homeland today, speaking their Euskara language that nobody else understands. You would think that the Basques could provide us with a direct link to Old Europe, before the Yamnaya herders made inroads west some 5,000 years ago, but nobody seems to be interested in embarking on that road.

One day, I would like to see a textbook of European history begin with the Basques. At least, one that mentions them. By any account, they are much older than the Greeks and the Romans, or even the Egyptians, and they are still with us, adhering to their ancient culture. Historians of today's large nation-states

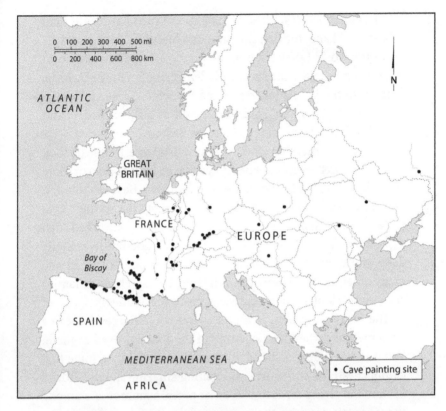

Map of western Europe showing location of paleolithic caves and cave paintings, ca. 15,000 BP, long before Europe was Europe. Recently, more Basque caves have been found with Paleolithic evidence, twenty in the Urdaibai estuary alone (Bizkaia), and near Donostia the Aitzbitarte Cave has figures dating to over 33,000 years, while the Atxurra cave contains over 100 figures of the Magdalenian period. Adapted from "Cave Art History," Royal Society of Chemistry. Cartography by Bill Nelson.

and cultures write for the rest of us from their national point of view. Since the Basques are a tiny minority, perhaps they think that they do not deserve analysis on the grounds that they have not contributed anything to Western traditions.

Speaking of which, Elko-born Vince Juaristi in his book *Basque Firsts: People Who Changed the World* (2016) attempts to remedy this oversight. He describes the histories of such Basques as Juan Sebastian Elkano, the first documented maritime circumnavigator of the world (after Elkano, the first to sail around the world *twice* was a Basque friar named Mallea); Saint Ignatius of Loyola, founder of the Jesuits (current Pope Francis is a Jesuit); Nevada Governor and Senator Paul Laxalt, son of a sheepherder; and other luminaries who happened to be Basque.

He does not mention who the first artists were, but if you look at a map of prehistoric cave paintings that go back 20,000 or more years, you will notice that many surround the Basque Country. You may also want to know why those artists risked their lives going into the interior of caves to paint? Has anyone asked such a question before? Basques believe that their goddess lives there, deep in the caves. Basques did not believe in sky deities, like so many other prehistoric people. Why not? For a prehistoric family, can you think of a more secure and protected abode than a cave?

The idea of a *goddess* living in a cave could harken back to a hazy memory when the ancestors of the Basques lived in them. What better place to spend winter, surrounded by a huge fire, eating chestnuts and acorns, and telling amazing stories? Stories of humans giving birth to babies, of prominent mothers among them, consistent with the concept of the Basque goddess, who basically is a mother and a wife. She may be a little more powerful, a little different, but still a woman and a mother. Basques did not believe in creator deities either, though they have stories of discoveries like agriculture and tools. For a Basque it makes no sense that the gods live in the sky, separated from the world they had supposedly created.

EQUALITY

There is one clear dichotomy between Western traditions that originated with the Greeks—in Eastern Europe properly—or the Middle East (such as Christianity), and those traditions original to the Atlantic West, which are still alive today. The latter has a more egalitarian view of society and that of the sexes, as opposed to a vertical, patriarchal one found imported from the East. A Basque woman does not surrender her family name and take on her husband's when she marries. That may be only a detail but a telling one. The Basque wife would be insulted if told that she belonged to the husband.

That the Basque society is more egalitarian is set in law. For example, in 1526 the Basque region of Bizkaia proclaimed that all Bizkaians were not just equal but also noble (it did not specify Bizkaian *men*). How long did it take the British to pass a similar law? In France legal equality came in 1789. The US Constitution states all men, meaning white, are created equal but only those with property could vote, and women, Black people, and the Indigenous populations were not included.

The Greeks gave us the word *democracy*, but they and the Romans did not believe that all humans were equal. Europeans are Christians, a religion that preached love among all people, but the Roman Catholic Church was hierarchical in nature, leading to a tough time making inroads among the Basques. It was considered a foreign religion and an instrument of Romanization. It preached a God who was a father figure, while the Basque deity was female. Followers of Christianity promoted a vertical society— God on high, the king/pope next, and everyone else below. This foundation stood in contrast to the locally based, mostly egalitarian Basque system of governance; the aforementioned Law of Bizkaia of 1526 barred Christian bishops from entering. Some Basque regions (Gipuzkoa and Bizkaia) did not get their own Catholic bishop until 1950.

LANGUAGE-BASED PASSPORT

In the old days, only kings and other prominent authorities could provide you with safe transit and letters of immunity, and the beneficiaries of such passports were other leading and notable people. The masses need not apply. Again, the Basques had other ideas, based on language. Euskara, their ancestral tongue, is their foremost distinguishing marker; they define themselves by their language. They call themselves Euskaldun (Euskaldunak in the plural), which means "speaker of the Basque language." They do not identify themselves by the country, their king, their religion, their nationality, or by the passport they carry. Language is the oldest human marker, and it is so simple and smart. If you speak the same language, we can understand each other, but if you do not, you are somebody else, a stranger—you are *erdeldun*. According to the Basques, the world is divided in two: those who speak Euskara and those who do not. Therefore, anyone who speaks Euskara, regardless of race or origin, is a Basque. Genius!

Another enigma is the blood of the Basque population. Even today, after living next to other groups for millennia, many Basques carry a distinct blood type, in fact the highest incidence of Rh-negative O in the world. The Mayans are another group with a high occurrence of O-negative blood. According to theorists, the Rh-negative blood did not come from Africa with *Homo sapiens*. So why does it appear in the Basque Country? Perhaps Basques are not part of the *Homo sapiens'* migration? Basque DNA too apparently distinguishes itself from neighboring populations, but there are arguments about it—after all, this is a new science. Luigi Luca Cavalli-Sforza contends that Basque carry unique gene mutations, but David Reich seems to mostly disagree, though he does not deal directly with the Basques. Latest research indicates that Basque DNA includes unique mutations but that it is not significantly different from their neighbors'.

The Oldest People of Western Europe

Before Europe had a name, before Rome, before Greece, there was a place called Euskal Herria, the land of the speakers of Euskara. Through millennia, the onslaught of Indo-European languages forced the Basque speakers to retreat into the Pyrenees Mountains and the Atlantic. There, thanks to the ocean and the mountains, they survived. Euskal Herria is like an Indigenous reservation in the US.

There are seven historic Basque regions, three in Iparralde north of the Pyrenees in what today is France—Lapurdi, Nafarroa

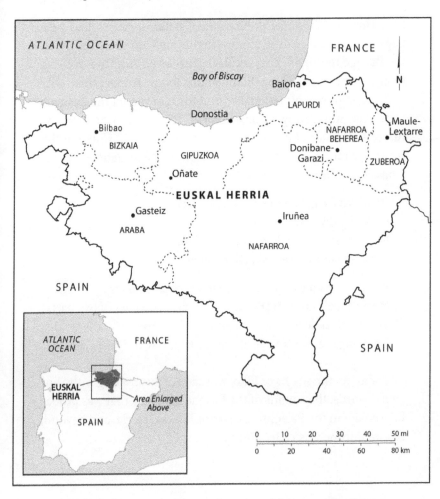

Map of Euskal Herria, the Basque Country, with its seven regions.
Cartography by Bill Nelson.

Beherea, and Zuberoa—and four in Hegoalde, south of the Pyrenees in what today is Spain—Araba, Bizkaia, Gipuzkoa, and Nafarroa/Navarre. You could say that there are six regions, because Nafarroa Beherea (Lower Navarre) was in theory part of the old kingdom of Navarre until 1659 when the kings of Spain and France decided to settle their differences by establishing a border at the Pyrenean crest, thus dividing the ancient land of the Basques in two. They did the same thing to the Catalan speakers, and perhaps that was the plan all along—divide and conquer. Despite it, the Basque motto of "Zazpiak Bat" (The Seven Are One) reflects their sentiment regarding their identity, today stronger than ever.

The geography of national boundaries prevented the Basques from communicating among themselves, which in turn accentuated the dialectal differences. A *bertso* (poetry) printed in the 1979 San Francisco North American Basque Organizations (NABO) Convention brochure states it well:

> *Hombertze euskaltzaile, urrunetik jinak*
> *Euskadi badago're, bi zati egina*
> *Jaia hunek kentzen du denen bihotzmina*
> *Bihotzez bat gaudela, hau da atsegina.*

So many Basque devotees, who have come from afar
Even though Euskadi [Basque Country] is divided in two parts
This Festival does away with everyone's sorrow
Knowing that we are one at heart, that is our consolation.

Today, on the streets of Elko, you can still hear, along with Shoshone words, the sounds of the Basque language that was probably spoken in the Paleolithic caves of Euskal Herria, and beyond, before Europe was called Europe.

CHAPTER 2

Accounting Everyone

Everyone makes history. An army general may get all the glory, but he needs soldiers to win the battle. The sheep rancher needs *artzainak* (literally, "sheep watchers"), who count every ewe and every lamb. In the Basque community every individual is somebody and worth counting, and American Basques have not forgotten it. When a Basque person dies in Nevada, their countrymen show up at the church en masse. Priests in Northern Nevada joke regularly that the church gets filled on Easter and Christmas, and at Basque funerals.

Funerals are ethnic opportunities for the Basques, especially those from the Old Country to get together, and the same is true at *mus* (card) tournaments, and at festivals. During such events, conversation soon drifts to one topic that for years now has been in the mind of every Basque immigrant: "Zenbat gara?" (How many of us remain?) Like the aspen trees they carved a century ago, the immigrant population is aging and dying. Whenever they meet, someone almost always says, "Have you heard? So and so died last week." Or "Have you heard that so and so is in the hospital? Not doing well." It means that there will be another funeral soon.

It's important for Basques to count everyone because they are only a few, about 3 million in Europe and another million or more scattered around the world. The other reason, a cultural one, is that Basques take pride in a horizontal society where every person is equal and mingles freely among compatriots. Basques take umbrage at someone who thinks—or appears to be and act—as if they are better than you. In Europe, neighboring societies were

more stratified, the Castilians, for example, and they did not welcome the Basques, who were often poor, pretending to be nobles.
Castilians made fun of them, principally because they could not
speak Spanish fluently. "Habla en cristiano," they would demand.
Yet, the Basques may speak several languages to the Castilians'
only one.

So, yes, count everyone in the tradition of the *auzolan* (a local
labor program, employed in rural areas) that required every farmstead to contribute a worker to fix communal roads and bridges.
Only widows and the elderly were exempt. Count everyone. Elko
Basques are familiar with the idea, because their parents and
grandparents counted thousands of sheep—every sheep, not just
the big fat ones.

THE NUMBERS

According to the 2000 Census, the Basque population in the US
was 57,793. This is one of the smallest minorities. States with the
largest Basque populations according to three US Censuses are

US Census	1900	1910	2000
CA	745	6,267	20,868
NV	180	971	6,096
ID	61	999	15,000
OR	no data	no data	2,627

On Elko Basques, the 1900 census reports 57; in 1910, 194; and
circa 1970, 1,000. In comparison, Winnemucca and Humboldt
Counties had more Basques than Elko early on, with 84 in 1900
and 275 in 1910.

The average marrying age at the turn of the twentieth century
was twenty-seven to twenty-eight for men and under twenty-
three for women, most of whom married within the year of arrival
from the Basque Country. In 1900, 62.5 percent of the children
in Elko County were born to Iparralde parents, and 37.5 percent
to Hegoalde ones, but this trend was reversed by 1910. The average number of children was two.

We rely on the census to count the American people, but, when Basques meet, one of their favorite pastimes is keeping track of individuals in their community. Who died, who married, whose child was born. It's their own census taking. Older Basques are still very much engaged in this exercise and will happily spend hours deciphering the levels of their kinship, for which they use Euskara, the ancient vehicle of their oral memories.

In 2018, I had an opportunity to test this notion with my ninety-five-year-old brother-in-law, Claudio Yzaguirre, and his wife, my sister Jesusa Mallea. Claudio arrived in Yakima, Washington, in 1948, and after his marriage the family moved to Hines/Burns, Oregon. That was in the 1950s and 1960s, and I asked them a simple question, "How many Basques lived in Burns and Hines during your time?" Within thirty minutes, the couple produced forty-nine individuals (and provided plenty of details), half of them with families and children. There were probably others who they could not recall after so many years had passed, but it was nevertheless a remarkable retention. Most of the Basques were ex-sheepherders, employed at the Hines Lumber Company, like Yzaguirre himself.

In Elko, I often used the same method to count people; for example, I would ask, "Who were the other sheepherders you worked with?" I have never once encountered an interviewee who could not remember any of his coworkers. With the Basque Club tracking its members, it was like having its own internal census. In 1971, there were about 1,000 Basques, about 15 percent of the town's population. In the 1970s, the club had a list of 650 adult individuals, and the remaining 350 were their children under eighteen.

I realize memories are fickle and can be wrong and partial, but a human memory is unlike data on a piece of paper, which can also be wrong and incomplete. Human memories are not cold but warm and interconnected with other memories, in our case with families, children, and relatives who provide a portrait of a community, a personal testimony of a time lived and remembered. You can ask people more questions and receive more details and nuances; that is the difference.

THE LAST ONES

Much of this study looks at the period 1970 to the present, and by then Basque sheepherder immigration had almost ceased. If most of the men were in their early or mid-twenties, today the age of the youngest ones is near seventy, but most immigrants alive are closer to eighty. At that age, the average Joe has started to take medications and to count his or her remaining years to live. Pedro Zabala of Burns, Oregon, used to say, "When a person starts swallowing *kernels* [Basque for "pills"] he is done for."

Out of the 57,793 Americans who claim Basque ancestry in the 2000 US Census, the immigrants alive today may number 2,000 to 3,000. Counting them in Northern Nevada would not take long. In Winnemucca, six were alive in 2018. In Elko, we counted twenty-eight in the summer of 2018 (see their names in the epilogue).

In the early 1970s, the percentage of the Basque population in Elko was considerably higher than it is now, but perhaps Basques' visibility and impact in town were about the same as today. But then, we have the problem of who gets to be counted as a Basque. I discovered that the herders moved around quite a bit, more than we were aware of, from ranch to ranch, from town to town, and state to state. An individual may have disembarked from the train in Winnemucca, as many did, and from there may have gone to herd sheep in Paradise Valley, Nevada, or McDermitt, and then moved on to Jordan Valley, and finally ended up in Boise, Elko, Reno, or California.

One reason for moving were the stories that herders eagerly heard through the grapevine of good and bad sheep bosses; who paid more and who less; who provided free wine; what outfit had horses or donkeys, tents, or sheep wagons. Almost all these people who moved frequently were unattached young men. The women were almost all married and settled in towns or lived on ranches with children, and they hardly moved. The young herders were footloose until they married or until they moved to town, where they might get a job or buy a business.

WHO IS BASQUE IN THE US?

Of the Basque Americans recorded in the census, the majority are not full-blooded, so their identity can vary greatly, but at least enough of the awareness survived to perceive themselves as Euskalduna, Basco, or Basque. Many are half-Basque because the father, the sheepherder, married a non-Basque woman. Linguistic compatibility, and availability, was the reason a sizable number of these sheepherders married Hispanic women especially in California, and as a result the children may speak Spanish but not Basque. In such cases, the cultural stock that the sheepherders bequeathed their children is meager. Even in cases when both parents are Basques, the number of their children who speak fluent Euskara is extremely low today. Fortunately, some of them learned to dance traditional dances, of which Basques are very fond. Some too learned to play mus.

Out of the 2000 population, my ballpark guess was that the members of Basque clubs in the US number under 20,000 and the active members perhaps 1,000. I decided to get an accurate count, and with the help of Kate Camino, Marie Petracek provided it in 2019. According to Ms. Petracek, NABO has forty-three member clubs with two in a dormant state. The total membership count of the forty-one clubs is 6,586, and of those 936 members are in Nevada. My estimates were exceedingly high.

The percentage of club members may be higher in smaller towns and lower in large ones like Reno. Basques aren't behaving any differently than other minorities. The reality is that the march to Americanization is unstoppable, as it must be, and in Elko we see it clearly.

WHO CAME? SAILORS AND OTHERS

Basques arriving in the early twentieth century were mostly from farming communities, but after 1950 we see a few townspeople among them who knew little about sheep. For example, an immigrant from Bizkaia in the early 1960s being interviewed by the American consul in Bilbao was asked if he had any sheep at home, and he answered, "Yes, and they all have new shoes." He was hired. This is not a joke; the herder himself told me the story in a 1991 interview. Mike Laughlin was probably joking about herders like him when he said that a sheepdog knows more about herding.

There is another group of sheepherders that has received no attention. An unsuspected number were sailors who had jumped ship. They were mostly Bizkaians with a long tradition of traveling the oceans. One was Ignacio Urrutia, who jumped ship in Wilmington, Delaware, in 1932. (Here was a man looking for a job during the worst depression in American history.) Through contacts, he arrived in New York City to plan the train trip across the country. He bought a business suit and a hat, and he was given sandwiches but told not to drink anything, because he would have to go to the bathroom and risk being detected. He bought a newspaper and pretended to read it during the day. Nobody suspected he was an illegal alien, and after three days he arrived in Boise, Idaho, where his relatives were waiting.

Speaking of which, Lopategui tells the story he witnessed in his sheep outfit, which had recently hired a Bizkaian sailor as a cook. One day, a herder from Zuberoa (or Xiberua) came to camp hungry, and the only victual he found in the kitchen was a single fried egg. His reaction was "Ala jinkua, pardieu, Bizkaino marinerua oilo puskar bat xanputrian" (By God [repeated in Basque and in French] this Bizkaian mariner has only one chicken fart in the skillet). With a little imagination you can translate that into vernacular Elko parlance today. There is no way to track down the number of sailors who became sheepherders, but from the stories that come up in conversation, I would guess a minimum of 5 percent.

Unifying the Basque Language in the Americas

It is probable that the Bizkaian mariner did not understand half of the words the herder from Zuberoa uttered, because the two were born at the opposite ends of the Basque Country and spoke different dialects. This incident introduces us to the subject of dialectal differences within the Basque language, which are based on regions isolated by geography and the lack of unified government. The main ones are three, but there are a dozen more subdialects. This is amazing in a country that is half the size of Elko County.

So, when Basques decided to immigrate to the Americas and met for the first time fellow compatriots from other regions, they often could not understand each other. Imagine a sheep camp in Elko, where the herder and the camp tender barely understood a few words of the other. It happened more than once. English was not the only foreign language; they found out that Basque was too.

When I asked herders about this translation issue, they confessed almost embarrassed that it happened to them, but they quickly added, "It only lasted a week or two before we assimilated each other's vocabulary." The result was that Batua, the Unified Basque language, was developed in the New World out of necessity by immigrants living together. It happened in places like Mexico, Peru, Cuba, Argentina, and so on. We ourselves are witnesses to this phenomenon in Elko County, where the blending of Bizkaian and Navarrese (Iparralde dialect is also Navarrese, except Zuberoan) started in sheep camps and continued in hotels and bars in town. You can hear Batua in Elko today. Jess Lopategui says he can converse with any Basque speaking any of the dialects without a problem. That's Batua. However, if you consult academic books, they will tell you that linguists in the Basque Country hammered out Batua in the 1960s. Yes, true, there was an earlier practical version being spoken all over the New World, but you've heard about it here for the first time.

Furthermore, when Basques in Elko and other cities with Basque clubs were able to understand each other, they gradually began to let go of old labels and started to regard themselves as Basques, not French Basque, Spanish Basque, or Navarrese. They realized that it was more important to be just Basques, but the linguistic unification was the main instrument of ethnic awareness. Even today in Elko, most Bizkaians do associate themselves with other Bizkaians, and the Navarrese with other Navarrese.

CHAPTER 3

The Pioneers—Altube Brothers and the Garats

The Altubes and the Garats came to Elko County for the land, and the Basques who followed them came for the same reason—they were attracted by the open spaces, like other settlers. Even today, except for the Reno area, Northern Nevada is mostly devoid of people except along I-80 and the paved highways, where you find 95 percent of the population. Beyond that there is nothing but land, huge empty dry flats enclosed within mountain chains. Imagine what it looked like in the 1860s before the railroad. Well, for the most part, you can still see it today. Elko County's main economic incentive was land, and it had lots of it. It also had some mining, but in 1900 most Basques wanted to raise sheep. Land was the first attraction because it was suitable for herding sheep. This was their *promised land* as Robert Laxalt put it, with freedom to run their sheep unencumbered by fences, highways, and towns.

LAND OF SURPLUS POPULATION

If survival is life's priority, you could say that the Basques have been good practitioners of it. In the last few centuries many families were large, and for most siblings this meant immigration to the Americas or joining the church. The Basque farm, typically small, was impartible and passed on to a single heir. This was the best strategy to guarantee the survival of at least some family genes. Other members had to find their own livelihood elsewhere; thus, since the beginning of history we find Basques looking for jobs, starting with the Roman Empire and accelerating with the

Spanish Empire in the New World, from the Pampas of Argentina to northern Mexico.

Basques were innovators and job creators as well. The kings of Spain depended on Basque iron manufacturing of things such as pikes, canons, and ships to fight their wars. The Dutch, the English, and the Norwegians learned commercial whaling from the Basques, who had established whaling stations in Newfoundland in the 1500s and dominated the production and sale of whale oil in Europe, so much so that Queen Elizabeth I forbade buying oil from them. Too much silver was leaving England, she complained.

South to North European Expansion

I am not going to describe here a full-blown chronicle of the sheepherder immigration, which has been told already by others (for example, *Amerikanuak*). But before we begin with the Altubes, we must remember where they came from: South America. Our story does not demand that we go that far, but we do have to take a detour to Mexico. We often hear only about the American expansion westward in the 1800s, but the European settlement in this part of the world was two-pronged, starting with an earlier one from Spain and Mexico in which the Basques played important roles.

In this context nobody ever mentions the first bishop and archbishop of Mexico, Joan Zumarraga (also known as Juan de Zumarraga), born in Durango, Bizkaia. He died in Mexico in 1548, and he can be truly and realistically considered the patriarch of the Basques in North America. In fact, he may have been one of the earliest—if not the earliest—Basque sheepmen in North America. Though he always claimed to be a poor Franciscan bishop, he owned—or controlled—land with 6,000 sheep on it. The meat and the wool went to meet the needs of the church (over which he presided), and his manager was a Portuguese man, whom the bishop praised for his ability. Strange, but as far as we know, he had no Basque sheepherders.

Zumarraga was an enlightened man; he not only brought the

first printing press to the New World and published the first books, but he also imported Basque female teachers to Mexico to instruct Aztec girls, something unheard of in the contemporary church. He brought over directly or indirectly through sponsorships more than a dozen families of relatives and Basque countrymen whose last names today are found all over Mexico and the American Southwest, even spreading into Nevada and beyond. One way or another associated with Bishop Zumarraga, we find such family names as Aguirre, Ibarra, Zabala/Zavala, Garcia, Ochoa, Mendiola, Abendaño, Urquiaga, Gamboa, Ortiz, Ribas, Salazar, Salcedo, Bergara/Vergara, Urrutia, Mallabia, Loyola, Legazpi, Mallea, Zaldibar, Archuleta, Echevarria (or Echeverria), Oñate, Aranguren, and more. Some of them had expanded into northern Mexico and the US Southwest by the 1600s.

Four Basque explorers discovered the silver mountain of La Bufa in Zacatecas in 1546, and soon thereafter Captain Francisco Ibarra pushed north into Sonora. By the 1560s, this territory was officially named Nueva Vizcaya (meaning "New Basque Country" and with Durango as its capital). Ibarra, like Zumarraga, was born in Durango, and he spearheaded the opening of the territory of northern Mexico for European settlers, ranchers, and miners.

Another influential Basque figure involved in the push to the north was Captain Francisco Urdiñola (born in Gipuzkoa 1550), who succeeded Ibarra in the governorship of Nueva Vizcaya. He was a true forerunner of the Altubes in Elko and other huge ranching empires that would develop later in the West. But Urdiñola was not only a cattleman, a sheepman, and a grain farmer who, just in Coahuila, controlled millions of acres; he also built cloth and hat factories and established the first commercial winery of North America in Parras de la Fuente.

Ibarra and Urdiñola attracted Basques and other groups from Spain. Basques pushed northward and contributed to the naming of one American state, Arizona, from *Aritz ona* (Good Oak Tree/s). New Mexico's first European settlement in 1598 was by colonists brought from the south by Juan Oñate Salazar, a Mexican-born

Basque, who founded Santa Fe in 1610. This type of settlement and expansion was replicated later further north by the Anglo-Americans pushing westward. San Francisco was founded on June 29, 1776, with settlers brought from Sonora by Juan Bautista (de) Anza, who probably spoke some Basque. His father, Captain Anza Sr., was an immigrant from Gipuzkoa. The two Anzas and half a dozen other governors and commanders in the two Californias, New Mexico, and Texas were of Basque descent.

The point here is that the Basques were in the West/Southwest long before Altube and Garat arrived in Elko in the early 1870s. Their goals and those of Ibarra and Urdiñola were the same.

The Altube Brothers

An obligatory starting point in the history of the Elko Basques entails the Altube brothers. The Garats arrived at the same time, but we will deal first with the Altubes and their Spanish Ranch in Tuscarora, Elko County. Pedro Altube and his brother Bernardo arrived from California in the early 1870s and established their ranching empire in the Independence Valley, some sixty miles north of Elko.

The brothers Altube Ydigoras were born in the farmstead Zugasti (or Zugastegi) in Zubillaga, a hamlet near Oñati in the Basque County. Their farm was typical enough, was mostly self-sufficient, and also had sheep. At the time, Oñati was an independent county and did not join Gipuzkoa until 1845. There were nine siblings (Carol W. Hovey—Altube's great-great granddaughter—says twelve, from two marriages), and Pedro was the eighth, born on April 29, 1827 (there are other attributable dates), and his youngest brother, Fernando, as born in 1831.

When Pedro was eighteen, he and Fernando sailed from Bilbao to Buenos Aires, Argentina, where they already had three brothers—Santi, Joxe Miguel, and Felix. With the discovery of gold in California in 1848, Pedro and other Basques quickly sailed to San Francisco from Chile (after crossing the Andes on horse with thirty-five other Basques, most born in Iparralde). Fernando

Pedro Altube, founder of the Spanish Ranch. Courtesy of Northeastern Nevada Historical Society and Museum, Elko, Nevada.

arrived in 1851, and for some reason he changed his name to Bernardo. By then, Juan Miguel Aguirre's hotel was there to welcome fellow Basques to California.

THE CALIFORNIA YEARS

At first, Pedro and Bernardo along with other Basques drove cattle from the Los Angeles area to the mines in the north. Later, they became partners with Jean-Baptiste Arrambide and bought a ranch in Calaveras. In 1858, Pedro married Marie Ihitzague from Iparralde, and two years later they were living in Santa Ynez, Santa Barbara County. Subsequently, with their friend Bernard Ohako, they opened a dairy and a butcher shop in San Mateo that lasted about five years. But ranching was calling again, and they bought La Laguna, a cattle ranch in Santa Barbara County. There they befriended other Basques, among them Ulpiano Yndart, who for a time owned nearby Nojoqui Ranch. Interestingly, his name cannot be found in the deed ledger of the ranch.

Even then, California weather was unpredictable, fluctuating from floods to drought, just like today, and the Altubes lost their ranch. They went to Mexico and bought several thousand head of rather skinny cows as well as horses. In 1870, the Altubes and the Garats trailed their stock east over the Sierra and into Nevada, and a year later they arrived in Independence Valley of northern Elko County. By 1872, the Altubes had set up what is probably the most celebrated Basque ranch in Nevada, the Spanish Ranch, which prospered and attracted Basque workers. Pedro owned two-thirds of the ranch and Bernardo one-third. The Altubes sold their holdings in Santa Barbara County in 1886.

INDEPENDENCE VALLEY

According to documents in the Elko County Courthouse, the Altubes bought the first property from several other investors who already owned land there, namely, Onis Peres (Louis Peres was Pedro's associate in California and owned one-third of the Spanish Ranch until at least 1880, when he was bought out), Pierre Depuy, I. L. Raqua, and others. In fact, the document seems to imply that the Spanish Ranch was already established and so named by these partners, not by the Altubes, who bought it and kept the name. Or it could simply be a matter of consigning the sale to paper a few years later and stating that the Altubes "bought the Spanish Ranch," which is what the document says. Carol W. Hovey states that the Altubes founded the Spanish Ranch.

The Altubes, like other settlers, became acquainted with the high desert of northern Elko County the hard way. With an average elevation of over 6,000 feet above sea level, the region can be unforgiving for the neophyte, and the brothers paid the price. After years of good progress was well underway, the Altubes lost most of their stock to the extreme winter temperatures of 1889–1890, when by one estimate 95 percent of the cattle in the county perished. It was after that when they started raising hay for the winter. Once again, the Altubes, with the assistance of Henderson

Bank, started over, bought more cattle, and with hard work prospered into one of the biggest ranches in the state, measuring twenty miles by ten miles (others say thirty-five miles by five to ten miles wide), plus the adjacent federal rangeland. The IL, the Thompson, and the Taylor Canyon Ranches belonged to the Altubes as well, and the holdings extended into the Idaho border. The Altubes' Tuscarora Meat Company products sold at most butcher shops in San Francisco, but sheep and Basque sheepherders too had a lot to do with their success.

Bernardo was the cattleman while Pedro oversaw the home ranch, according to Theo Dierks, who was at the ranch in 1902. The two were "charitable" people and kept their old employees until the ranch was sold. Dierks also says that in 1902 Pedro was feeble, but Bernardo was still strong (he was almost four years younger). Both had white beards. Pedro was "irascible and quick tempered" with "dark-brown piercing eyes." Bernardo was just the opposite, according to the seventeen-year-old Dierks, who was spending time at the ranch.

Some observers described Pedro Altube as a "Spanish grandee," in part because of his imposing figure (he stood six feet five inches tall—Carol Hovey says six feet eight inches—and was known as Palo Alto, "tall stick") and because he liked to be portrayed riding a beautiful mount in full regalia. But I doubt the Zubillaga-born Altube would agree with such a characterization of himself. He is also quoted as saying, in the manner of a feudal lord, "I ride my horse all day and I do not leave my ranch." Funny that this immense ranch had no house for its owners, but in 1885 a two-story house was moved from Tuscarora to the ranch. The Altubes' habitual residence was in San Francisco, where their families lived in a four-story mansion with twenty-one rooms comprising half a block.

The original log cabin at the Spanish Ranch was built by the Shoshones from the nearby reservation, but it no longer exists. Other buildings are the bunkhouse and the blacksmith shop. This bit of information checks with stories of later Basque sheepmen in the McDermitt, Nevada, area who employed Paiutes for sheep shearing and other chores. The Altubes may have hired a few Sho-shones for other seasonal work.

The Altubes ran cattle at first, but around 1900 they added sheep. It has been pointed out that one reason was John G. Tay-lor's sheep, but it could also be that the Basques were arriving in high numbers and Altube had ready-made herders. Nobody knows the exact stock numbers they owned, but one Elko paper wrote in 1880 that the Altubes had 5,000 head. According to sheepman Jess Goicoechea, the county tax collector required the operators to report at least 50 percent of the sheep they owned; could this be applied to the Spanish Ranch as well?

The Altubes hired about twenty full-time cowboys and many more during haying. Their ranch was a Little Euskal Herria (Basque Country) for the countrymen working there and gave them a footing in Nevada and in Idaho. These sheepherders and cow-boys provided something extra for the Altubes: land. One way the Altubes increased their ranch holdings was to have their workers apply for the 160 acres under the Homestead Act, and then, after proving ownership, the workers would sell them to the Altubes. The Homestead Act was intended to benefit the common man, but in many cases the wealthy land operators profited from it. The Altubes and the Garats had an agent in San Francisco, J. B. Arrambide, who was also their business partner in California, and he would contact people to apply for homesteading in the Inde-pendence Valley and then buy the land from them to sell to the Altubes and the Garats. Many of these so-called owners lived in San Francisco. At the Elko County Courthouse there are many documents of transactions executed by J. B. Arrambide.

~

Pedro Altube and Marie had six daughters. Pedro died in San Fran-cisco in 1905 at age seventy-eight and was buried in Colma, Cali-fornia. The Spanish Ranch was sold two years later along with its stock. Theo Dierks tells us that at the time a single head of cattle sold for $39.50. According to *The Reno Journal*, the ranch was sold to a syndicate comprised of W. H. Moffat, R. G. Humphrey, Peter Garat, and L. L. Bradley for $1 million, and included 20,000 sheep, 20,000 cattle, 2,000 horses, and 400,000 acres. Peter Garat, son of Jean B. Garat, became the manager of the new company they called Palo Alto Cattle Company.

According to the same Reno paper, the Altubes had first arrived in Elko with 500 horses, which they traded for cattle. A few days later, *The Elko Independent* reported that according to a prominent Elko citizen, the sale figures coming from Reno were a "50 percent lie." The ranch sold for $450,000 and included 10,000 sheep, about 10,000 cattle, and between 500 and 600 horses. The property came with 42,000 acres (Hovey says 74,000) of patented land and 8,000 acres unpatented. The paper reported that these figures are more believable because the county assessor had valued the ranch at $230,000. That is about half of its value, which checks with Goicoechea's statement from above. Carol W. Hovey says the Altubes received a total of $225,000 from the sale.

However, they kept the Thompson Ranch, Taylor Canyon Ranch, and IL Ranch until 1918 or 1919. Freddie Francisco claims that the town of Palo Alto was a land grant named after Pedro Altube, but a letter by a member of the Altube family casts doubt about the story, though not about Pedro's height.

As a corollary, the P-Bench cattle brand that some say was used by the Altubes was not so, according to Jess Lopategui. It was originally owned by a man whose ranch was purchased by Moffat and his partners and who in around 1960 sold it to Sam Etcheverry and Frank Arregui. The two partners (owners of the Elko Blacksmith Shop) requested that the P-Bench brand be included in the sale. A plaque of the P-Bench brand, complete with its history, still hangs on one of the walls of the Ogi Deli in Elko. The brand is owned by the Arreguis, Lugeas, Lopateguis, and the Wines of Elko.

~

In 1960, Pedro was the first cowboy in Nevada to be inducted into the National Cowboy Hall of Fame in Oklahoma City, Oklahoma.

In 1984, Pedro Altube was inducted into another Hall of Fame in Elko, which I will describe in chapter 12. Bernardo Altube and his wife, Marie Recarte (born in Iparralde), had two sons, Jules and Felix. Jules married Pedro's daughter Amelia and died in 1945. Bernardo returned to Argentina to visit his brothers but returned and died in Berkeley on March 17, 1917. Before that, he built the Bernard Hotel on Powell Street in San Francisco.

EMPLOYEES OF THE ALTUBE RANCH

Workers don't make news unless caught in some accident or an extraordinary event, and the historian is bound by that rule. Among the twenty people or so they hired—forty according to another account—were a few Mexicans, who probably came driving the cattle from Mexico. Roger Butterfield wrote in *Life Magazine* that the Altubes paid the Mexican vaqueros in yellow gold, and on paydays they would take off to town whooping and shooting their guns on half-broken mustangs. Some of them ended up dead or in the calaboose. Such an account makes for colorful classic tales about the heyday of the true Wild West, but is it accurate?

Americans were also hired, such as "Shorty" Johnson, who was seven feet tall; Jim Tunnell; and George Davis, who died in a mowing accident in 1897. Charles Fuller, a foreman, is mentioned in another accident. Al Buker, a Mormon, and Al Shannon, a cowboy, are mentioned in Dierk's letters, as are others of different backgrounds—Gene, an Italian; Pat, the Chinese cook; one Joe (there were several); a vaquero cook; and Old Dan.

BASQUE EMPLOYEES

There must be a reason why Pedro Altube is viewed as the "Father of the Basques in West." Clearly, the epithet doesn't refer to California, though even there he seemed always surrounded by countrymen, but it may apply better to Nevada and Idaho. Theo Dierks mentions Ben Loinez (probably Loinaz), as the bookkeeper at the ranch (Pablo Loinaz, Pedro Altube's brother-in-law, was his bookkeeper in California). Ben Loinaz moved to Winnemucca after the Altubes sold the ranch and went into the sheep business, and he even owned a saloon. Incidentally, he may have had relatives there, as there was another business in town owned by a Loinaz.

Ramon Lugea, born in California but raised in Navarre, was the blacksmith of the Spanish Ranch in 1902. John Mentaberry worked for the Altubes from 1903 to 1906, when he bought his own sheep in Humboldt County, according to Ruby Yrueta, Mentaberry's granddaughter. Other Basques were Jose Urias, Joe Yraguen, Pete (Pedro) Orbe, Jose Sustacha, and J. Francisco Goicoechea, the one of the "enormous build," says Dierks. Joe Anacabe started by cowboying for the Altubes in the early 1900s, and later he would own businesses in Nevada and California. Cruz Bilbao toiled for the Altubes, as well, a cook named also Bilbao who could be his relative.

Dierks, who became an undertaker in San Francisco, visited the Spanish Ranch several times in the 1930s and 1940s and found it totally changed; he did not recognize the place. The Garats were still there at the YP Ranch (see next section), but the old folks were all dead, he wrote. Dierks had befriended Ramon Lugea in 1903 and wrote him at least six letters, the last one dated March 1956. It is not known if Lugea, who died in Elko two years later, answered any of them.

The Altubes probably had a dozen Basques employees, or more. In one contemporary photograph we can distinguish some Basque physiognomies. The *Daily Independent* of Elko reported on June 10, 1907, that two young Basques (no names) had left Altube's ranch with a team to come to town for supplies when the horses were spooked by a car. One of the men jumped and sprained his ankle and was brought to Elko. The other, after picking up the supplies, had started back toward Tuscarora when the team got stuck in the mud. While trying to unload a whiskey barrel, he lost his balance and the barrel fell on his hand, cutting off the tips of three fingers. Mr. Altube (probably Bernardo or Jules) was notified by telephone, the paper reported.

In 1912, after the Altubes no longer owned the Spanish Ranch and John Garat was the manager, Bilbao was still the cook at the manager's house. His chauffeur was also Basque by the name Sabino (no last name). Whenever he encountered horses, Sabino would shut off the car until the horses were gone because they were frightened by the noisy monster.

GARAT-YNDART AND THE YP RANCH

Jean B. Garat (French spelling for Garate), with wife and sons, practically followed the Altubes from California into northern Elko County, arriving before 1872, and established their YP Ranch northeast of the Altubes in Independence Valley. Garat and his partner and relative Jean Yndart were from Iparralde and their friends, the Altubes, were from Hegoalde. A sizable number of Altube's Basque friends who came from Chile and Argentina were of Iparralde origin, all of them practically hailing a few miles from Garat's birthplace, Larretxo, where he was born in 1826 and

Jean Garat and wife, Grace, founders of the YP Ranch. Courtesy of Northeastern Nevada Historical Society and Museum, Elko, Nevada.

married Grace Marie about 1845. Garat and Jean Yndart (he was known as Juan in California) had a third partner, J. B. Arrambide, also from Iparralde. Both Garat and Yndart arrived in California soon after the Gold Rush, but rather than mining they became cattle ranchers.

The Garats trailed approximately 1,000 cattle over the eastern Sierra through Bridgeport, California, and spent over a year crossing Nevada before they found their place at the Salmon Point of the Owyhee River, where they purchased about 320 acres from the estate of Captain Stiles, according to Edna Patterson. Later, they kept buying more land and acquiring it by the same methods as the Altubes by taking advantage of the 160-acre Homestead Act. In many of these transactions, Arrambide in San Francisco acted as their agent and even partner. For example, an 1890 Elko County Courthouse document reveals that Arrambide sold 17,500 acres to Peter and John Garat, at purportedly one-quarter of its value.

YP RANCH

Garat-Yndart settled in the areas known as White Rock and Edgemont, Nevada, now a ghost town. Their YP brand was in use in California in 1852, was recorded in Elko in 1872, and is believed to be the second- or third-oldest brand in continuous use in the US. Upending stereotypes about Basques, YP ran straight cattle, no sheep. They say out West that cattlemen get more respect than sheepmen, but for some reason, there is considerably less information about the Garat-Yndart outfit at the Elko Museum than about the Spanish Ranch that still runs cattle and sheep.

In the harsh winter of 1889–1890, the Garats suffered heavy losses, 90 percent, like all other stockmen in the county, which forced them to put up hay for winter feeding. That meant hiring dozens of extra people in the summertime, like the Altubes did.

The Garats had four sons—Pete, John, George, and Henry. In 1895, John Garat married Matilda Yndart, thus firming even more the family and business ties. In 1910, the Garats bought the SL Ranch and moved their headquarters there. The YP outlasted the

Spanish Ranch by over thirty years. It sold in 1939 and included 75,000 acres, 7,500 cattle, and some 500 horses; today it is known as the Petain Ranch.

Jean B. Garat died in 1939 in California and was survived by his widow. We have an insightful detail told by Mary Urriola Smith, who as a young girl grew up near Jack Creek, where her parents had a store. She vividly remembers that "one cold winter Mrs. Garat died. Her three sons brought the body to our place where they fed their horses, had coffee and sandwiches before proceeding to Elko 60 cold miles away."

GARAT-YNDART EMPLOYEES

Often it is the Altubes who get the credit for attracting fellow Basques, but the Garat-Yndart outfit deserves nothing less, if not more, as we see below. Many Basques worked for the YP, one reason being that the ranch was in operation when increasing numbers of Basques were arriving in Elko County. Gregorio Aldaya of Lesaka, Navarre, was the blacksmith in 1905. In 1915, he married Graciane Etcheleku of Luzaide and moved to Elko. He associated himself with the Heguys, who owned property near the Telescope Hotel and allowed him to set up his own blacksmith business. Blacksmith Ramon Lugea became a Garat foreman in Edgemont. He had a Basque crew working under him. One of his daughters was born there in 1913. Lugea worked for Garat until 1918, when he bought an eighty-acre ranch in Lamoille, where he lived some years with his wife and three daughters.

The following Basques worked at the YP Ranch:

- Urizar, a cook, obviously Basque (one Felix Urizar died in 1957; he was a rancher outside Burns, Oregon, and he had two other brothers)

- Peter Garat, 1898 (a relative, cattleman in White Rock, Elko Co.)

- Julian Erquiaga, 1900

- Sotero Erquiaga, 1900 (Julian's brother)

- Jose Goitia, 1900

- Tomas Jayo, 1902

- Jose Sustacha, 1910 (later established a ranch in Lamoille, still in the family)

- Cruz Bilbao Arejita, 1917 (worked first for Altube)

- Pedro Bilbao Arejita, 1917 (brothers)

- Pio Juaristi, 1917

- Rufino Juaristi, 1917 (Pio's brother)

- Eustaquio Villanueva, 1917

- Martin Lekumberry, 1918

- Gregorio Arrate, 1918

- Jose M. Arrese, 1918

- Benito T. Etulain, 1918

- Norberto Obieta, 1918

- George Garat, 1920

- Henry Garat, 1920 (relatives, brothers, who managed one of the Garat's ranches)

- B. Monasterio, 1920

- Luis Yturriaga, 1920

We may assume there were others, especially before 1900, but more research is needed to uncover their identities.

~

Mike Laughlin, of Elko, says, "the Basque stockmen were cattle-men who brought to Nevada the customs and traditions of the

Old California Spanish vaqueros. The customs and traditions that these Basque cattlemen brought could well have been the start of the buckaroo tradition in Nevada, as we know it today."

Funny thing is that literature extols ranch life and finds many heroes among the earliest ranchers living in the wild. In fact, it seems that the wilder the place is, the more valuable fodder for historians. But what happens to all these wild country heroes? Eventually you will find them in town, where a civilized community of people live. The Basques did the same.

CHAPTER 4

Counting Ranches

With the success that the Altubes and the Garats enjoyed, other Basques were eager to join them in acquiring ranches and raising stock. Some of them got a start by first working for the two pioneer ranchers and saving their wages. We have some information about the Altubes and the Garats yet almost nothing on those who followed their footsteps. Though activity and sheepherding were going on, few details are available until the early 1900s.

In 1906 R. B. Wilson of the US National Forest wrote a report on the Bruneau, Jarbidge, and Mountain City areas. Apparently, this was a prime grazing district, because Wilson says at least forty-three sheep companies, large and small, used it in the summer, with a total number of 392,350 sheep. His spelling of surnames is atrocious, but we can identify thirteen of the sheepmen as being Basque: John Etchevery (Etcheverry), 3,800 sheep; Arimosby (probably Erramouspe), 4,000; J. Bengelcher (Bengoechea), 11,600; J. Altube, 11,250; Bicente and Co., 4,000; P. Laca, 3,900; M. Hasquet, 5,800; P. Corta, 2,500; Irigoyen, 2,500; G. Sabala, 12,900; M. Satica, 2,800; J. Bentaverg (Mentaberry), 2,800; Lopex (Lopez) brothers, 4,600.

The names of seven more companies that Wilson mentions are problematic, but some of them could be Basque: Othalepo and Co., 3,100 sheep; Tellerforo (Telesforo), 4,700; Motta, 3,400; M. J. Triguerro (Triguero), 5,500; Frank Triguerro, 3,000; Amarel (Amaral), 4,500; and Eyran, 4,000.

We suspected as much—that after the 1880s the Basques in Elko had already jumped into the sheep business—but until now, we lacked details. Now we can put on the map the names of these early Basque sheep operators, the size of their herds, and the location of their summer range. Wilson states that in this area of extreme northern Elko County, among the sheep operators "nearly all the small owners (are) nomadic 'Bascos' with no ranches of their own and paying no taxes." He reflects the frustration of the more established ranchers who raised mostly cattle in his complaining about the excessive number of sheep, but he adds that some of the large sheepmen were well connected politically and economically and there was not much that could be done about it, except government regulation in the form of allotments.

Wilson goes on to state that the nomadic sheepmen are from the Basque Provinces in the Pyrenees Mountains and that they are not US citizens; their only aim, he says, is "to live here until they have made enough money to go back home."

We can call his last statement inaccurate. Of course, Jules Altube was well known in the area, but Wilson may not have known Jose Bengoechea, who at one time owned or controlled 100,000 sheep in Idaho and who in Mountain Home built one of the finest hotels west of the Mississippi. His new home was Idaho, where he was known as "the King of the Basques." As far as the rest of the "tramp" sheepmen, Erramouspe is in California, and Laca, Satica, Mentaberry, Corta, Hasquet, Lopez, and the Sabala families are still around in Northern Nevada if not Elko. Frank Triguero may or not have been Basque, but he homesteaded in southern Idaho.

There are aspects not yet researched regarding early Basque ranchers. For example, did they get a start by homesteading? How many acquired ranches after making money as "tramp" sheepmen? How come banks loaned them money without their being citizens? The obvious answer is trust. It appears that some—I would say many—bought property by pooling their money or by means of partnerships. Brothers becoming partners was one observable practice, as was partnership between those who hailed from the same town back home. The Altubes, Garat-Yndart, Saval brothers, and the Goicoecheas fit the description.

That the Basques raised a lot of sheep is not up for debate. There was a Scottish observer who described them as not really the best sheepherders but certainly the most dependable. To be sure, a Basque will be hard-pressed to admit defeat when it comes to doing his job. The need to be considered a good worker, and not lazy, is ingrained in the Basque psyche.

There is an appropriate song, "Ezkontarazi" (Forced to Get Married), that depicts how Basques feel about resolve. It tells the story of the young couple whose parents forced them to marry, though there was no love between them. The last verse says: "I am looking to the future and to springtime when the fields will bloom again. Though we did not love each other, they forced us to get married, so . . . *we must* love each other." Here is that warped Basque sense of duty. If it is expected from us, we must do it, and not fail. Most sheepherders lived by that credo, and when they became owners themselves and when faced with challenges, many persisted.

Those who know western rangeland will tell you that most of it is better suited for sheep than cattle. More important, sheep provide the owner with two annual incomes—one in the spring with wool and another in the fall with lambs. Normally a rancher makes more money with sheep. So then, why were cattle so popular? And more important, why did cattlemen hate, attack, and kill sheep and sometimes sheepherders in the West? As sad as the reading of that history might be, it's amusing that many of these sheep haters, when the economy demanded it, were not above switching from cattle to sheep. As, the saying went, "Raise cattle for prestige, sheep for the money. A cowboy hat beats a sheepherder's beret any day."

Some of these issues are difficult to understand. Many of the cattlemen came from European backgrounds where sheep raising was accepted and important to the local economy, such as in Ireland, Scotland, England, and so on; but people from those countries seem to act differently in the American West. To justify their behavior, some argued that the sheep were smelly, that cattle would not eat the grass where sheep had trampled, that the woollies destroyed the grass by eating it down to its roots, for example. Nowadays smart ranchers run both sheep and cattle because they feed on different grasses. Sheep will also eat grasses that are harmful to cattle, and they will chomp on blooming weeds, like cheatgrass, before they go to seed, thus cleaning the range.

Cattlemen's hostility toward sheep and sheepmen was in part rooted in ethnic and cultural bias. If we trace to the beginnings, when Anglo settlers expanded into the West, no domesticated sheep existed on the land, except in the Hispanic territories. Texas had millions of sheep during the colonial and Mexican periods, and so did New Mexico, which was the premier exporter of the woollies into the lands Americans acquired in 1848. The herders were non-Anglo with no knowledge of the English language, and those differences surely set the stage for conflict. Religion was another factor for friction, but control of the resources was the ultimate reason for conflict.

Sheep could have prevailed over cattle in the West, but their need for care was the main reason it did not. Sheep always need a herder because they are easy prey for coyotes, wolves, cougars, and bears. On the other hand, cattle can be driven into pasture or into the mountains and left alone for weeks and months at a time. Basically, cattle are cheaper to run. Today, the old quarrels are history, and, voila, sheep are almost having a second life. Formerly viewed as causing devastation to the range, they are now regarded as saviors, cleaning machines, and aids to carbon sequestration. In parts of California and Nevada, sheep and goats are used to cut down the brush and decrease the fire danger around cities. Somewhere an old Basque sheepherder is smiling and saying, "What took you so long?" In May 2019, the *Reno Gazette-Journal* published a letter by a reader blaming the fires on the lack of wildlife such as elk and deer, but the writer forgot sheep—the primary mowing machine. Their absence most certainly has exacerbated the recent devastation caused by the fires in the West.

~

Elko is a premier ranch country, blessed with adequate-to-good range and enough water for stock. The weather could be better, for it can turn from winter to summer-like and reverse itself just as fast in the high country. As the snow melts, nutritious grasses and blooms that sheep love abound. Before the federal government took over the public lands, some Basques made more money than they had imagined possible by simply driving their sheep from place to place. And because they owned no land and paid fewer taxes, the more-settled ranchers, who themselves enjoyed the same free public lands, detested them. Fortunately, most of the time Elko County stock operators chose harmony for the common good.

Family Ranches

As mentioned earlier, from the 1870s until the early 1900s, there is a dearth of information—other than Altubes and Garats—regarding the hundreds of Basques who had already arrived in Northern Nevada. A camp tender working in the Columbia Basin told me in the 1960s that he had seen an aspen tree in Beaver Creek carved by someone named Vicondoa and dated 1889. That would be the oldest carving we know of in Elko County, but I do not remember hearing of any Vicondoas (though once I visited the Vicondoa Ranch in Surprise Valley, California). No carvings by the Altubes have ever been found, but I recorded one in the Copper Basin by Ramon Garat, dated 1901.

In the early 1900s, half a dozen Basque sheepmen and ranchers settled between Elko and the Idaho border, roughly a distance of 100 miles. In Jack Creek near Tuscarora, beside the Altubes, there were several small ranches owned or rented by Basques, such as Urriola, Achabal, Bilbao, and Laucirica, but this generally happens after 1910.

It appears that early Basque ranchers made a little money, though some more than others, and the following song often heard at Basque festivals, may be telling their story:

Nevadara joan nintzan
Xentimorik gabe
Handik etorri nintzan, maitia,
Bost milioien jabe.

Txin txin, txin txin,
Diruaren hotsa,
Haretxek ematen dit, maitia,
Bihotzian poza.

I went to Nevada
Without a penny
From there, my love, I came,
The owner of five million [pesos or dollars].
Chin chin, chin chin,
The sound of money,
That is the thing that gives me, my love,
[bis] Joy in my heart. [bis]

I know a few immigrants who could be the authors of the song, except that most of them did not return to the Basque Country.

SAVAL RANCH

Saval Ranch was the earliest in Elko County after the Altubes and the Garats, as far as I know. A good number of the early Basques in the county worked there or had business with it. In that sense the Saval brothers are comparable to the Altubes and the Garats. The "Saval Ranch" signs on the Mountain City Highway are still up today, even though the original owners are long gone. Situated on the eastern foothills of the Independence Mountains, the ranch was established by three Zabalbeascoa brothers—Juan (John), Jose Manuel (Joe), and Gabino (Guy). Two of their sisters also came to Nevada. They were from Ispaster, Bizkaia, and Sol Silen says they arrived in 1892 and went to Winnemucca. Joe was born in 1874, according to his daughter Josephine, who liked to spell her last name Savalbasquoa. He was fifteen when he came and for years worked for the Scotsman John G. Taylor in Rye Patch, Nevada.

Joe met Jesusa Guridi in Golconda, Nevada, and she was swept off her feet by the dashing and smartly dressed gentleman. She was twenty-seven, from Gallarta, Bizkaia, when she arrived, and they were married in 1917 in San Jose, California. The Urriolas and the Beitias of Elko were her kin, as well as the Garamendis and the Aranos. The Savals were related to Corta, a sheepman of Jiggs, Nevada, and to Pio Achabal of Jack Creek. It was a tight-knit group from the same area in the Basque Country. As Josephine Saval put it, "The Basques are related to everybody."

Joe Saval's home base ranch was in Buffalo Meadows, Lander County, Nevada. His daughter remembers a big house with a big porch covered with grapes. The Savals employed twenty-five to thirty, mostly Basque men, and wife, Jesusa, cooked for all of them meat, potatoes, beans, and veggies (with bread and wine, no doubt). Shearing the sheep began in Buffalo Meadows and continued in the trail north 100 miles, ending at the Indian Creek.

Joe died in 1938 and Guy two years later. Joe's widow had to learn ranching business 101 in a hurry, but learn she did. Jesusa Guridi lived in Battle Mountain and took over the operations, which was still in business in Lander County in the 1960s, lasting until 1990. (For additional information, see Koldo San Sebastian.)

John Saval married Carmen Aboitiz in 1903 and acquired his own sheep ranch in Smoky Valley in 1917, but in the following year he died in a car accident in Pine Valley. It's not clear whether the early ranch and livestock acquisitions of the three brothers were a common venture or individual enterprises (after 1918, obviously, only Joe and Guy were in business), but Josephine Saval says that Joe and Guy had the Snow Creek Ranch near Jack Creek. It had 300 acres with irrigated meadows, where they built "a gorgeous house," according to her; however, it later burned down.

The Saval Ranch, mentioned earlier, is about fifty miles north of Elko and some ten miles south of Goicoechea's Ranch. The ranch was in operation by the early 1900s, because among the workers was Francisco Goicoechea, whose son Jess was born at the ranch in 1909.

Between the three Savals, Guy was the better known and the youngest, but all three engaged in ranching and owned much property and livestock, especially Joe and Guy. After the establishment of the ranch and making money with sheep, a pattern developed among the Basques to settle in town or at least to buy a house or a business. Guy did just that, as he co-built a hotel in Elko, and shortened his last name to Saval.

Whirlwind Guy went on to other activities and didn't stay long with the hotel (see chapter 10). Perhaps with cash from the sale of the hotel, Guy bought several ranches near the Idaho border that included 19,000 sheep and horses. He bought another ranch in White Pine County, and the two brothers ran thousands of heads of sheep and cattle in several counties of Nevada, employing many Basques. One document I saw at the Elko Museum stated that Guy Saval was known as the "Basque King." The man certainly had to have money or credit, or both. Today, an immigrant would have a tough time buying ranch after ranch as he did. The Saval business is a classic example of brothers starting as partners and then diversifying and going into business separately. The difficulty is knowing the details: who owned what and when.

On September 19, 2021, I had a lucky encounter with two ladies in Winnemucca, Nevada. The older one, even before I could introduce myself, told me: "I am Guy Saval's niece." It was as if I had hit a jackpot in the local casino, and instantly, through her, I felt transported back to 1900 Elko.

Goicoechea's Ranch

The Goicoechea brothers—Pete, Francisco, Domingo, and Fernando—came from Bedarona, according to Sol Silen and Koldo San Sebastian soon after 1900. Initially Francisco, who was a large man, worked for the Altubes, and later the three brothers were employed at the Saval Ranch. In 1908 Francisco married Juliana Arechabaleta by proxy, and their son Jess Goicoechea, who would personify the Basque sheepmen in Elko County, was born at the ranch. A year or two earlier Francisco and Juliana moved to Elko and bought into a partnership of the Telescope Hotel.

In 1911, Pedro/Pete Goicoechea accidentally shot himself in the foot while working at the Saval Ranch. Pauline Mendive stated that Pete was one of the Basque pioneers in northern Elko

Entrance to Goicoechea's Ranch.

County. Two years later, he married Guadalupe Ybarlucea, and they had three sons, Julian, Benny, and Ray. Ybarlucea died soon after giving birth in 1918. These three siblings eventually bought a ranch in Eureka, and Pete Goicoechea, longtime politician and current Nevada state senator of Eureka, is the son of Julian. Today, the senator runs the Goicoechea ranches in Eureka.

In 1912, Francisco and his brother Pedro homesteaded an area between the Mountain City Highway and Beaver Creek, known as the Home Ranch, according to Larry Goicoechea. Later they acquired the Beaver Creek Ranch from Pedro Corta, but in the meantime, in 1913, suddenly Francisco (everybody called him Patxi) died, and two years later his brother Fernando married the widow, Juliana. Out of this union was born Elias, who would run the Goicoechea cattle operation, while Jess ran the sheep part of it.

Edna Patterson says that Pete Goicoechea, Frank Hoye, and

others started buying parts of the ranch before 1907. In that year they sold it to the Williams brothers for $15,000. Fernando Goicoechea finally bought it back in 1928, and it is still owned by the Goicoecheas.

By 1919, and perhaps before, the Goicoecheas were running their own sheep and had secured a forest permit in the Copper Mountain area, south of Jarbidge, Nevada. They were issued this permit until Jess sold the sheep in 1976, plus additional permits on BLM land. They ran between 6,000 and 8,000 sheep, plus cattle. About this time, there was another Goicoechea—Esteban, from Mendexa, Bizkaia—working in the Rubies, where on August 15, 1918, he carved his name on an aspen in Rattlesnake Canyon. His hometown was not far from Bedarona, and he may have been related to the Goicoecheas, whose operations were eighty miles away.

Jess Goicoechea was a man totally immersed in the sheep industry. There was no one like him in the county. He was friendly and treated his herders well. His wife, Mariana Lugea, baked many a pie that she took to the sheep camp. In the late 1960s, Jess already knew that his business did not have a bright future, that in fact it was coming to an end, which is what he told me then. Fifteen years earlier, the grazing permits were cut in half in the state, and the operators had to reduce the stock numbers accordingly. It was the beginning of the animosity of the stockmen versus the federal government regulators that would last decades, in fact, until today.

The Goicoechea herders were almost all Bizkaian, and I met some of them in 1968—Juan Antzamendi, Gontze, brothers Jose Manuel and Luis Jayo, Joe L. Mallea, Edorta Arrate, Juan Juaristi, Mañukorta (a popular *bertsolari* poet), Julian Arrillaga, Javier Ascazibar, and the brothers Felix and Ramon Zugazaga. One, Jose Echarte, was from Lesaka, Navarre, and another was from Iparralde. Jess Goicoechea sold the sheep in 1976, and soon after he and Mariana (together they had three children) took their first trip to the Basque Country. While there, in the company of Lopategui, they attended the World Aizkolari (Woodchopper) Championship in Donostia, Gipuzkoa (see chapter 15).

For years Elias Goicoechea used to host a big BBQ at the ranch on the Fourth of July, according to Fred Beitia Sr. Elias married Alice Larios; her father owned a large ranching operation on the Nevada-Idaho border. Her mother was Eizaguirre (Matilde Jauregui's sister) from Berriatua, Bizkaia. Today, the ranch's ownership and operation are in the hands of Elias Goicoechea's grandson, Mitch Goicoechea, who, after an absence of forty-one years, jumped right back into the sheep business in 2017. He owns 3,000 ewes that spend winters in Fallon, Nevada, and summers in Copper Mountain. The Goicoecheas have held on to that forest allotment for over a century.

SUSTACHA RANCHES

It started with one, but there are two Sustacha ranches today, situated in the idyllic setting of Lamoille, Nevada. Jose Sustacha, born in Luxua near Bilbao, arrived in 1910 and found employment at the Garat Ranch until he gathered enough capital to start a ranch of his own. He married Francisca Arambarri in 1916. She was born in Berriatua in 1891 and arrived in Elko in 1913 and worked at the Overland Hotel until her marriage. They had three children: Jess, born in 1922; Jose (Joe); and Fermina, born at the Star Hotel in 1917. Today, the Sustachas comprise four generations of Joses (Joes).

Around 1915–1920 Sustacha bought Cecilio's ranch, a couple of miles from Lamoille on the road to Elko. I have no information on Cecilio. After some years he sold it and bought a place above the Community Church in Lamoille. This is the main Sustacha ranch that extends to the very foot of the Rubies. He soon bought Hereford cattle in Tulare, California, according to Jess Sustacha, but his widow, Marilyn Kane, says it was at the University of Nevada Ranch in Reno. The cattle arrived by railroad, and still today in 2025 the Sustachas run nothing but registered Herefords, some of them black.

As the ranch prospered, they hired between fifteen and twenty American workers during haying time, according to Fermina Sustacha. From their prime snow-watered meadows they put

Original Sustacha ranch house, Lamoille.

up over 1,200 tons of hay for the winter. The stacker had to be a strong and able man, the best paid—$2–3 a day with three meals and two snacks every day. Pio Aguirre was one such man, an ex-boxer, and a stacker at Cross Ranch. Francisca Eizaguirre had to cook three square meals every day for the workers, which included baked pies and snacks.

Growing up at the ranch, the Sustacha children learned to do chores early. As soon as Jess was able to jump on a horse, he sold vegetables, flowers, and garden seeds to their neighbors. When Fermina and Jess started school, they spoke only Basque. They were lucky that Edna Patterson, the premier local historian, was the first-grade teacher in Lamoille.

The Sustachas ran sheep as well, as many as 10,000 in the 1930s and 1940s and eventually 800 cows. Jess remembers how at a young age he delivered supplies to the Basque herders. Joe Sustacha added to his ranch by buying more property below it but separated by less than half a mile. Today, the two Sustacha ranches comprise about 10,000 acres, mostly deeded, with some BLM grazing land. The land was divided in 1966 between Jess's two sons, who run both parts today. Finally, it is noteworthy that the Sustachas and the Aguirre tribe of Elko are related through Francisca Arambarri.

Dinner House Ranch

The Dinner House Ranch, located at the junction of Mountain City Highway (225) and the Tuscarora Road (226), was built in 1869–1870. Emilio Jayo lived there in the early 1900s, according to granddaughter Leslie Madigan. Her grandpa told the story of an incident in 1909, when a buggy going to the Spanish Ranch plunged into a creek with a trunk valued at $1,000. Jayo was working there and tried to help but could not retrieve the buggy until the following morning.

The Yraguen brothers—Basilio, Jose, and Roman—owned the Dinner House Ranch. Born in Natxitua, Bizkaia, they went to sea by age ten and had traveled the world before arriving in Nevada, first in Paradise Valley, where they worked for Reese Evans for over twelve years. Few details are known of their ownership of the ranch from 1926 to 1949 (or from 1924 to 1940, as per another source). They apparently ran some cattle, and the place was also a roadside inn, as its name implies.

Basilio Yraguen married Benedicta Apraiz from Ea, Bizkaia, before coming to the US, according to their son Frank Yraguen, who in Elko was known as the "Irish Basque" because of his red hair. One day at the ranch a horse kicked Basilio and broke his leg, and he moved to town. Frank—born in Sacramento, California, in 1931—was the first quarterback of the Elko High School football team (1948), and he also played in Elko's all-Basque softball team. Frank only spoke Basque at first, but as he grew up he learned Spanish, Italian, and then English. He even spoke some Chinese. These were the languages spoken in the neighborhood where he grew up. Elko used to be an ethnic stew, and we could say that it still is.

SAM FURNACE RANCH

The Aguirres lived at the Sam Furnace Ranch in Ryndon, fourteen miles east of Elko, where Gabino "Guy" Aguirre and his wife, Angela Odriozola (born in Gernika in 1903), raised eight children. She was kin to Celso Madarieta, and after arriving in Nevada, she cried for a month. She would have returned to Gernika right away. . . "if I had money to buy a ticket." Guy, born in Muxika, came in 1914 at eighteen, and married Angela in 1923, the year she arrived. Half of the Aguirre family would eventually work for the Southern Pacific Railroad, like Guy.

The *Elko Daily Free Press* of April 27, 1925, reported Angela's bravery at the Ryndon Ranch, when she saw a cow being branded gone berserk and running straight to where her three-year-old, Johnny, was standing. She only had time to push the boy off the path of the charging cow. Unfortunately, she got hit and her arm was broken, but the boy was saved. In her later years, Angela moved to town and became the Amuma (grandmother) of her many grandchildren. She lived to be ninety-seven.

WILDHORSE RANCH

The Aguirres was an involved bunch of American Basques who seemed to be all over town. One of them, Manuel, wanted a bigger ranch and he found one in Wildhorse, about seventy miles north of Elko. Johnny Aguirre, the first president of the Basque Club, grew up in that location. In 1938, Manuel sold 600 acres of the ranch to the US Forest Service for $40,000. The condition was that he had to move out within six months because the government was going to expand the nearby Wildhorse Dam, built in 1937. He still had the rest of the ranch, but had to vacate the area of the dam, which was enlarged only in 1969. Manuel moved his house to the east side of Highway 225, where there was a store as well. The store along with the ranch were sold in 1944, at which time the record shows that Manuel Aguirre had a partner.

Speaking of the Aguirres, Jess Lopategui says that a book can be written about them for they comprise a large band in the county.

What is more, other distinguished Elkoans—like Pete Jauregui, Calixto Laucirica, and Lopategui himself—came from the same hometown as Guy Aguirre: Muxika.

Finally, Wildhorse Dam is a popular destination for anglers during the summer and for ice fishing. As an aside, we could add that few people are aware that this corner of Nevada is not part of the Great Basin; that the water from Wildhorse flows into the Pacific via the Snake River. Indeed, once salmon used to migrate all the way up to this corner of Nevada. Another peculiarity of Wildhorse is that in winter, it registers some of the coldest temperatures in Nevada.

Mendive Gold Creek Ranch

Mendive Gold Creek Ranch, located twenty-five miles north of Wildhorse Dam, is a bit higher at almost 6,300 feet elevation, and it may even be a colder spot than Wildhorse. The Humboldt-Toiyabe National Forest has a ranger station nearby. Prudencio Mendive and his wife, Paula Ybarlucea, were living in Battle Mountain, Nevada, in 1927 when they bought the Gold Creek Ranch, which entailed 2,500 acres. Prudencio arrived from Bizkaia quite young and finished high school in Battle Mountain, where he later worked as a miner at the Betty O'Neal Mine.

After marriage, with five children in tow, the Mendives moved to Gold Creek, where two more boys were born. They ran sheep and cattle, and Jose Ybarlucea, Paula's brother, was a partner in their sheep operation. After World War II, Jose returned to the Basque Country, so the Mendives bought him out and switched their main income to mostly cattle. Their brand was P5. After Prudencio and Paula's passing, the sons managed the ranch, which expanded to 3,500-deeded acres plus BLM and US Forest Service allotments. It was sold to Ellison Ranching Company in 2000. At the time, it contained the ranch house, shop, and calving shed.

Elko has quite a few isolated ranches like the Mendive, where electric power lines arrived only in 1974. Until then lights had come from diesel run generators. Telephone, however, came in much earlier; the switchboard to Jarbidge and Charleston was at the Mendive Ranch.

Finally, it must be mentioned that Toni Marks, a young woman from the Los Angeles area, married Raymond, one of the Mendive boys, and immersed herself head-on into Basque-style ranching on the Elko northern outback. She loved ranching and living in the wild, most of the time. Toni now lives in Elko, and she has been running the research section of the Northeastern Nevada Museum from May 2005 to the present. She contributed considerable information on Gold Creek Ranch.

CORTA SHEEP RANCH

It was established by Pedro Corta (Cortabitarte) from Gizaburuaga (a weird geographical name in Bizkaia meaning "the place of human skulls"), and it is located not far from another Basque ranch, Zaga's. He, Pete, first worked for Saval and was able to buy a place sixty-five miles north of Elko, which he sold to the Goicoecheas. He bought the Cedar Hill Ranch of 1,120 acres in Jiggs in 1911, where he ran 6,000 sheep. His partners were Manuel Nachiondo, Domingo Calzacorta (Sr.), and Martin Amestoy, but eventually he bought them out. From 1940 to 1943, Corta and Alex Heguy also ran sheep together. In 1935, Corta acquired Vicente Juaristi's forest permits. Both were born in Gizaburuaga.

After World War I, sheep and wool prices slumped, and for a time sheepmen were in trouble, as were the banks. Not only did the military buy far less wool than before, but also there was foreign competition. In 1920, sheep that had sold for $25/head could be had for $5. Wool sales were stagnant and remained in storage. Pete Corta was the first rancher in the county to sell his 1920–1921 wool (250,000 pounds) at 15 cents a pound. Before it was selling at 65 cents.

Pete Corta married Juanita Gortari in 1910, and their sons Pete and Henry continued with the ranch of 9,000 acres with 4,500 sheep and 175 Herefords. Their US Forest Service allotments were Corral Creek and Mitchell Creek in the Rubies. Some of his herders were the Leniz brothers of Gizaburuaga, who worked for some eighteen years, and Jose Fagoaga of Aranaz, Navarre, among others. Henry's son Ray Corta sold the ranch to Canyon Construction of Elko, and he went to live at his other ranch at nearby Twin Bridges in South Fork. He was living there in 2025. He is third-generation American Corta.

ZAGA RANCH

The Zaga Ranch is in Jiggs, thirty-three miles south of Elko. Federico Zugazaga (better known as Fred Zaga) came to America in the 1920s at age sixteen. After herding sheep for some ten years, he married Livia Orbe and became a government trapper. Livia was born in Elko, Nevada, and Fred in Lumo (Gernika). In 1942, the Zagas bought the ranch where they ran cattle. Harrison Pass in the Rubies was Zaga's forest allotment.

When Fred became a citizen, the clerk at the Elko County Courthouse unceremoniously shortened his name to Zaga. Strangely, his son Freddie, on the other hand, born earlier, retained the Zugazaga name, but today his sons go by Zaga.

Though I knew and visited Fred and Livia regularly in the 1960s, I neglected to ask questions. Now that they and their son Freddie are deceased, we depend on Freddie's widow, Simone Young Zaga, to inform us of the details that she remembers. Food celebrations on the year's great holidays, such as Christmas, are some of the things she has not forgotten. It was a special time of the year when life around the ranch subsided under the heavy snow and the cold provided more leisure time for family life and visiting. Christmas dinners were exceptional, alternating among the Basque families in the vicinity, one being Livia's sister Anita Mitchell, married into a ranch a few miles south in Mitchell Creek. When it was Livia's turn, you were assured a gourmet feast with *makailu* (salted cod fish), tongue, clams and rice, pies, and other goodies—all washed down with red wine and cups of coffee.

BEITIA RANCH

The Beitia Ranch was another isolated Basque ranch in the Charleston area, some eighty miles north of Elko, established by John

Beitia (Guerricabeitia). He was born in the hamlet of Jaio (now a ghost town) in Munitibar, Bizkaia. He ran sheep and died in 1946 in a haying accident. His son Fred married Pauline Mendive of Gold Creek Ranch. They ran cattle, sheep, and horses, and for about five months they were mostly snowbound. At times, supplies and mail were airlifted and dropped on the snowy meadow near the ranch house.

To give you an idea of the ranch's remoteness, Fred Jr. says that outlaws in wool chaps used to show up at the ranch toting sawed-off .30-30s. "We used to fear them, we used to call them Vets. Dad would invite them in for a cup of coffee, but not Mom. She would say: They don't have to come in, they can drink the coffee out there." Fred added that these outlaws used to hang out in the Bruneau Canyon, and he presumed they bolted to Idaho when convenient, and back again to Nevada.

Fred (in 2018 he is Sr.) was born in 1946, came to Elko in 1967, and worked for the city for thirty-seven years, many of them as parks director. At heart, he still thinks like a rancher inhabiting what many would call the *wild country*. "A lot has changed from the Rubies to the Idaho border," he says.

> When I was young, we had deer, but now we have deer, elk, and antelope. They overwhelmed us. There are thousands of elk now. My uncle Frank Beitia worked for the Forest Service, and he told the Fish and Game people that we do not need to import elk; they would come on their own, but they did not listen. They imported some and now we have thousands. Mustangs are not a problem. You ride them or use them for something. When I was young there were a lot of people in Charleston, but now only a few. When my dad and uncle passed away, we were able to divide the ranch, but I do not know what our kids are going to do when we are gone. Are they going to continue putting up hay? Some of them like to hunt.

Beitia continues, "When dozens of deer were eating the alfalfa my dad used to complain to the Fish and Game, and they would say,

'Do whatever you have to do, Mr. Beitia.' So, the Indians came, and took the meat and they made moccasins, gloves, and chaps." Fred misses the people he knew in Charleston who had later left. Now only the Pruntys are there. He remembers Pete Ytcaina's big outfit; his sheepherders gave the Beitias the lepe lambs, bread, and wine too.

PETE ELIA RANCH

Pete Elia was born in Navarre on April 6, 1897, and came to Nevada, where he married Leoni Etchegoyhen. The two had a daughter, Isabel, born in Winnemucca in 1934. He came to Elko, and for a time he ran some 20,000 sheep, according to papers in Northeastern Nevada Museum's Family Archives. Somehow, he weathered the Depression of the 1930s; in fact, in 1933 he got 12.5 cents/pound for wool, the highest price paid in Elko at a time when it was difficult to dispose of wool. In the 1950s, he bought the Felipe Yribar Sheep Company in Pashimeroi, Idaho, and later he sold it to Bolen Uresti (probably Urresti).

Elia ran some 10,000 sheep of his own, but with his partner he ran more sheep and cattle. The Northeastern Nevada Museum has a lot of photos of Mocho, one of Elia's herders, and some of other companions, but their names are missing. Elia's nephew Juan Martin Erro, ninety years old, lives behind the Star Hotel and has a big garden. I visited him in the fall of 2019, and his garden was still in production. He said that ladies from the nearby brothels come to buy produce, and they always paid him more than the asking price. "They are very nice," Erro said.

Elia, Celso Madarieta, the wool merchant, and sheepman John Carpenter—who later was a Nevada assemblyman—were good friends and major players in Old Elko. From time to time, they hosted BBQs for their friends and business associates. When Elia retired, Carpenter bought his sheep. Pete Elia died in 1979.

HEGUY RANCHES

The Heguy Ranch, based in Charleston, was another large Basque operation, established by Alex Heguy that ran only sheep. His grandson Bob Heguy is a retired CPA in Elko, and he says that his grandfather was born in Jatsu, in northern Basque Country, in 1884 and came to the US in 1905. Bob says he received a bedroll but no tent, and it snowed on him on his first night as a sheepherder. After some years afterward, he and Allen McBride partnered and ran sheep in Jiggs, up to 16,000 heads, but during the Depression the bank took over, and they split.

Alex Heguy established the Snow Creek Ranch, then moved to Terrell Ranch in Charleston. He married Emily Etcheverry, born in Baigorry. Edna Patterson says that Martin Elgora (?), Martin Segura, and Gracian Bidaurreta were associates of Heguy, who started with 1,000 ewes bought from Guy Saval and 2,000 lambs from Mike/Miguel Lostra.

At the time, sheep were trailed long distances, all on foot. The Heguy trail was Kinsley Mountain, about 250 miles from the Idaho border, and it proceeded to the Rubies, through the Secret Pass, Stagg Mountain, and on to Jarbidge. Sheep are labor intensive, especially during the lambing season, Bob Heguy says. You get up at 4 a.m., go out, and check to see how many lambs were born. Docking, shearing, cleaning their eyes in the desert, the sheep dip . . . it is a lot of work and care.

The sheep were dwindling by the 1970s, followed by cattle, and the Heguys sold out in 1975, at about the same time as the Goicoecheas. By then, the Heguys had accumulated tens of thousands of acres of private land. The ranch was sold to the federal government for a conservation project. With the money, the Heguys bought a place near the town of Elko. Bob says his father was "tough as nails"; he could do anything, no give, no quit. He laments that there are no such people today. Bob says being Basque is being responsible, having integrity, showing honesty, and being family loving more than anything. We are the same people as those who came from the Pyrenees. "I trust Basques, because if I need help and call them, they will come."

YTCAINA RANCHES

Pete Ytcaina (should be Ytçaina or, in Basque, Itzaina) was born in Aldude, Iparralde, and arrived in the US in 1898 at age seventeen.

He became one of the biggest sheepmen in Elko County. They say that he owned over 20,000 sheep of his own, plus another 60,000 with his partner Servel, a sheepman from Idaho. Ytcaina was a tough guy who encroached and pushed to get ahead in business. During the Depression, in the spring of 1933, his wool sold for an amazing price of 20 cents/pound, when a month earlier it had sold at 12 cents. His main ranch was in Currie, Nevada, but he also had other ranches and corrals in the Mary's River area north of Halleck, says Lopategui. His summer range was up in the Rubies, east of Secret Pass. He owned thousands of acres that were sold at more than $1 million. Ben Allustiarte, of California, bought his sheep in 1958.

BASKOVILLE (YTCAINA CAMP)

A man told me about Baskoville while I was documenting aspen carvings in the Independence Mountains in 1990. I said, "Baskoville? I have never heard of it. It sounds like a big place; where is it?" The man was vague but thought it was somewhere north of Halleck. It was intriguing news to me, though when I asked around about the name and the place, none of the Basques seemed to know anything. When I inquired at the local Forest Service office, they had no information. Fred Frampton, who in the 1990s was the Forest archaeologist in Elko, told me that he knew of an oven and a cabin somewhere in the vicinity of Mary's River.

Bob Heguy's family ran sheep in that territory, and he thinks that Baskoville must have been Ytcaina's main summer camp and, he added, also Heguy's. These outfits were large and hired so many Basques that camp tenders stationed there had to provide provisions to many sheepherders scattered for miles around. Therefore, the locals named the place, accordingly and correctly, Baskoville—a historic site that was never rendered on the map. One more Nevada ghost town, I guess, but this time not mining-related, instead sheep-related. Furthermore, Bob Heguy said Ytcaina homesteaded somewhere in the vicinity, at the lower Mary's River basin, where two sheep trails come together: the Jarbidge and the Sun Creek trails. He thinks it could be the site of Baskoville.

Mike Inda, a longtime Reno resident, herded sheep for Pete Ytcaina in the 1950s, but he never heard of Baskoville. Of course not; the name was used only by American ranchers of the area, not by the Basques themselves.

Ytcaina was quite a character, and Elko people still talk about him. He supplied his herders with five-gallon coffee containers that were good for holding water after the coffee was gone (by then the coffee probably tasted like chicory). He usually did not pay his herders until they quit. His nephew Jean Ardans can attest to that. In fact, he had several nephews working for him (one said that he had not been to town in forty-two years), and when they finally quit, their uncle paid them one lump sum. Lopategui knew them and can vouch for the story.

Coming straight to town from the range, Pete often looked scruffy, even like a bum. Sometimes he may have had too much to drink as well, like one night in 1959 when he entered a bar located in what used to be the old Overland Hotel. The barman refused to serve him, telling him that he already had enough, and ordered him to get out. Among the Elko Basques this episode has several versions. In one, the bar was the Telescope and, in another, the Silver Dollar, which Pete had owned since 1942 or 1943, or some other joint that Ytcaina entered that night. Lopategui has seen the paperwork at city hall, and he can set the record straight for us: Ytcaina bought the bar that later was named Sandpiper, but I am getting ahead of the story.

Ytcaina had recently sold his outfit; at the time, gloating in money, he was greatly annoyed by the barman's refusal. The following day he went to the Commercial Hotel Casino to look for Red Ellis, the owner of the bar. Cutting the preamble short, he told Red that he wanted to buy the bar. Ellis told him that it was not for sale, but Pete would not take a no for an answer. Name a price, he told Red. He was so insistent that finally Ellis gave in and sold the bar.

The following day, or soon thereafter, Ytcaina could not wait to return to the bar and order a drink from the same barman. Apparently, he still looked rather unkempt, and the barman again

Historical photo of Pete Ytcaina.
Reprinted from Sol Silen.

refused to serve him. That was the moment Ytcaina was waiting for, the tale goes; "I own this place, so now you get out," he told the barman. That was in March 1959, but he did not enjoy his new acquisition very long because he died on June 5, 1959, a day before the commencement in Sparks of the Western Basque Festival, which he was planning to attend. He was seventy-nine, and *The Salt Lake Tribune* called him "One of the West's most colorful characters." Two years later his wife sold the bar back to Red Ellis, who sometime later named it the Sandpiper.

BARINAGA RANCH

Pete Barinaga and his wife, Elvira Pena, owned the Barinaga Ranch, and they had four children. Pedro/Pete Barinaga was from Markina, Bizkaia, and after coming to Nevada he herded sheep at various ranches, including the Saval Ranch. The Barinaga Ranch is in Lee, twenty-six miles south of Elko. A creek runs through it, and in 1991 I saw that some fruit trees were still standing on the nearby meadow, still healthy and producing. Pete Jr., born in 1926, served in the Korean War and later was injured in a logging accident, thus becoming a paraplegic. At the ranch, Pete Jr. was another Basque who hosted an annual picnic and BBQ for his many friends and acquaintances. Pete had the reputation of being a very good mechanic and passed away at eighty-eight in 2014.

NICK GOICOA

Nicolas/Nick Goicoa was from Orbaizeta, Navarre, and acquired a ranch in Clover Valley, on the south side of the Rubies. Earlier he was in partnership with Allen McBride; after the dissolution, he ran around 5,000 sheep. I remember visiting his main camp below the "Hole in the Mountain" in 1969. Quite a view from up there. Nick bought the Chicken Ranch in Clover Valley, where he hosted an annual Fourth of July picnic. Goicoa, like other Basque sheepmen, sold out in the 1970s or before.

Nick was married to his cousin Mercedes Lugea, and they had a son, Ray, who became a lawyer. Ray married Kitty Tenille and died young at forty-two, leaving behind a large family. Ray was one of the early presidents of the Basque Club, in 1962 and from 1965 to 1967.

VICENTE JUARISTI

Vicente Juaristi from Gizaburuaga, Bizkaia, was born in 1880, and after arriving in the US in 1899 herded sheep in Winnemucca. He bought Jake Minola's place of 640 acres located south of Jiggs and ran about 6,000 sheep. He was one of the early prominent Basque ranchers. In 1912, he married Mary Walthers, whose parents had a ranch in Jiggs, which Juaristi operated for years. After the sheep industry slump of 1920, Juaristi was the first in the county to sell his 50,000 pounds of wool at 25 cents/pound in 1922. He was the uncle of Jose and Juan Juaristi, brothers who arrived in Elko in 1948 and 1955, respectively. A photo of Vicente is found in Sol Silen's book (no page).

OLABARRIA RANCH

Pedro Olabarria was born in Markina in 1878 and arrived in the US in 1901. In 1911, he married Simona Bastida, and they had two children, Albert and Laura. The couple established a ranch in Gold Creek near Rowland with his partner Ignacio Madariaga (Patterson says Joe Madariaga, but that was after Ignacio died). They had two winter bands, which means four summer bands, or about 4,000 ewes. The ranch was located by Bruneau, and it was called Rattlesnake Ranch or Olabarria Ranch. Somewhere in the area there is an Olabarria Canyon, as well, says Valerie Olabarria Rodgers, Pedro's granddaughter.

Ignacio Madariaga, Olabarria's partner in the sheep operation, was originally from near Markina. After Madariaga committed suicide in the 1930s, his brother Joe Madariaga became Olabarria's partner. The Olabarria Ranch sold in 1948.

LARIOS RANCH

Larios Ranch, a sprawling property located at the Nevada-Idaho border, was owned by Manuel Larios. A California Mexican, he held a land grant that was lost to the Americans. He came to Nevada with the Altubes and worked for them, even though he was addressed as "Don Manuel." In 1907, his son BB married Daniela Eizaguirre, a Bizkaian lady, and together they had several children. Larios died in 1944, and his wife continued managing the spread until 1952, when she sold out and moved to Elko. She died there in 1957, killed by the train as the car she was riding stalled on the railroad tracks.

JAVIER GOYENECHE

Javier Goyeneche, whose origin was in Lesaka, Navarre, bought a ranch on Lindsay Creek south of Jiggs and ran several bands of sheep with Felipe Eizaguirre and others. Goyeneche's grazing ground was mostly in the Rubies, but in 1914 he also ventured north into the Gold Creek area, which was already crowded.

DOMINGO CALZACORTA

Domingo Calzacorta (Sr.) was born in Markina, Bizkaia, in 1884. After working for the Williams brothers, he started ranching by partnering with Billy Moore, and the two ran 9,000 sheep and 1,000 cows in Newark Valley. Calzacorta also partnered with Pedro Corta of Jiggs. He bought a ranch in Battle Mountain, which he later sold to W. T. Jenkins. Calzacorta married Anita Marisquirena, and they had three children. Their daughter Margarite helped many Elko herders with their paperwork. She spoke Spanish, even though both parents spoke Basque. Their son Domingo Jr. became a mining engineer and worked for Newmont, as told. Domingo owned the Amistad Hotel with Celso Madarieta, who was married to Anita's sister. In 1931, Calzacorta and Pete Jauregui bought some sheep, but by then the two were more into town life and hotels than into ranches, and the venture didn't last.

ALZOLA RANCHES

Faustino Alzola, originally from Ispaster, arrived in the US circa 1900 and married Eusebia Elguezabal; both were from Bizkaia and together they had five children, sons Arsen, Frosty, Jim, and Eugene, and one daughter, Sara. Faustino Alzola was one of the founders of the Bruneau Sheep Company, along with Frank Gedney and others, and they raised sheep and cattle. The company was run as a corporation, and after the parents passed away the Alzola brothers tried to keep it, but in 1943 it was sold to J. R. Simplot with its 12,000 sheep.

Arsen Alzola and his brothers bought homestead properties that were relinquished, and in 1946 they acquired the Sunflower property from George Rizzi, a successful rancher of the area. They raised sheep, cattle, and horses. In the same year, Bernard Yribarne, who ran sheep in the JP Country, sold his ranch to the

Alzolas and went back to his birthplace in Iparralde. The Alzolas sold out in the 1980s, but the deal fell through, and the brothers took the ranch back.

This is the so-called JP Country—the area of Bruneau River, Mountain City, and the Owyhee. According to P. B. Kennedy, in this territory more than 60,000 sheep from Idaho were grazing in 1902, but the actual count was closer to 100,000.

Pete Paris Ranch

There were three Paris brothers who arrived in Nevada and worked in Elko for the Williams brothers sheep outfit. Beltran Paris established the Paris Ranch in Cherry Creek, White Pine County, Nevada, where Pete was born and raised. After growing up Pete came to Elko and went into ranching. He first bought sheep from his cousin Paul Inchauspe of Silver Creek Ranch, north of Austin, Nevada. Later he bought Henry Corta's sheep and ranch in Jiggs. He sold the sheep but still has a ranch between Jiggs and Lee, Nevada, with 700 head of cattle. He also bought Bob Right's property. Around 2010, he sold/leased his sheep to a man from Idaho, who also bought nearby Zaga Ranch.

Basque Ranches in Lamoille

The Basques, like others, recognized the beauty of Lamoille and its assets for ranching, with abundant water to irrigate the meadows below the Rubies. Lamoille had a flour mill, a bootlegger, a beaver farm, a school, and a church, according to Jess Sustacha. His father, Jose Sustacha, was one of the earliest Basque ranchers there. Besides him, there were at least five more Basques—Lugea, Bastida, Laucirica, Cecilio, and Urriola—who owned ranches. These were not your classic huge Nevada ranches in the desert but more like "a nice place to live in the country" prime real estate ranches. Having said that, Calisto Laucirica did run cattle with his partner.

Lamoille attracted more than ranchers. Marisquirena, a Navarrese father and his American-born daughter, built a bar restaurant, the Pine Lodge, which is still in operation today.

LUGEA RANCH

The Ramon Lugea Ranch in Lamoille was also known as the Seventh Canyon Ranch, which Lugea purchased in 1918. We already met Lugea working for the Altubes and then for the Garats. The ranch he bought was small by Nevada standards, eighty acres, but he ran it more like a Basque farmstead. He planted an orchard with several kinds of fruit trees; he made cheese, canned vegetables and fruit preserves, and brewed cider that tasted like champagne. He sold lamb, fruit, and even ice at 25 cents a chunk. The family raised so much food at home that they only came to town twice a year to shop and to buy supplies.

Every year, the Lugeas hosted a picnic to which Basques were invited. The Elks had their barbecues there as well. There was no need to hire musicians either, because Ramon Lugea played accordion and guitar. Lugea's parents came with Altube from Argentina but went back to Navarre before they returned to the US. The American-born Ramon married Grace Eyherabide, a lady from Iparralde, and they had three daughters.

The Lugeas sold the ranch during the Depression for $14,000. Ramon died in 1958. The sisters Mercedes, Elena, and Mariana married three Basque men—Nick Goicoa, Frank Arregui, and Jess Goicoechea respectively—and their progeny endures today in the county.

LAUCIRICA RANCH

Calisto Laucirica owned the Laucirica Ranch in Lamoille. He married Pilar Arambarri of Berriatua, Bizkaia, in 1922, and their daughter Mary was born in 1925. In the 1930s, they were living in Jack Creek, and from there they moved to Lamoille. Mary shared that at the ranch they had lots of cows, chickens, and pigs and made chorizos at home. They also had a garden with fruit trees and strawberries. This first ranch was lost during the Depression, but after leasing Elko's Star Hotel for five years, Calisto bought another ranch, and they lived there until 1949, when they finally moved to town.

OTHERS

There were many other sheep operators in Elko County, some lasting longer than others, such as Juan Quintana, Jean-Pierre Mariluch, Serafin Barrainea (Barainca?), Joe Berrueta, Luis Alacano, Joe Echegaray, Pete Etchart, Pete Arrascada, Pio Aguirre, Ralph Gamboa, and Pete Ordoqui, whose ranch near Currie was still standing in the 1990s. Several of his naked figures were carved large on the aspen groves above the ranch. Each of these sheepmen ran at least several bands of sheep, approximately 5,000, and most of them owned or leased a ranch. As seen, there is much more Basque history left to tell in Elko County.

CELSO MADARIETA

Then there were individuals like Celso Madarieta, not a sheepherder and not a rancher but always around sheep and ranches. He was a wool and lamb merchant serving Elko. Born in Ea, Bizkaia, in 1891, he arrived in the US in 1906 and herded sheep for Andy Little of Idaho for a short time. He came to Elko and tended bar for the Jaureguis at the Star Hotel. Later he went into business with Domingo Calzacorta (Sr.) and owned the Amistad Hotel.

Celso married Agustina Marisquirena of Etxalar, Navarre, in 1913, and laid the foundation of Celso Livestock Company that made him a well-known figure in Elko County and beyond. They say he knew the value of wool and sheep like few other people ever did, which is why he was successful. Someone like Madarieta was very useful to Basque sheepmen because they tended not to be as aware of market trends as their American counterparts. Celso was a popular figure in Elko, where he died in 1966. He and Pete Elia hosted popular barbecue affairs at the Pete Barinaga Ranch in Lee, as well as in Lamoille, and in Elko itself.

ALLIED CATTLE AND LIVESTOCK COMPANY

The Allied Sheep Company was definitely not a family-owned ranch, and it was not considered a Basque outfit per se but operated in Northern Nevada, precisely in the area of the Garat-Yndart cattle ranches. In fact, Jean Garat and his partners are believed to be some of the original founders of Allied. In the 1960s, its central office was in San Francisco (J. B. Arambarri was one of the Garat partners stationed there), where the monthly checks for the sheepherders were issued. At the time, most Elko sheep companies did not pay by check.

Allied had about 10,000 sheep and as many cattle in five or six ranches, some of them on the Oregon side, with Basque herders, such as Jose Recondo, who was the foreman from 1966 to 1974. Recondo remembers how one 1965 winter day twenty-eight Allied sheepherders converged on the Winnemucca Hotel in Winnemucca. Of the twenty-eight, twelve were originally from Lesaka, Navarre, like Recondo himself. The hotel almost ran out of food on that day, but not drinks, he quips. One can only imagine the atmosphere at the old hotel on that day. The noise, the laughter, the singing, the dancing . . . perhaps even some improvised poetry. Too bad there was no one to video-record it.

Jess Lopategui worked on two sheepherding contracts for Allied until the mid-1960s, when you could call it a thoroughly Basque-manned company. From 1950 to the 1970s, at least six of the foremen were Basques. The following is a partial list of the Allied workforce provided by Lopategui and Recondo, who today owns a ranch in Selah, Washington: Manuel Arbillaga (foreman, 1950–1961), Pete Ampo, Fernand Sorhondo, Jean Iribarne Sr., Jean Iribarne Jr. (more on him in chapter 8), Antoine Lascaray, Louis Laspade, Marcel Inda, Michele Inda, Eugenio Ullibarry, Miguel Arbe, Jose Manuel Jayo, Luis Jayo, Pedro Guerricagoitia, Luis Monaut, Tomas Bilbao, Pedro Artola, Ramon Gavica (foreman, 1961), Domingo Calzacorta Jr. (foreman, 1962), Antonio Mindeguia (foreman, 1963), Antonio Urrutia, Jose M. Urrutia, Pedro Goyeneche, Jose Goyeneche (foreman), Francisco Juanicotena, Nicolas Perez, Jose M. Ozamis, Gabriel Goya, Jose Ramon Zubiria, Miguel Inza, Santiago Marichelar, Hipolito Apezteguia, Alfonso Zubizar, the Lasa brothers, Javier Bereau, and Fermin Alzugaray (foreman in the 1970s). Finally, the trapper attached to Allied was Santy Mendieta.

The tally amounts to forty individuals. I met a dozen of them in 1968 when I visited their main camp located at the Columbia Basin, in northern Elko County.

Counting Sheep and Wages

We have not dealt much with sheepherder wages, which naturally did not remain constant, but were adjusted to the vagaries of the economy. When meat and wool prices were up, the rancher could afford to pay more, and whenever there was a bump on the road, wages suffered. Bixenti Astoquia carved an aspen on Telegraph Mountain in 1901 to tell us that he was earning $100 a month, which can be considered good wages. A 1906 Forest Report of northern Elko County indicates that the average wage for a sheepherder and a camp tender was $30 to $40 a month. During the 1921 sheep collapse, wages were cut to $60/month. In the 1960s most herders in Elko made between $225 and $250 a month. Today some Peruvian herders in California are demanding over $4,000/month with overtime.

Finally, after this ranch count, let us try to arrive at a very ballpark figure of counting sheep. In the early 1900s, Nevada had over a million woolies, and Elko County had the most. In 1930, during the great recession, Nevada still had more than 800,000 head, and Elko had a major part of that. In 1909, the Humboldt National Forest in Elko County received grazing applications for 560,000 sheep and 330,000 cattle. Lopategui in a 2014 interview said that during his sheepherding days (1950–1960), Elko and Eureka counties had half a million sheep. Sheepman Jess Goicoechea estimated 300,000 sheep pasturing north of town and about 100,000 more in the Ruby Mountain area during his time (1925–1975). I do not have the figures from the Bureau of Land Management, which manages most of the grazing land in the county, but the sheep numbers would be about the same.

Alfonso Ygoa, born in Txomineko Borda in Lesaka, Navarre, managed John Carpenter's sheep outfit in Lee, Nevada, in the 1960s, and on February 25, 2018, I asked him if he could help me round up the number of sheep in Elko during his time. His answers came in quickly: Carpenter, 22,000 (sold in 1976); Jess and Elias Goico-echea, 5,000–6,000 (but I also heard 7,000–8,000); Joe Echegaray, 5,000; Ellison's Spanish Ranch, 12,000; Allied Sheep Co., 12,000; Nick and Ray Goicoa, 5,000; Sorenson, 12,000 (NNM Papers say 13,000); Corta brothers, 5,000; Heguy Sheep, 5,000; Julian Goico-echea, 5,000; Pete Ytcaina, 10,000 (but I usually hear much higher numbers, 15,000+); and Bruneau Sheep Co. (Simplot), 12,000.

Ygoa's numbers are lower than Lopategui's, but of course the count is not exhaustive, as Ygoa blurted these numbers almost automatically, and he was not including Eureka County. These are comprehensive numbers supplied by the experts, and I am confident of their accuracy.

CHAPTER 5

Sheepherders' Happy Hour

Happy hour? Seriously?

In this chapter I am going to annotate some misconceptions and lacunae in the extant literature about sheepherder life. Elko newspapers only occasionally covered the Basque herders and their lives, which is understandable because their activities took place away from town and the public view. But there was another aspect to this omission. The herders were all foreigners, so they attracted less attention. We can say that much of the news that caught the attention of the media in town starting in the 1970s related to accidents, weather, and such. As the Basque presence in town became more noticeable, so did coverage of the Basques by the media.

Newspapers seldom emphasized the lonely lifestyle of the sheepherders. Historians and writers, on the contrary, highlighted the isolation and their solitary lives, even though many of them had never set foot on a sheep camp, much less followed a sheepherder up and down the hills and deserts.

Another noticeable void is that authors who dealt with the Basques wrote about sheepherding and ranching and overlooked their compatriots living in town. The premise is that the Basques were sheepherders, period. The reality was that 80 percent of the time, more Basques lived in town than on the range. This was one considerable misconception. Finally, a third blank in the record is the following: Most writers totally ignored Basque women, whether living in town or on ranches.

Elko serves as a good example of this. By the early 1900s to 1910, when according to M. P. Arrizabalaga, Basque immigration mushroomed and presumably all came to herd sheep, there were several Basque-owned businesses already established in town. Data is limited, however, because the Census counted the Basques in town, but do we know how many others were not counted, especially among the so-called tramp sheepmen? The aspen carvings might have been helpful here, if only we had recorded them before they disappeared.

TIGHT-LIPPED

Books on sheepherders all agree that their lives on the range were solitary, so much so that some of them went crazy. While it's undeniable that theirs was a lonely occupation, too much hay—or shall we say, sagebrush—has been made over it already. We do know that many ex-herders were close-mouthed about their lives on the range and refused to say much, even to their own children, no matter how often they begged for information. "Oh, there is nothing to tell," was the excuse of many a father. Perhaps those years were not happy or easy, and it made sense to keep quiet. In speaking with members of the Basque community, this topic indeed comes up often, where children were genuinely curious about their father's sheepherder occupation, but their curiosity remained unmet.

I have had the opportunity to talk with sheepherders for hours, and I would like to inform their probing children that their lives in the mountains were often far from boring or painful. It was a time when in their own minds the immigrants "passed the test," the test of growing up and becoming a man. We found that some arrived in the US as teenagers, sixteen-to-eighteen-years-old who had never boiled water in their lives. Imagine when overnight you had to manage a thousand ewes and their lambs, making sure that they did not go hungry—after all, that was your job. But besides that, you had to cook, so that you did not go hungry yourself, and do the dishes and laundry, besides that. These experiences were not all boring, not to many sheepherders.

To many young immigrants the sudden immersion in sheep

husbandry entailed a pivotal but transitional time, the process of growing up and eventually becoming "American." Many did not enjoy it, because their goal was elsewhere, like living in town and raising a family, but I met a good number of ex-herders who genuinely enjoyed their time alone in the mountains; they loved sheep and their sheepdogs. Having said that, I found more arbor-glyphs with statements like "Shit to you, Sierra," than "I love the Sierra"; yes, indeed.

After recording more than 25,000 aspen carvings in several states, I can say that for many herders approaching a tree with knife in hand amounted to a high point of the day, like their happy hour. They were about to document something import-ant to them. The aspens were like their diaries, their confidants. Some carved statements that speak to their high sense of humor. One new immigrant arrived in Columbia Basin, and the camp tender took him to a place with nothing but thousands of sheep. He was told: This is going to be your camp for a couple of weeks. The herder said that the so-called camp amounted to a tent, a dog, and some provisions. The following day the new sheepherder went to a tree and carved this in Spanish: "Hotel Suddenly, still open three days a year."

High up on Copper Mountain, above the Goicoechea Sheep Camp, in northern Elko County, I found the following aspen carv-ing dated 1915 with an amazing message by JZ, which later I found out was Jose Zaracondegui, originally from the Bizkaian coast:

Len neskatan (Before I used to chase girls)
Oin arditan (Now I am chasing sheep)
Beti amesetan (I am always dreaming)

Zaracondegui, who was a bertsolari (improvisational poet), spelled out in concise and beautiful poetry what a sheepherder's life was all about: Chasing sheep but with a lot of time left for dreaming. So, when the herder told his children that his life was not "interesting," what he really meant was that he spent a lot of time dreaming, which is a very personal activity. All along he had been dreaming of a future life in town among other human beings. Approximately 5 to 10 percent of the herders have no regrets and confess to having enjoyed their lives on the range. That still leaves a lot of unhappy people, but some of them went on to own sheep and ranches, so what is there to gripe about?

In my opinion, it was sad that most ex-herders decided not to share with their children their good and bad times in the mountains; by doing so, a lot of history was sent to limbo. There were exceptions, however. I am sure that Joe Sallaberry of Turlock, California, was one of them. With the help of his two daughters, he published the story of his life. Mattin Etchamendy of Bakersfield, California, was another, and he too published his story in the Basque dialect of his hometown Ezterentzubi. The well-known Salt Lake City musician Jean Flesher is translating Etchamendy's story. Arriaundiaga, born in Lekeitio, Bizkaia, wrote in the 1930s about his sheepherder life in Idaho; he dressed like a cowboy, packed two pistols, and had shoot-outs with real buckaroos. These three men certainly have no regrets about their years on the range.

There were good times at the sheep camp, but perhaps the father thought they were not suitable to share with his children. What happens in sheep camp, stays in sheep camp. Such stories will remain untold until the audience is right and familiar. No stranger should expect to get the whole scoop from a Basque in just a couple of interviews.

The Not-So-Lonely Sheepherder

First came the radio, then the pickup truck, and the two changed considerably the sheepherder's life. Before that, there were horses that allowed them to get around and get together, albeit for a few hours. Some of them did not have horses, but a mile was nothing for a young person used to walking miles every day.

Some sheepherders have no qualms about telling stories, especially while eating and drinking among familiar faces. It was not always boring: We had some good times too, to paraphrase.

Loneliness was real but relative. As one put it, the sheepherders also had their own happy hour. I had to laugh. Basques need little excuse to get together for food, drink, and banter. It's true that certain things are best left unmentioned when the audience is not intimate, but eventually they do tell. The phrase often heard that there are few secrets in the Basque community is very true.

On the range, any day could be a Saturday or a Sunday—all you needed was the impulse, a horse, or just two strong legs to cover a few miles to meet at a neighbor's sheep camp with a couple of other herders. The sheep would be bedded down, and until early morning there was no need to be with them. Summertime in the high country can be exhilarating, with nature at its best, when herders rightfully felt like "lords of the range," as one author put it. Who was there to oppose them?

The story one "famous" Bizkaian herder used to tell after he returned home is totally befitting here: He claimed that in Nevada he became the boxing champion of the world. His old friends in Europe were amazed by the news and pressed for details, and he was happy to oblige. He said, "One day while herding sheep I climbed a high mountain and at the top of my lungs I shouted that if anyone wanted to fight me, now was the time. I listened for an answer and hearing none I repeated the challenge three times to be sure, but nobody showed up, so I became the champion."

These were the "good time junctures" that you catch when you visit sheep camps or spend enough time talking to herders at their own level and in their own language. While eating and drinking—without the two there is no conversation—the two main topics at these "happy hour" gatherings were herding and women. Herding was by far the biggest issue, though I also heard them say that they talked mostly about women at the sheep camps when they were among sheep, and about sheep when they were in town among men and women. In Elko, many people will tell you this is totally true.

Being alone in the mountains was far from being boring if you knew what to do. For some who didn't have any previous

Goicoechea's herders enjoying their "happy hour," 1968.

experience with sheep, it was a liminal time: a time to sink or swim. Men under twenty had no previous experience frying an egg, much less washing their own clothes. They had to learn in a hurry the chores their mothers used to do for them at home in Europe. Some herders took to cooking with gusto, like having coffee routinely before 5 a.m., watching the sunrise. But washing dishes? Not so much.

Older herders often offered help to the newly arrived, though I also heard that they did not. Old-timers believed that the young ones would learn quicker from personal experience and through suffering, which is an intriguing Basque methodology. These new experiences weren't all bad—far from it—because later when some of them got married, their cooking experience translated into their taking over that task that forever had been the duty of wives.

The radio changed sheep camp life by bringing it closer to the rest of the world. I have heard many herders declaring their enthusiastic anticipation of the *Basque Radio Program* on Sundays on KELK of Elko, and the one broadcast from Boise. One or two herders told me they had to dance when hearing the music—they could not stay put. These were the weekly sheepherder happy hours.

Before radio, the most common pastime was singing, whistling, and bertso-making (poetry). Even after the radio, whenever two bertsolari got together, poetry improvisation was instinctive and attracted an eager audience. After all, it was one of the favorite entertainments in rural communities of the Basque Country. It did not matter if the poet's message carried a warning. The camaraderie of the occasion made up for it.

This is what happened in a California sheep camp in the 1920s, something that could have happened in Elko as well. The bertsolari poet, fortified by companionship and food and drink, felt inspired, and in sixteen verses he counseled his compatriots on several relevant topics. He admonished them about the dangers they might encounter in town interacting not only with Americans but also with their own countrymen—hard to believe.

As soon as you land in town, they will invite you to a drink, then to the mus card game. At first, they will let you win, but they are in cahoots with your partner, and eventually you will be sorry you ever went to town. You will return to the mountains *larru gorri* (without clothes) after losing all your wages.

This poet probably spoke from personal experience and though his message was not very entertaining, it was educational and instructive. These get-togethers were probably repeated in other towns and sheep camps, including in Northern Nevada, but this historian missed that train. Another frequent pastime in sheep camps was card games. Wherever Basques get together, in town or in the mountains, food and drink follow and a mus card game is not far behind. The only options are playing for fun or for money. Thus, for the young herders the hours passed happily until the hint of a new day in the eastern sky told them it was time to break camp and hurry back to their respective herds.

Jess Goñi, "Naparra," the bertsolari who is well known in Elko, is fond of reminiscing about his sheepherder years in Idaho, when he and Jesus Urkidi sang improvised poetry many weekends and for years at the Basque restaurant in Rupert, Idaho, to a packed audience of fifty to sixty people. And if the bar was too far? No problem—the poets could still sing in the hills for their fellow herders.

The other great change maker and isolation breaker was the pickup truck. It shrank the sheepherder's geography in a way that the horse never could. I've been told of sheep owners rationing gasoline or taking the keys away so that the herders couldn't go to town, especially on weekends. There had likely been escapades before, and probably after as well, as one aspen tree carving some sixty miles south of Elko seems to show: "We cannot hold our dicks any longer; tonight, we are going to the whores. Hurrah!" A trip like that would be unthinkable without a pickup.

Those working in the California Valley often herded in fenced-in areas with traffic and towns all around. Even in Idaho, towns were generally closer than in Elko, and the trips from the sheep camp may have been more manageable. Only the cooperation of an obliging camp tender—the man usually in control of the pickup—was needed. Securing that, herders could sneak into the nearest town, away from the *damn* sheep, to have a few drinks in a bar—any bar would do—in Jiggs or in Mountain City, for example.

The point here is to shed light into the never-ending litany of sheepherder loneliness found in literature. It's time to talk about the occasional breaks they enjoyed—which I call happy hour—after all, happy hour in town doesn't last forever either.

At this point I am going to take the reader 600 miles away from Elko to Parker, Arizona, where I spent the 1970–1971 winter. To my surprise, I discovered that it was sheep country. I met about fifteen sheepherders wintering their sheep in lettuce fields that had been harvested. From them I learned that Idaho Secretary of State and sheepman Pete Cenarrusa, among others, had his sheep some fifty miles south in the general area of Blythe, California. I was used to only isolated sheep camps in Elko County, and it was surprising to find that the sheepherders in Parker worked and lived near populated areas. The herders could and did go to bars and sometimes even to the movies. In certain bars it wasn't difficult to find other pastimes, such as the presence of Hispanic women, with whom most herders could interact in Spanish. Therefore, we can say that not all sheepherding jobs were created equally.

Finally, we seldom think of the sheepherder's responsibility. We know that he was young, full of life, and loved company. But the rancher had entrusted him with considerable property: 1,500 ewes plus their lambs, no less. I think the Basque sheepherder was very aware that the value of his sheep amounted to more money than he ever had, and caring for them was his utmost priority. It was unlikely that he would try to go to town every weekend, even if he could. It might endanger his charges and jeopardize his job to boot.

Despite the "Fokken cheep" and such messages I read on aspens, bragging about not having lost a single sheep in the high country was a standard claim I remember hearing. Some owners gave out extra pay to such herders and to those who raised the heaviest lambs. That was something to be proud of. It was a happy hour.

CHAPTER 6

Life on a Remote Ranch

You jump on a horse and ride ten to forty miles a day on the open range. If hungry you go to a sheep camp and eat, even spend the night. The same in a cattle camp. In the wild country 100 miles from nowhere, when you find someone, you appreciate that we are human beings. These are the thoughts and words of Bob Heguy, who grew up north of Elko in the Nevada outback. Life was very different on an isolated and remote ranch. "You were snowbound most years from November to April," said Fred Beitia Jr., raised on a ranch in Charleston, Nevada. (Today Charleston is a place, not a town.)

Ranch life in the late 1800s and early 1900s had few amenities. Electricity was not available and indoor plumbing was a luxury until the 1930s, even for the well-to-do ranch families; outhouses were the rule. Telephones became available much earlier than electricity, first generated by diesel power. Houses were not well insulated, and the wood stove had to be fed through the night to counter the brutal winter temperatures. Extra wool blankets were luxuries and necessities.

Some Basque families lived on ranches built quickly from scratch at great sacrifice, mostly of lumber, which was in short supply in Nevada. It must have been a shock to those accustomed to living in solid stone houses in the Basque Country, where wooden houses were history. Most Basque-ranch families, however, lived in homes built by some earlier owner. Cabins found in sheep camps, on the other hand, were mostly built by the sheepherders themselves.

Constantina Bengoechea, better known as Mrs. Gabica, arrived in Winnemucca in the early 1900s and died there as a centenarian. Her husband brought her from Europe during a cold Northern Nevada winter to live in a half-built ranch house. Like Angela Odriozola Aguirre of Elko, she spent many days and nights crying and would have returned home in a heartbeat, if only she could have. We can almost bet that a few other women in Elko County endured similar circumstances.

Such living conditions were particularly hard on pregnant women and babies. In 1900, the average lifespan in the West extended from mid-forties to fifties, and although the Basques usually exceeded that average, in these parts of Nevada one had to be extra careful to make it to a ripe age. A walk among the Elko cemetery headstones can be an eye opener on many lives cut short.

On these developing early ranches, backbreaking work from sunup to sundown was the norm. It was no place for lazy people. It was usually Old Man Winter, as if taking pity on humans, that forced them to slow down, giving them time to think. But if you had sheep, neither winter nor summer made a difference; you had to care for them and feed them. Elko's cold climate provided no winter feed for sheep, which were trailed south to the slightly warmer desert lowlands for several months, a trek that could last several months each way.

Once winter was over, springtime was a busy—busier—time at a ranch: fix fences, shoe horses, repair irrigation ditches, and get ready for the brief summer. As April approached, pregnant ewes were ready to drop their precious lambs, through which the herder expected to earn most of his income. But springtime weather in Elko County can be unpredictable, and, in some years, you could be lambing in a blizzard, endangering the lives of the newborn lambs. (I have witnessed snow on the 4th of July and on the 23rd of August in Elko County.) Lambing required extra help because if you lost too many of them due to bad weather or the predation of coyotes, you were not going to make money in the fall. Experienced herders made all the difference during lambing.

Summer months were just as busy—if that were possible—but

supplying the outlying herders once a week was the most important task. Most provisions for herders had to be purchased in town, but small operators strove to save money by growing as much of their own food as possible. Most immigrant sheep owners believed in frugality in earnest but the next generation not so much. Horses were essential for most ranch work, such as haying and of course riding, but they too had to be fed. In the fall, shipping the lambs was always a happy time for both sheep owners and herders—the owners got paid, and thus they could afford to pay the herders. Before the 1950s, some outfits paid only once a year, right after shipping the lambs.

Female Chores

Meanwhile, life at the ranch house was mostly the domain of women. They had to do all the housework, of course, and laundry was one of the most onerous tasks. A "large tub [was placed] on the kitchen stove" for hot water, the technology of the day. It would take several loads of soapy tub, and "[t]he final rinse was [done] in the creek," said Mary Urriola. What if you did not have a creek close by? Water made all the difference in Nevada's desert climate. Lugging water from anywhere was a chore, often reserved for teenagers. The Beitias did not raise much of a garden, for lack of water, which was an anomaly for most Basque ranchers.

Food was even more important than laundry. Women had to prepare food for winter, make chorizos, and can vegetables for a family to survive. For that they had to have a large garden spot, fertilized with plenty of manure to grow onions, carrots, cabbage, potatoes, leeks, and so on to carry the family through the frigid months. They tried to raise tomatoes and peppers (essential for chorizo making), but it was a struggle in Elko's high desert climate. Raising one or two pigs around the garden was easier and necessary.

If that was not enough, some women did much more, like Elko's Ana Sorhondo Hachquet, one of the few Basque women who lived in the sheep camp with her husband (something Hispanic women in New Mexico did traditionally). "I did the work of a man," Ana told me laconically.

FOOD

Winters were long, cold, and dreary, and because of the elevation many of these ranches were snowbound for months. We're lucky to have accounts from several men and women who grew up in those conditions. Raised on a ranch in Jack Creek, Steve Urriola gave the following eyewitness account:

> Ranch food consisted in killing a heifer and hang it in the barn for drying and to freeze. You cut a piece of it for the week. You grew potatoes, onions, and hang cabbages upside down. Before winter sets in, you go to town to buy supplies: 100 lbs. of beans, 200 lbs. of sugar, 500–600 lbs. of flour, and dry fruit in 5 lb. kegs. We had milk at home, so butter as well, with lots of bread baked daily to fill the stomach. We had chickens and eggs. Toward spring meat would be low, so we kept a few sheep to slaughter then. Sheep keep fat better. We also ate non-laying chickens during this time.

Some ranches had the advantage of a creek nearby. Running water anywhere in Nevada is better than gold. Back in the old days, creeks like Jack Creek were full of fish, and ranch boys knew how to catch them. Fresh fish was good for you and supplied a change from the everyday diet. Women dipped the fish in egg batter first, then in breadcrumbs, and fried it in plenty of oil or fat. That is how Livia Orbe Zaga used to cook and serve fish in Jiggs.

Florence Erquiaga Black, one of the early dance instructors in Elko, grew up in Denio, a hamlet in the Nevada/Oregon border, with thirteen other siblings. Their mother baked fourteen loaves of bread at once in a big Mississippi stove. The family butchered two pigs a year, had four to five cows for milk, had chickens, made chorizos, and cured hams. Furthermore, they did a lot of canning for winter meals. They picked apples and made them last through the winter (*sagar ximelak*, dried-up apples), like in the Old Country.

Already we have seen examples (see chapter 4) of enterprising ranchers like those in the Lamoille area who tried to replicate some of the foods, such as apples, pears, cherries, and strawberries, found in the Basque Country. Ramon Lugea, for example, made *sagardo* (apple cider) and cheese. Homemade bread was a necessity, and we can assume that baking it was one of the main chores ranch women engaged in.

Simple Lifestyle

The greater lesson we learn from these ranch stories is that life was very spartan and work hard and constant, but if endeavor did not always bring success, at least there was the satisfaction of having tried. Mary Urriola said that her family grew up sturdy and healthy with strong neighborly ties. She had only one dress, made larger so she could wear it longer—at least two years. By the third year, it was well worn out. Her mom made a blouse for her to look more feminine, but she did not care much about it; boys and girls wore bib overalls and played together. At these ranches, there was no room for idle people. Even children of well-off ranchers had chores to do, such as pulling weeds in the garden, gathering eggs, taking care of the chickens, and even milking cows, said Josephine Saval.

Many other Basque-ranch women likely did the same to survive the early pioneering days in remote places. In fact, the fare of these families at their ranches, though more varied, was not that different from what sheepherders ate most days at their camps. We have enough such accounts (I have seen and tasted what the herders ate), but the inventory that Grace van Dalfsen Erskine provides is a little different: spaghetti, macaroni, beans, rice, flour, canned veggies, canned milk, lots of garlic, potatoes and onions, a variety of dried fruit, wine, and two–three pounds of tobacco. She added that the herders killed deer for variety from mutton. Her list seems to be an improvement on the diet most Basque herders ate. Grace was married into the Griswold family and took an interest in the Griswold Sheep Co. She briefly described the inside of a sheep wagon also: a twelve-inch diameter pot-bellied stove, a bed, two chairs, an icebox, and a table. She wrote that Griswold had a Portuguese cook in camp at Spruce Mountain, Elko County.

CHAPTER 7

The Forgotten Basque Woman?

Not here with us contributors and coauthors. Let me begin by saying the obvious: The historical omission of the role of women. Until the twentieth century, 50 percent of the human population, women, had little or no history. A woman had to be a goddess, a queen, a courtesan, a murderer, or a saint to deserve the historians' attention. This glaring absence applies to the Basque women of Elko as well.

When all the attention is on sheep and sheepherders, it is easy to overlook women, because 99.9 percent of the sheepherders were men. Sol Silen did have photos of married couples, men and women, and families, but his undivided attention was on the men who had sheep, cattle, and ranches. Some of their spouses were attractive and deserving of praise, but none were prominent.

More recently, other writers did not fare much better than Sol Silen. Douglass and Bilbao's *Amerikanuak* covers a lot of geography, covers the Basques in North and South America, and has an extensive index, but *women* are nowhere to be found. Jeronima Echeverria came to the rescue, blazing the trail in *Home Away from Home*, in which she dealt with Basque hotels. When dealing with hotelkeepers, homemakers, cooks, and cleaning and laundry workers, you cannot ignore women. Echeverria not only gave them their due; she put them on a well-deserved pedestal.

Nearly 100 percent of the Basque women in Elko were wives and mothers, and caretakers, cooks, housekeepers, and certainly all-around good neighbors. In fact, it seemed like the immigrant women came out from a single mold, that of their mothers and grandmothers in Europe. I did not find any colorful figures among them, such as the notorious Susie Raper, the horsewoman from Tuscarora, for example. Therefore, little attention was given to them.

Naturally, life today is not like it was a century ago, and there is a lot more diversity among the younger generation of women, the majority of whom do not live on ranches but in town. Though they may be of Basque descent, their daily lives are like that of many other women in Elko. They work outside the home; they may be single or married to a non-Basque, belong to the club, or not, go to a Basque restaurant, or not. But they probably have Basque friends with whom they socialize. As Sara Sabala Ghrist said, "Basques love to get together, swap stories, and find out we are all related."

EQUAL?

Not even close, if we read the extant literature. Even today women are still fighting for equal rights in our own country. But my query is: What if that literature had been written by mostly women, rather than mostly men? It would be very different. Not so many stories of battles and of wars of conquest. Fewer male gods and male heroes. More stories about children and their care, no doubt, and about women's responsibilities and other issues, such as pregnancy and giving birth, cooking, sewing, and mothers, grandmothers, and queens. It would contain a lot of old stories and legends. In other words, if would be a very different history.

Women are mentioned throughout the present study, but we—the authors—too depend on earlier histories and cannot escape present reality. Some observers view Basque society as matriarchal: Women are not only equal, but perhaps a notch above that. Indeed, there are documents—written by men—that to an extent vouch for that. But if you ask the women themselves, they may question it. They will surely point at their never-ending chores. We often heard women say: I come home from work, and I cannot sit down, relax, or have a drink, like men usually do. I must keep working, cooking, cleaning, laundering, or whatever. And who takes care of the children?

It is the old story of division of labor that could be—or is—unfair to women. However, that division makes Basque women unquestionably the queens of the kitchen and in charge of the household, and most everything concerning the children and their welfare. They teach children to walk and talk; they take over their education more often than men do. Many oversee the day-to-day household finances as well.

The Basque community in Elko is a mixture of cultures in a state of flux, the old from Europe and the one they encountered in the US. If both husband and wife are immigrants, there may be less dissension than when one of the consorts is non-Basque. Even when both are Basque, but one is immigrant and the other American-born, arguments are more likely to occur. We can say that after witnessing the many divorces of the sheepherders who married non-Basques.

In this sense, it is remarkable the agreement among several American-born Basque women, who advise their Elko daughters, "Don't marry a Basque." Should we be surprised, or shocked even? This doesn't happen today in 2025 but did a few decades back, and the reason appeared to be that Old Country men were not particularly undesirable; rather, they were set in their old ways and not sensitive enough to the American reality. Was that one of the reasons why a number of Basque women married Italian men? Or vice-versa, Italians married them because of the culinary skills that Basque women were known for? I have not met one individual, male or female, who told me that their mother was not a good cook. On the contrary: Without exception, I heard nothing but praise for their mothers' cooking.

HOTEL MAIDS

Young Basque women arriving in the US in the early 1900s came to get married, because their other likely alternative in Europe was to become a nun or to stay single. About every one of them in Elko started out by working at one of the Basque hotels in town. Many already had a contact or a relative guiding them to their destination, which was a necessity because they had no money and no knowledge of English. What they had in abundance were the skills needed by an all-around maid unafraid of work. We are reminded of Matilde Eizaguirre's fortunate encounter with her future husband, Pete Jauregui, at the Elko train depot. She went to the Telescope Hotel, where she started working right away. That is how it was for many immigrant-Basque women, until they were *swept off their feet* by some young man, often born very close to her birthplace.

Basque hotel maids were seldom paid wages. For most, the arrangement was *tripa-truke* (work for room and board), and they could count on long hours and short sleep nights. Teresa (born 1911) and her sister Anita Jauregui grew up at the Star Hotel, and they provide eye-witness accounts about these newly arrived women, most of them about twenty years old.

At the Star Hotel there was always plenty of domestic work to do, such as sweeping, cleaning, and kitchen-related chores; cooking; and washing dishes three times a day; however, laundry was the hardest task with the rudimentary equipment—or none—back then. It took two strong women to wring the sheets and hang them to dry. Blankets were heavier and harder to wring dry. But where? Elko has brutal winters, with many days of temperatures well below freezing. The kitchen was the only warm place available. The Star made their own chorizos that had to hang dry for a week or more, but where? Again, the kitchen was the only warm place. We can assume there were times when chorizos and sheets hung together. The Jauregui sisters, as they told their stories, joked about the delicious smell of the sheets.

From their account, we can understand, too, why the sheets were changed once a week by alternating the rooms. It was nearly impossible to wash and to dry the sheets more often. The Star had twenty-two rooms and two bathrooms, so chamber pots were de rigueur in each room. Emptying them three times every day was another task for the women.

There were some positive aspects in the lives of hotel maids: The atmosphere was thoroughly Basque, as if they had never left their hometown except now they were hearing Basque dialects they had never heard before. The hotels were mostly crowded in winter, with idle sheepherders in town. Whenever the boarding-house owners hosted a party, a birthday, or a wedding, music and dancing went with it, the maids were the first in the circle danc-ing and the last ones out. They had youth, energy, and joy, which were also good for business.

Many women married rather quickly, and children and house-keeping usually followed. According to the Jauregui sisters, many Basque women who arrived early in the US lived on remote ranches with their husbands, while a few settled in town. Unfortunately, history has provided us with little information on either group.

A Ranch Woman's Day

In chapter 6 we already covered a similar topic, but we need to look at the subject more broadly. Housewives, whether in town or on a ranch, made history like everyone else; it is preposterous to think that these women did nothing of interest or significance. Let us begin with mothers giving birth and caring for children. We take it for granted, even though it is the most fundamental to human existence. Now consider doing it in 1900. The mothers often gave birth in Basque hotels; those on isolated ranches were lucky if a friendly female neighbor helped them. The doctor may be sixty miles away, or if a blizzard were blowing outside, forget it. Florence "Flossie" Erquiaga Black's mother had fourteen chil-dren and lived 100 miles from the nearest doctor, so she deliv-ered her own children. Early on, many Basque families averaged around four children—fewer than their parents had back home—but after the 1960s, when most Basques lived in town, that number was drastically reduced.

I have walked around the headstones in the Elko cemetery sev-eral times looking for Basque surnames. You realize that a century ago, life was precarious and short. So many infants buried there! JG, for example, had four stillborn babies and three who made it to adulthood. Other headstones tell the story of the mother dying after giving birth.

We can hardly imagine what a woman's day was like a century and half ago on a faraway ranch, with no indoor plumbing and no electricity. You had to feed the wood stove all day every day for cooking and during the winter for heating, as the stove was the only source of warmth in the subzero nights. Dry firewood was a daily necessity. Water had to be carried in from a well if you were fortunate enough to have one near the house; if not, you had to fetch it from a spring or the creek, often a woman's chore. Nevada is not a friendly place for year-round running creeks. Frank Aguirre of Ryndon had seven siblings, and he says that they had to pack in water for a quarter mile.

Shock at Arrival

When I was a boy in Europe, I remember one phrase I used to hear, "Amerikan be txakurrek ortozik," which means "Even in America the dogs [still] go barefoot." This statement usually came from the mouths of some homebound sheepherders from the US, perhaps disappointed after all the hype. Constantina Bengoetxea would certainly agree. The young wife came to Orovada, Nevada, where her husband had a sheep ranch around 1900. The house was under construction, without windows, and it was winter when she arrived. Freezing wind blew in mercilessly through the openings, though they tried to stop it with bed sheets. "Nora etorri naz ba ni?" (What kind of a place have I come to?), she would tell herself often. She was ready to turn around and go back to Europe, "If only I had been in Gernika, so that I could walk home," she told me in 1992.

Angela Odriozola Aguirre arrived in Elko in 1923 and could thoroughly agree with Constantina/Mrs. Gavica, even though she had relatives in town. "If I had money to buy a ticket back home, I would have gone right back," she said. Angela did not think much of Elko with cows in the street. She cried for a month. There were 1,500 to 2,000 people in Elko then, and you could say it was a rough frontier town. You could also say that Angela became a frontier woman; she had to. She raised eight children on a ranch in Ryndon, and when she became an American citizen in 1958 the judge asked her to "Sign here, Republican"; thereafter she always voted Republican.

When we think of a ranch, we reckon it is a man's domain, but much of it revolves around the house, which is the domain of women, the wife, and others. The others may have included hired-female helpers—by better-off ranchers—but more often they were relatives. A big garden was essential to pull the family through the long winter months, and that meant lots of canning and other methods to preserve food. Onions, potatoes, and carrots could be stored in the cellar. Often, these were female chores.

I am not suggesting that men did not help, however. They surely helped make chorizos, something many Basque families prepared for winter protein and for a quick meal or snack. Several ladies shared how difficult of a job it was cleaning intestines, which are necessary for chorizos. It is long and tedious work that requires plenty of scarce running water. The slaughtering of pigs, sheep, and heifers was strictly a male task, but women collected their blood that was saved for making blood sausages.

For the most part, women's lives were stationary, tied down to their homes. Their husbands might travel but wives did not, because of the children. For most women, even those living in town, life involved a long list of chores to do: cleaning, cooking, laundering, mending clothes, and so on. All this, besides raising children.

Some women did much more if that were possible, as Ana Sorhondo Hachquet told me in 1990. Born in 1898 in Aldude into a family of ten, she was the youngest. She came to the US in 1925 and was working at the Overland Hotel in Elko when she met Martin Hachquet. They were married the following year, and the two ran sheep in Elko and Eureka counties for many years. She lived at sheep camp with her husband, coming to town only to deliver the babies. After she moved to town, she boarded ranch boys and girls who were attending high school. Ana became naturalized in 1946. Her husband died in 1960, and she passed away thirty-eight years later as a centenarian. I guess wielding an axe to break ice four inches thick in the creek to water the sheep, which Ana did often, may be the recipe for a long life.

Mixed Marriages

Among the Basques arriving before or soon after 1900, we hardly see intermarriages. Basques wed Basques because Basque women were available. This pattern changed after World War I, and marriage to non-Basques accelerated when the Immigration Act of 1924 that US Congress passed established national quotas. There were also other reasons as well. Women living in town, for example, or those more educated, were not attracted to ranch life and to Basque men working there, so they married non-Basques (This happened in the Basque Country itself starting in the 1960s, when women refused to marry farm-owning bachelors). Today, of course, it is a different story. Those full-blooded Basques who marry another full-blooded Basque constitute a minority. But a part-Basque still partners with another part-Basque more often than not. Basques served in the military during the two World Wars, and after returning, especially after World War II, they were more likely to move and to marry non-Basques. Speaking of mixed marriages, the following is one woman's story. "My name is Georgina A. M., and I was born in a mining camp in Nevada between Austin and Fallon. My parents were Bizkaians and we didn't speak any English until school. We prayed and sung in Basque. Mom was a cousin to Jimmy Jausoro's mom, a Mallea. Mom had wonderful voice; Uncle Juan played the flute [*txistu*] and we played *pandero* [tambourine]. Dad was a great dancer, and my son played accordion. I met my husband, an Italian rancher, in Fallon. He was fifty-two when he died; I have been a widow for forty-four years."

There is something intrinsically healthy and natural, and undeniably attractive, in Georgina's lifestyle recollections; she died in Elko at age ninety-three.

In Elko we find quite a few Basque-Italian marriages, more than, say, Basque-Anglo ones. The reason could be religion but also some culture, like food and drink. For example, both nationalities are bread-heavy (in the form of pasta for Italians), they both use garlic and tomatoes, and they both drink wine. Anita Anacabe Franzoia in chapter 20 tells us of such Basque-Italian marriages, though we find fewer Basque men marrying Italian women. Frank Aguirre says that when Basques married Italians, they called them "Basco Wasps" ("Wops"?), and it could indicate a little resentment.

Earlier I mentioned cultural differences among immigrants and American-born Basques. Such differences emerged even among the American-born, and they had to do with education and lifestyle. Teresa and Anita Jauregui were college-educated and confessed that they wanted to marry Basque men, but their lack of educational level was a drawback. Besides, most were working on ranches helping their parents, while the sisters lived in town, Anita said.

> There wasn't much to choose from. We both dated Martin Gastanaga, and we played with the Corta Boys, Pete and Guy, all the time as kids. Teresa said, I think my parents would have liked me to marry one of the Cortas. They wanted us to marry in church, which we did, but neither of us married a Catholic. . . . Our parents had a big gathering at the Elko Hotel and at the El Dorado on Gabon Gaba (Christmas Eve) when they invited the whole town. You could meet people then, but later when we were teenagers, we had less chance. We had an uncle, Philip Echegaray, who played piano, danced, and sang with everybody. He was full of fun. He was a popular bachelor.

Angela Odriozola Aguirre had her own priorities when it came to marriage. One day she pointed at a nicely dressed woman and told her son Frank, "That is the kind of girl you want," and Frank said, "I agreed, and married one."

Larry Moiola had an Italian father and a Basque mother, and he married a Basque. He explains the Basque-Italian marriages that abound in Elko: "Basques and Italians like to party, and they put on a good party." They also like food, and the Star offered some Italian food, like ravioli, which Larry said was good enough. One consequence of Basque-Italian marriages was that the children would grow up mostly monolingual with just English. No Basque. No Italian.

Hotel and Motel Queens

Women were the queens, who took excellent care of the hotel business and its customers, and with little fanfare. Jeronima Echeverria already called attention to these extraordinary women who worked untold hours every day, especially on weekends. Elko had its share of them, with Matilde Eizaguirre perhaps the queen of them all (but only because we have more information on her than on any other). And yet when it comes to the Star Hotel, it is her husband, Pete Jauregui, we hear about. We are fortunate that it is their daughters, Teresa and Anita, who set the record straight for us. According to them, it was their mother, more so than their father, who was all business. She exuded energy and she had the brains. She was not meant to be a housewife. "Mom was boss, but dad was king," the sisters declared politely, yet cheerfully. Like saying: Mom was the CEO, and Dad was the president. So now we know the real story behind the often-repeated tale of Pete Jauregui, who gets all the glory when we talk about the Star Hotel. From what the daughters tell us, it was their mother, Matilde, who in most cases was the driving force. The father would have been happy to retire and go fishing, they observe, but their mother was never happy being a homemaker.

After they left the Star Hotel for the second time in 1942, they could have retired, yet she was not ready. They bought a grocery store, the International Market, though that venture lasted only a few years. They sold it but she could not stay idle, so they built the Elko Hotel and hired a manager to run it. Again, they had that for three years, because it was during the Depression, and they lost money. The Elko Hotel left them with a bad experience, but they nevertheless decided to build the first nightclub in town with a cocktail lounge, bar, and dancing. To run their nightclub, they hired Johnny and Fernando Arrascada.

After that they bought the Masonic Hall, then started another hotel with a restaurant and a bar with a few rooms upstairs. They named it El Dorado, and Pete was the bartender. The dining room at El Dorado could seat thirty-five to forty-five people, but business was not good. About the same time during the Spanish Civil War, the Nazis on behalf of Francisco Franco's Nationalists bombed Gernika, where Pete's brother Tony had returned from Elko. The town was destroyed, and Tony lost everything. The Jaureguis brought him and his wife over, and they worked at the El Dorado. They also sponsored Pete's sister Mercedes Jauregui Lostra and her brother Tony Jauregui to the US. Tony was a mechanic, and Mercedes was a waitress.

Teresa and Anita said that their mom was bossy; also, cooks would quit, and she then had to do the cooking herself. Francisca Lostra was one cook, and she was wonderful.

> So, our parents sold El Dorado and built a motel, The Travelers, on the corner of Idaho and 12th Street. Motels were a big thing then and Elko didn't have many. Mom saw that motels were making money, and they had not at El Dorado. They had the motel for two years. Matilde would be on call 24/7. She would get out of bed and rent a room to someone showing up in the middle of the night. Dad was afraid but she was not. Mom even helped clean the rooms. Later they built several more motels: El Neva on Idaho Street and 7th. The builder was Sauveur Elizagoyen, and after a short time they sold it back to him. In 1967 the Jaureguis, Elizagoyen, and his sister Leone (married to Leo Morandi), built the Marquis Motor Inn, the finest on Idaho Street.

Leone was another motel queen, and she and Leo ran the motel until 1984, after which Matilde's business career ended. She then stayed home and went fishing with Pete, and when he died she lived with her daughter Teresa, cooking until her 100th year and lasting four more years. Teresa died in 1912 at age 101, and her sister Anita also made it to beyond a centenarian.

The roles played by Pete and Matilde are not an anomaly among the Basques. It is not rare that the mother is the mover and the shaker. Gregoria Garteiz may have been one too. She was some-one Matilde knew well because they were both in the hotel busi-ness, married to Dan Sabala of the Overland Hotel. A trustworthy local source told me that at least two other Basque women she knew in Elko fit Matilde's model: Margaret Olave, the second wife of Joe Anacabe, and Mary Yspizua Etcheverry (also known as Mary Jayo or "Erreketa."). Both were immigrants who increased their considerable holdings by buying property.

Charlene Sabala Shobe was more ambivalent about her own parents: "We thought Mom was the boss, but we found out Dad was." Denise Arregui Lopategui added, "We women are the hub of the house, but he wears the crown."

There were other motel managers, like Marguerite Odiaga Ozamis. After running the Star Hotel for some years, she and her husband, Domingo Ozamis, invested in a motel, the Stam-pede, built in the 1960s and located at the western entrance of downtown Elko.

PACKING SCHOOL LUNCHES

This item came up in too many a conversation to be ignored. We have seen that many American-born Basque kids spoke no English when they started school. Pete Bengoechea, born at a ranch in Coffee Creek and a Humboldt County commissioner, was one. In 1990 he told me that his imaginative teacher put him between two cousins who already spoke some English and acted as interpreters for him. Such ad hoc methodologies alleviated somewhat the already-tough teaching job. But in general, it took several years before these mostly ranch kids caught up with their Anglo-speaking mates. Parents who took a proactive role in their children's education made a huge difference, while the children of parents who cared less took longer to catch up.

Many kids who lived on faraway ranches attended one-room, state-sanctioned schools. Even though the buildings were usually centrally located, some ranches could be miles away. The only available transportation then was a horse, and in that sense the Basques were no different from other kids. Fred Beitia Jr., of Charleston, was one of those who rode a horse to school miles away. The Sustacha kids similarly rode horses to school in Lamoille, and so did most others who lived out of town. Basque mothers had to make sure that their children had adequate clothing for the ride, which in the winter could pose a serious problem. In some cases, part of the ride took place in the dark or semidarkness, when the kids carried lights.

Another interesting detail about Basque kids attending school concerned lunches. The mothers made sure that their children did not go hungry, so they tried to pack nutritious lunches, prepared with whatever was available at home. But what they were packing was so "foreign" from what other kids were eating at school, that Basque kids were made fun of. Imagine the predicament: Not speaking good English was enough of a handicap; they didn't need to be embarrassed about lunches. This happened to the Lugea sisters—Mercedes, Elena, and Mariana—attending primary school in Lamoille. The daughters went to school with delicious ham and bean sandwiches that their mother, Grace, prepared for them, only to be made fun of by other kids.

An interview with Ken Barrenchea corroborated that this was not an isolated and unique case. He and his siblings attended Fallon school, and their mother packed lamb sandwiches with big chunks of homemade bread. Their schoolmates made fun of them, simply because they were not eating peanut butter and jelly sandwiches. More than once the Barrencheas chose to go hungry rather than face ridicule, and they would chuck the sandwiches in the ditch before arriving at school. It would not be hard to discover that other Elko Basque kids experienced similar reactions to their sandwiches.

BASQUE CLUBS AND WOMEN

Having been around several Basque clubs, I know that women work as hard as men do, whether during the festival or at any other event. I bring this up because in the fifty-seven years that the Elko Club has been functioning, I see that only three women have been chosen presidents versus twenty-five men. My question is, why?

One woman I interviewed said that women's voices in the club do not carry the same weight as that of men. A woman offers an idea, and nobody takes it seriously, she said. A man does the same thing, and he is acknowledged. But Cassandra Torrealday, an active member, does not think the club is sexist. "If you have good, solid ideas, they will listen," she says. So why the disparity? Women certainly are capable of the job. Do we doubt that someone like Matilde Eizaguirre Jauregui could handle it?

One board member said that women simply do not sign up to run for president. Why not? Is it because it is a tough job requiring long hours, and women have less free time than men, as hinted already? Possibly. There is no question that it takes commitment to run a Basque club, because the president knows that he and a couple of other colleagues will end up carrying the heaviest workload. That is usually the way it turns out. One Elko woman said that, indeed, men spend more hours running the club.

Immigrant women never have been afraid of work. They used to be the ones who usually peeled twenty pounds of potatoes for the lamb stew, prepared the veggies and the salad, and clean the pots and pans after the festival was over, though some of the pots are so big and heavy that men take the job over. The lack of women presidents, however, could be understood by tradition. If we recall several statements already cited, in the public arena Basque women appear to choose to defer to the men, and that is the reason why few of them have been presidents. The same pattern can be seen at Winnemucca and Reno Basque clubs. It is indicative of the traditional culture, which assigns different chores to men and women. That makes sense, just like mothers oversee rearing the children and taking care of their other needs. This practice is attested by Elko women speaking about their mothers.

TRANSMITTING THE CULTURE

Basque mothers are keen when it comes to the education of the children, and this is true even when the woman is less educated than the man or is less fluent in English. Thus, the children of many immigrants went to college and got degrees, and Elko is not lacking in such examples. Having said that, Elko today is a peculiar town; for a young man freshly graduated from high school it can be conflicting to choose college versus working in the mines making a high salary.

Finally, we arrive at the topic of cultural transmission and preservation in the US. Older Basques in Elko want to know if their culture and traditions will survive. In October 2019, an eighty-year-old immigrant told me that he did not have long to live and to him that was the end of the culture. For him Basque culture meant the one he brought over from Europe, and it was ending in Elko. His wife was of Basque descent, and their children had Basque names and were dancers in the club, but they do not speak the language. In his opinion, the Basque community does not represent the culture anymore. They are American Basques, more American than Basque, he said, and I have to agree.

As reported earlier in this study, Basques define themselves by language and not by ethnicity. Therefore, speaking Euskara is a premium, but to what extent? What is culture, anyway? It is an open question. How much of the language is enough or not enough? I found that many American Basques of Elko do appreciate their culture, which they see as special. Women told me that strong family ties among Basques were something to hold on to. They mentioned hard work, honesty, and being a good neighbor as well. So, yes, they recognize these traits in the Basque culture as positive, desirable, and worth keeping. Euskara did not come up in the mix.

Who transmits culture and language? It is primarily the woman, the mother—we see it over and over. When an ex-sheepherder marries a non-Basque, the children will grow up learning their mother's language. Generally speaking, I have only known a few immigrant-Basque fathers with the gumption to ensure his children grow up speaking Basque. They see that mostly as the mother's role. After all, she spends more time with them. Thus, language is the first and main casualty in Elko, not only in mixed marriages but also in marriages of 100 percent Basques. Many of the fathers came from Europe believing that Euskara was worthless for finding a job and making a living; that was what the teachers taught them in school. Therefore, to try to speak it in America was a waste of time. They instead encouraged the study of Spanish or French. Today, this thinking is less prevalent because the parents are more educated, but it is undeniable that in Elko you need English, and even Spanish, much more than you need Euskara.

Many mothers will talk to the baby in Basque for the first few years, and of course in a ranch environment of old, Euskara used to be the only language spoken in the house, but those days are long gone. Besides, after the children started school, neither the father nor the mother pushed the native language. To the contrary, the father would say, "We are now in America, and we speak English." Several sources attributed those words to the father, but interestingly, nobody mentioned the mother uttering them.

Let us admit that swimming upstream is tough. Parents cannot fight necessity and reality. That is why in Nevada today you can easily count the children and young people who speak Basque. The number of those who understand it is considerably higher, and I often meet people who regret not being able to speak the language. Some of them blame their parents.

CHAPTER 8

Government Trappers

Not all the Basques associated with sheepherding and living in wild places like nomads were sheepherders. Some of them were trappers. Though trappers were an integral part of sheepherding, I do not remember reading much about them, much less about Basque trappers. This is another lacuna in the literature. Though their jobs were very different, they often ate and slept in sheep camps with the herders. In fact, trapper Steve Moiola not only looks back on his trapper days with pride, but also says that food tasted different—and better—in a sheep camp. Authenticity counts, he says—lamb, big round loaves of bread, red wine, and the great outdoors.

Trappers were able hunters, a group of unrecognized people deeply involved with ranching, particularly sheep. Unlike cattle, sheep have many predators that need to be controlled. That was the job of a trapper, an endeavor that started in 1885 by the Wildlife Services, a federal agency. Today, ranchers get reimbursed fully by the government for every cow or sheep killed by predators, but no such benefit existed in the old days.

Most trappers in Elko were not Basques, but a few were, some of them immigrants and some American-born. The list made up of the following sections, however, may not be complete. The earliest trappers out West may have been the Hispanics of New Mexico, but many more historians have covered the tracks of those doing business with the Hudson Bay Fur Company in Vancouver, Canada. They trapped for pelts, but here in Elko we mainly consider the trapping and killing of predators, specifically coyotes who preyed on sheep. When the coyote was killed, the trapper—or the government—kept and sold its pelt; therefore, the job was twofold.

In a 1950s–1960s photo of Elko trappers I saw at the Northeastern Nevada Museum, there are about twenty individuals. Those were years of high sheep numbers on the range, and control of coyotes was paramount. There were two kinds of trappers: the old-traditional type working in the wild country on foot and/or on horse. In the early 1960s, they started using 4x4 pickup trucks, and sometimes the horse was given a ride in the truck that couldn't go all the places a horse could.

The traditional method to control predators consisted of setting up traps or using poison. Starting in 1973, a radically different type of coyote control was employed using airplanes and helicopters. This came about after President Richard Nixon forbade the use of poison on federal land. Poison was very effective, too effective: It killed all sorts of wildlife, including valuable sheepdogs.

RUFINO "BENA" BERRUETABEÑA

In 1969, I interviewed Rufino "Bena" Berruetabeña, who was born in Markina, Bizkaia, in 1899. By then he had retired and was living in Twin Bridges, south of Elko. After enduring the fated years of sheepherding, he became a government trapper. The job requirements included owning a horse, a gun, and a bedroll for the nights spent under the stars, and, more important, having a special calling for living in the wild. Large sheep companies had a trapper assigned to them, and Bena worked for the Griswold Sheep Company, though he was not the only one. Big companies required more than one trapper. According to Grace van Dalfsen Erskine, Bena was "a fine Basque gentleman . . . much respected." One area of Bena's territories included Spruce Mountain in southeast Elko County, where Griswold lambed in late May.

Bena married and had a daughter. He told me that he had killed more than 120 cougars, as many or more bobcats, and thousands of coyotes, too many to remember, though somewhere he had a piece of paper with the exact number. Each pelt was worth money, about $5 and as much as $20–25 each when demand was high. Bena died in Elko in 1976.

SANTY MENDIETA

Santy Mendieta was an Oregon-born American Basque, who in the 1960s appeared in a magazine photograph among sheepherders playing his accordion. Born of Bizkaian parents in 1914, his sister was married to the well-known Arock, Oregon, rancher Freddie Eiguren. By 1948, Mendieta was a government trapper working with the Allied Sheep Company. He was an old-type trapper using a horse and his legs for transportation and poisoning the vermin. He lived in Winnemucca, but during the summer he brought a trailer to the Columbia Basin camp, where his family spent the season. He retired after 1965 and owned and managed the Pyrenees Motel in Winnemucca, Nevada. He died in 1884.

FRED ZUGAZAGA

Fred Zugazaga (later known as Zaga) was born in Bizkaia, in 1904. According to his daughter-in-law Simone Young, after arriving in the US, Fred worked as a sheepherder for either Corta or for the Goicoecheas. In his first job, they gave him 300 rams, a burro, and a "basko map" (lines traced in the dirt with a stick). He married Livia Orbe in 1934 and took a job as a government trapper in the vicinity of Roberts Creek.

Zaga always dreamed of owning a ranch, and his ticket was going to be trapping coyotes and gathering and selling enough pelts. However, one wintry day to his misery someone stole all the pelts hanging in his shed. But being a trapper came in handy, for he tracked the thieves and recovered all of them. With that money he and Livia bought the Zaga Ranch. Afterward, he gave up trapping and took up ranching. The Zagas are the grandparents of the current (2025) Basque club president, Choch Zaga. Fred Zaga died in Elko in 1987.

Jean Iribarne

Jean Iribarne (Jr. unless otherwise noted), born in Arnegi, Iparralde, came to the US at age seventeen. When he sat for the interview with me, his first words were "Euskeraz ein behar dogu!" (We must do it in the Basque language!). He mixed his native dialect with the prevailing Bizkaian spoken in Elko. In 1961, after eleven years herding sheep with his father for the Allied Sheep Company, he became a naturalized citizen and secured a job as a trapper for the Fish and Wildlife Service Control, staying with them for twenty-one years. According to Lopategui, Santy Mendieta assisted Iribarne with the application paperwork. Like Bena and others, Iribarne used strychnine and cyanide in killing coyotes. After 1972, when poison was outlawed, Iribarne migrated from the ground to the air and shot coyotes and other vermin from airplanes.

Iribarne plays the clarinet and has spiced up Basque festivities for four or more decades with his friend and accordion player Bernardo Yanci (1926–2016). Along with playing music, the two musicians taught Basque dancing—quite a switch from trapping. Jean also baked the sheepherders' bread—those huge round golden loaves—in the Dutch oven for fifty years. In 2024 Iribarne was living in Elko.

Steve Moiola and Mitch Moiola

Steve Moiola and Mitch Moiola, two cousins from Elko and fresh out of high school, were offered unexpected trapping jobs in 1974. Why them? I asked. For several reasons: They had gone to sheep camps, they were hunters, were Basque Italians, and knew the country. It was the kind of trapping for the government that entailed using airplanes and lasted just a few years until 1978, the tail end period of the Basque involvement in sheepherding.

After poisoning coyotes in public lands was outlawed, ranchers were losing many animals to predators. According to Alfonso Ygoa, a camp tender for many years, the coyotes took an average of 250 lambs from each sheep herd in Elko in the 1960s, and

Steve Moiola and his cousin Mitch Moiola were aerial trappers; here Steve uses the traditional horse for his work in the Rubies. Courtesy of Steve Moiola.

that was when they were using poison. The ranchers demanded urgent corrective action from the Department of Fish and Game. That is when aerial trapping (killing) began, and the Moiola cousins got the plum jobs. Well, sort of. They loved shooting, but the job paid 14 cents per mile for their pickup transportation, $25 a month allowance for the horse, and a salary of $440 a month before taxes. From that they paid for bullets, tires (that lasted only 10,000 miles), gas, motels, and food on the road. In 1974, prices for coyote fur skyrocketed from $25 per each coyote to $70 and up, so there was a lot of trapping going on. In that year the aerial gunners sent 883 furs to Seattle. After that, the government who owned the pelts started giving trappers six boxes of rifle shells and a brick of .22 bullets.

The Moiolas shot coyotes, bobcats, badgers, and rattlesnakes, which were considered vermin. Snakes could bite a dog, and the herders would lose a valuable assistant. They could also bite humans. Mitch worked north of Elko, and Steve sometimes worked on foot in the Rubies, where there were few roads but many rattlers. One summer he killed forty-one, and five within thirty minutes in the Echo Trail area.

At the time, the county's immense range was mostly off-limits to 95 percent of people. There were a few 4x4 vehicles, but conquering the wilderness was difficult. Imagine then a machine that can fly over everything—the Rubies as well as the valleys. From up there you could see a lot more, such as coyotes mixed with the sheep in the herd, looking for the choicest morsel, and the herder and the dogs totally unaware.

The Moiolas shot many coyotes, and after a while Mitch became a supervisor under coordinator Mike Laughlin. The legislature provided $250,000 every two years for helicopters. They flew thousands of hours, and you could not rule out accidents. One time, a helicopter's engine quit, and the crew landed in a meadow near Lamoille on two feet of snow. Helicopters needed to take a break after four to five hours of flying.

In the winter of 1974 to 1975, Steve recalls, "Mitch and I were in Wendover, Nevada, as sheep were coming in from Utah. We landed the chopper next to a motel and we tried the walkie-talkies, which were a new thing. We could not make them work, so we grabbed our bags, our two guns and we were walking toward the motel when we found ourselves facing the Nevada Highway Patrol, the county police, and the Wendover cops with guns drawn and aiming at us. They thought we were up to no good, but it all ended amicably."

The aerial program grew with more money coming in, but it did not last. Many big sheepmen in the county sold out, and before 1980 the Moiolas were left without sheep and without a job. The coyotes lived happily ever after, and the Moiolas retained the memories.

Vicente Bilbao

Vicente Bilbao, born in Bizkaia in 1897, came to the US in 1914 and worked for a sheep outfit in McDermitt. Three years later, he and two other Basques traveled on horseback to Elko to take jobs at the Spanish Ranch. He started trapping in 1928, and in 1932 he set up a home in Lower Jack Creek. Bilbao married Paula Eguilior, and they had two children; they moved to Elko in 1956, and he died there in 1983.

Bilbao learned to trap in the Independence Mountains and stayed with it for over forty years (1928–1969). He supported his family by trapping beavers, bobcats, and coyotes. Coyote pelt was worth a low $5 to a high $15 during the Great Depression. (Bilbao is another guy who could claim, "Hurrah for the Depression" such as the herder Frank Rodriguez did on an aspen tree carving in 1932.) Beaver fur fetched anywhere from $40 to $75.

Bilbao was self-employed and during his many trapping wanderings, he also took an interest in rocks and mining claims that later turned into gold mines (see chapter 19). Bilbao did not work for the government and did not agree with those who were protecting coyotes: "They do a lot of damage to livestock," he said. In 1932, Dan Saval, who was a herder for Balbino Achabal—another Basque sheepman—brought him three coyote pups found near a lambing corral. They were about two days old, two females and one male, and they opened their eyes eleven days later. One female left the yard and killed a lamb when she was four months old. Bilbao killed her but spared the other two, whom he kept chained and penned for three years. The two teamed up to hunt mice and rabbits. The male would run around and spook the rabbits, and his sister would hide ready to pounce and kill. Bilbao says the coyotes were as tame and as domesticated as the dogs, but they would attack any stranger who showed up. Eventually, that forced him to destroy both of them.

Vicente Bilbao, trapper and prospector, 1977. From
obituary, *Elko Daily Free Press*, November 10, 1983.

Furthermore, Bilbao refutes the idea that coyotes only kill the
sick, the lame, and the old. On the contrary, he said, "they kill the
best and biggest." The sheepherders I spoke with about this issue
agree with Bilbao, but immigrant herders don't write; therefore,
the prevalent view by the experts contradicts them. Sure, on lean
days they may have to feast on the lame and the sick, but whenever possible they would pick the best in the herd. The following is
the description of how it happens, according to one sheepherder:
"The biggest lambs are the strongest and they are likely to venture
outside the herd or wander in the periphery, where the coyote

waits in ambush. After the kill, they only eat the choicest parts of the prey. They kill pregnant ewes and eat the unborn lamb."

Once, Bilbao saw a coyote eat a calf as it was being born. He also saw a coyote kill a full-grown healthy deer: the deep snow slowed her down, and the predator could run on the frozen crust without sinking. Bilbao also said that the coyotes do the most damage because they also eat the eggs of birds that nest on the ground. According to the US Department of Agriculture, in 2020 in Nevada coyotes killed or injured 253 cattle and 596 sheep, down from 1,332 sheep in 2019. (For more on Bilbao, see https://sheepherdingin-northernnv.wordpress.com/vicente-bilbao-oral-history/.)

Nick Landa

According to Steve Moiola, Nick Landa was born in the US, became a trapper, and stayed on the job for thirty years. He leased a small place of about 400 acres from John Carpenter, located four or five miles east of city of Elko, where he ran a few cows. He and his son were living in Elko in 2021. Frank Arregui and Jess Lopategui bought the ranch from Carpenter in the 1980s.

CHAPTER 9

Basque Hotels in Elko

By 1900, Elko was not the same town that the Altubes and the Garats found in the early 1870s. The railroad had been running for over thirty years, and Elko could even boast of being the only university town in Nevada for eleven years (1874–1885). Furthermore, Elko was the main stop between Salt Lake City and Reno. More important, sheep and cattle ranching had taken firm root in a county blessed with good grazing, adequate water, and spectacular mountain ranges that offered prime hunting. No wonder the Basques were flocking to Elko in droves and that by 1907 Elko already boasted of two Basque hotels.

Jess Lopategui has researched the Elko archives to get the details on the history of the early Basque hotels, and he will be our guide. Just as relevant or more so is that two of the hotels in town were owned by his relatives who were born in his own village, Muxika.

THE SAVAL HOTEL

The Saval was owned by Guy Saval, the youngest of the three Saval brothers from Ispaster, Bizkaia. He may have started his plan for the hotel as early as 1906. In that year, Miguel Ballarena from Lesaka, Navarre, bought lots 1.2.3.4 of Block U on Silver Street from Mr. Crane. Ballarena had a sister, Concepcion Ballarena, who may have acted as the intermediary, for a year later in 1907 Saval married her. By then the hotel was built and it included a *pilota* (handball) court, where in November of that year a famous match took place: the first handball championship in Elko between John Etchebarren, the Nevada champion, and Andres Ripa, the California champion. As a side note, Hank Samper of Elko said that Pongo Rena built the Telescope in 1908, but he offered no further details.

Jeronima Echeverria wrote that Saval and Pete Jauregui owned and opened the hotel in 1907. She adds that it was the first Basque hotel in Elko where Pete Jauregui may have been one of several proprietors with percentage ownership. In fact, there is a paper at the Northeastern Nevada Museum stating that even Pedro Altube was for a while involved with the Saval Hotel, but he had died in 1905. The document may refer to the initial planning of the hotel.

TELESCOPE HOTEL

Saval's hotel tenure was short, perhaps a couple of years, and he probably had partners. Around 1909, the range wars between cattlemen and sheepmen were heating up and they scared the recently arrived wife of Francisco Goicoechea, Juliana Arechabaleta. Juliana convinced Francisco to leave the ranch (he was in business with Saval) and move into town. Goicoechea bought the Saval Hotel with his partners Martin Inda, Pedro Orbe, and some other individual and they renamed it the Telescope Hotel. Whatever that may be, Goicoechea soon returned to ranching.

On August 27, 1926, a fire was reported at the Telescope causing some damage, and it was duly repaired. The hotel had many owners, the same as the Star. Mariano Jauregui ("Parranderu") was one of them, and during Prohibition he lost it. The sheriff sold the Telescope at an auction, and Dr. Hood bought it for $8,063,23. Hood had loaned the money to Jauregui, and he did not want to lose the property. Hood put Enrique Samper in charge as manager.

In 1943, Hood sold the hotel to Samper, who was from Navarre and married to a woman from Iparralde. In 1951, the Sampers removed the handball court and installed an eight-lane bowling alley. At the time, Calisto Laucirica owned the Nevada Hotel next door and when the Sampers needed one extra foot at the alley, Laucirica obliged, selling them the portion they needed. Samper's son Hank and his wife owned the Telescope and the bowling alley until about 2000. As late as 1995 or so, the hotel rented rooms and had boarders. Since then, there have been several owners, and it is a pizza place as well.

THE OVERLAND HOTEL

Domingo Zabala (Sabala), from Gizaburuaga, Bizkaia, built the Overland in partnership with Eulogio Onaindia in 1907–1908, when they were already paying taxes. The recording of the lot's deed on which the hotel stood is dated 1911. Elko Lumber was the previous owner of the lot, and its sale price was $2,400, which the Basque partners probably finished paying in 1911. Onaindia may have been the father of Joe Onaindia, who was an American-born *morrosko* (corpulent man) and a barman at Laucirica's Nevada Hotel. In fact, Jess Lopategui thinks he may have been a relative of Laucirica.

Dan Sabala and wife, Gregoria Garteiz, builders and owners of the Overland Hotel. Courtesy of Gretchen Skivington.

The Overland was located across the street from the Commercial Hotel on Fourth Street, and it had three stories and twenty-four rooms. At the backside of the hotel there was a handball court just like at the Telescope for playing pilota.

Domingo Sabala changed his name to Dan and married Gregoria Garteiz from Winnemucca. They were the grandparents of Gretchen Skivington, professor of English at the Great Basin Community College (GBCC) until her retirement in 2020. Ramon Iriondo owned the property attached to the hotel, the Gaiety Theater, a silent-movie house, which he sold to Sabala for $5,000 in the 1930s. The Great Depression hit hard many businesses like the Overland, and in 1937–1938 the bank repossessed Sabala's property. (For more information, see Gretchen Holbert's 1975 article on the Overland Hotel.)

In 1936 Joe Anacabe came to town, and he too had something to do with the Overland because his property was attached to it. The store he opened was not a hotel, however, and we will return to it in chapter 18.

THE AMISTAD HOTEL

The fourth-oldest Basque hotel was apparently the Amistad, later renamed Cloud 9. Celso Madarieta and Domingo Calzacorta (Sr.), both Bizkaians, were married to the Marisquirena sisters from Etxalar, Navarre. The brothers-in-law built the Amistad three years after the Star Hotel in 1913. It was located just west of the Star on the same block on lots 17 and 18. It had a bar and between thirteen to sixteen rooms.

The early history of Amistad (meaning "friendship" in Spanish) is fuzzy. Hank Samper said his father "originated" it, but he does not know if he built it. Cruz Bilbao, an old-timer, said that the Amistad has a long history, but he does not remember "exactly what" that is. According to Elkoan Adelita Viscarret, the Sampers built the Amistad. The *Elko Daily Free Press* reported that Celso Madarieta built it. Echeverria says that Joe Marisquirena built the Amistad in the 1920s, and John Lostra says it was in operation before 1926. Those are the comments and the memories.

In any case, Madarieta and Calzacorta sold it in 1919 to Emilio Dotta for $2,000, and it was managed by Marisquirena. Dotta in turn sold it to a Chinese (person or people) in 1923 along with lots 17 and 18, 13 dressers, 21 chairs, and 16 beds. Official papers incorrectly state that Marisquirena owned it; he was just its manager. These discrepancies could be ironed out by researching further in the local archives.

Clifton House Hotel

The Clifton, located on Commercial Street, was also an old building built before 1914, though not by Basques. It was, however, owned by Basques after 1932, when Emeterio and Concepcion Plaza bought it. In 1960 Jack Errecart and wife, Barbara, an American involved in the local government, bought it, but the deed is dated 1971. Errecart was born in Busunaritz, Iparralde, in 1908; came to Elko in 1930; and worked with sheep for fifteen years. Before buying the Clifton, he managed the Telescope for some years. Today the couple's son Jack Errecart, an architect, owns the Clifton, which has a bar and leases rooms for events.

Nevada Hotel

The Nevada Hotel, located on Silver Street, was built more recently. Miguel Arregui was from Errea, Navarre, and he owned the lot on which the Nevada was built. In 1927 he sold the lot to Anastasio Vizcarret (later Viscarret), who built the hotel and put it in his wife's name. In 1943, the couple sold it to Williams, who in turn in 1947 sold it to his wife. In 1950, she sold it to Red Ellis. At the time, Ellis owned the Stockmen's, which he wanted to expand, but the Nevada Hotel was located where he wanted to carry out the expansion. His solution was to sell it to Calisto Laucirica, or he may have simply given it to him just to move it away.

Laucirica found someone to move the hotel across the railroad tracks in 1951. He then bought two more lots from Alex Heguy to expand his hotel. According to one account, Laucirica sold the ranch he owned in Lamoille and opened the Nevada

The Nevada Hotel. Courtesy of Northeastern Nevada Historical Society and Museum, Elko, Nevada.

Hotel Restaurant, which had eleven rooms. Jess Lopategui spent his first days in America at the Nevada Hotel because Laucirica was his uncle.

Silver Dollar

The Silver Dollar, located on Commercial Street, was just a bar, not a boardinghouse, but it is worth mentioning here for its long history under Basque ownership. It started as a bank, until Marcel Inda bought it early on. The famous sheepman Pete Itcaina owned it after 1942 or so, and Jack Errecart and Ralph Fagoaga bought it from him. Fagoaga was born in Lesaka in 1928. After arriving in the US under contract from the Western Range Association, he worked five years as a sheepherder. In 1960, he bought out Errecart, and he and his wife operated the Silver Dollar for many years.

The place became known as the Baskos' hangout, according to Lawrence Moiola. The bar was open twenty-four hours, and at times you could see Bing Crosby, who owned a ranch sixty miles north of Elko, drinking there. Fagoaga died in 1996. He was a history buff and had a subscription to the *Voice of the Basques*, a periodical published in Boise, Idaho, in 1974–1977.

CHAPTER 10

The Star Hotel

The Star Basque Hotel and Restaurant epitomizes the spirit of the Basques of old Elko County as much as the Altubes, the Garats, and the Savals. This statement may not be fair to the other Basque hotels in town, some of them older, but the Star is still going strong in 2025, more popular than ever, while the others are no more. For example, the Winnemucca Hotel in Winnemucca, older than the Star by about half a century, ceased to operate on October 18, 2010. By December 2019, that 156-year-old building was demolished, and the Winnemucca Hotel along with so many Basque memories were over. (A reminder that much of what is written here about the Star can be applied to other Basque hotels in Elko, for they operated in a similar manner.)

There is a reason for introducing the Star before the Euzkaldunak Basque Club. For decades, the club has been known for staging spectacular festivals, but the early versions of the large festivals attended by every able-bodied Basque in town started soon after the Star opened in 1910 thanks to the foresight of its owners. The festival format was different, but the idea was the same: to gather, to meet old and new friends, to eat, drink, sing, and dance. The dances, forever the most important feature of all Basque festivals, especially today, are the same now as those performed during the early festivities at the Star; they include the jota, *porrusalda, arin-arin, aurresku,* and so on.

THE JAUREGUI BROTHERS

The Star was the byproduct of Basques who came to live in town after they made money elsewhere, or perhaps they had little money but a lot of ambition. Some bought ranches and stayed on the range, but others came to town to live or to set up businesses. It is tempting to say that the story of the Star began in California with Martin Jauregui, who came to the US circa 1895 and stayed until 1925. He was the father of the three brothers in Elko—Pedro (Pete), Alberto, and Tony Jauregui—and according to a report, he owned a dairy in California (though Lopategui is skeptical). We do know, however, that he was employed by the Altubes. (Source: Tony Jauregui, who was married to Lopategui's aunt.)

Jeronima Echeverria says that Pete Jauregui's financial backer was Emilio Dotta, who at the time owned a lot of property in town, and Matilde Jauregui says that much. In addition, the Jauregui brothers could also have financed part of the hotel from the proceeds of a gold mine they owned in Barinaga Ranch Canyon in Lee, according to Lopategui. And, perhaps their father helped too. I agreed with Lopategui that Pete could not have made much money managing the Saval/Telescope Hotel, because he did not stay there long enough to amass wealth.

Dotta sold Pete Jauregui lots 23 and 24 of block V in the city of Elko on October 10, 1910, but the deed was recorded only on February 2, 1920, possibly when the loan was paid off. Jauregui built his hotel on this site in less than three months and opened it in December 1910, when his two brothers may have been partners. By this time Jauregui had married Matilde Eizaguirre, an enterprising business partner in her own right; they had two daughters, Teresa and Anita. At first, Pete wanted to name their new hotel Australia—one wonders why—but they settled on "The Star." The star, such as *goizeko izarra* (the morning star), has great symbolism in Basque culture. A girlfriend and beautiful women are often compared to stars, which explains why sheepherders carved so many stars on aspen trees.

The construction of the hotel cost $11,000 (Matilde says $10,000), and when completed it had eleven rooms and a bathroom. Two years later, business being extra good, Pete found out that he needed a bigger hotel, so he expanded it by 100 percent

Historical photo of Star Hotel, ca. 1920. Reprinted from Sol Silen.

to twenty-two rooms (Matilde says "about 25") and another bathroom.

The Star is not just another Basque hotel/boardinghouse. The Winnemucca Hotel, for example, can more than compare in the role it played among the Basques of Humboldt County and environs, but it was not built or owned by Basques until the 1920s. The Star, on the other hand, was always owned by Basques and thereafter became an iconic landmark in the history of Elko itself.

The Jauregui (today spelled Jauregi) brothers were from Muxika, Bizkaia. Pete was born in nearby Gernika, Bizkaia, on September 27, 1880, and traveled the world as a seaman before coming to the US in December of 1898 according to Sol Silen, but his daughters say it was circa 1893. After working a few years in a dairy (his father's?) in California, he arrived in Elko. The year is disputed, but according to Silen he had arrived by 1905 and married Matilde Eizaguirre Calzacorta. Silen also says that he and Guy Saval co-owned the Saval Hotel, but Pete's daughters say that he was just

Historical photo of Pete Jauregui and wife, Matilde Eizaguirre, who built the Star Hotel in 1910. Reprinted from Sol Silen.

a manager. Koldo San Sebastian says that Matilde was seventeen when she arrived in Elko in 1908, so in 1905 she was too young to get a marriage license.

Matilde was born in Berriatua, Bizkaia, in 1895 according to her daughters but more likely in 1890 according to other sources. Her daughters also stated that she arrived in Elko in 1908 and that she married later in that year, but Matilde says she married two months after arriving in Elko. She had two other sisters in Elko County, and before emigrating she worked as a nurse's aide, though she herself does not mention it. Therefore, she was not a typical *baserritarra* from a farming background like most of the Basque women who arrived in Elko at that time. Suffice it to say, she was not the typical homebound wife either, content with cooking or raising children.

LOCATION

The Star Hotel was strategically located facing the Central Pacific Railroad and very near its depot on the other side of the tracks. Today, the old street to the train station is Ormaza Alley, as Ormaza Construction Company owns the Old Depot and the large building across the street. This used to be the Grand Central of the Basques, where so many alighted. The Star was one minute away and others, like Overland, were no more than five more minutes away. The Basque *ostatuak* (boardinghouses) run by their countrymen were, as Jeronima Echeverria says, "home away from home" for hundreds of Basques who arrived barely speaking one word of English. If some rancher was looking for a sheepherder, he made a beeline to one of the hotels—the Overland, the Star, or other. If a sheepherder was looking for a job, he went to the same locations. If a cowboy wanted a job in Elko, on the other hand, he went to the Commercial, five minutes away.

Teresa and Anita Jauregui remember that the Star was always packed with Basques—and *packed* could be taken literally. According to Constantina Bengoetxea at the Winnemucca Hotel, where she worked for decades, there were times when beds were rented not for the night but for eight hours, as sheepherders were waiting to jump in as soon as the previous customer's time elapsed. We do not know if the Star was ever so jammed with customers, but *packed* is the word to remember.

The two Jauregui daughters growing up at the Star were lucky that they could interact with young women freshly arrived from the Old Country. Many of these women came to find a husband and as soon as they arrived, they started working as hotel maids, usually *tripa truke* (in exchange for room and board) but not for long. "It was like a marriage hotel," Anita said. This further means that the man proposing marriage had a job in town or at a ranch. It could hardly have been a wandering sheepherder.

The rooms at the Star were especially packed when sheepherders came to town during the winter layoff. Others arrived for a short vacation or to recover from some health issue. Room and board were $1 a day, and it stayed that way for many years. Jose Fagoaga and Ramon Lastiri were the last Basque borders as of November 2018. They paid $700/month for room and board and three square meals a day, according to Scotty Ygoa, the owner of the Star. Quite a deal in Gold Country, where prices can be inflated.

HOME OF THE PICON PUNCH

Today, the Star is mainly a bar-restaurant, often busy, and always crowded on weekends. Most of the patrons come to drink a *picon* or two, which is an aperitif, and to fill up on the abundant and delicious food they serve. In 2017, according to Ygoa, they sold 16,000 picons.

If you are not from Northern Nevada, you may not know what a picon is. It originated in France, but the Basques in the West have made it their own. Several years ago, there was a story in the media about people wanting to make the picon the Nevada State Drink, but it did not materialize. It is a somewhat-bitter drink made with herbs and other ingredients; supposedly it is an aperitif, but Basques drink it before, during, and after meals, and it looks like many Elkoans agree with them. The picon can be mixed to suit one's taste, that is, sweeter or more bitter. The picon recipe, as served at the celebrated Winnemucca Hotel, required club soda, but since the late 1950s the Star has served it without.

Scotty Ygoa's picon recipe, slightly changed:

> Ice
> 3 ounces of Amer Picon
> 1 ounce of club soda (Winnemucca's version)
> Dash (1/4 ounce) grenadine
> 1/4-to-1/2-ounce brandy
> Lemon twist

> Fill a glass with ice (some bars have special picon glasses), add a dash of grenadine (more if you like it sweeter), Amer Picon, and club soda (optional), leaving slight room on top. Stir the ingredients. Top off the drink with brandy. Swirl in a slice of lemon. Finally, the real tough part: drink it. "Osagarri!" (In Winnemucca, "Zaku!").

OWNERSHIP

Even though the Star was always owned by Basques, the list of its owners is a long one, and it offers some interesting details. On October 5, 1922, after twelve years of grueling work, Pete and Matilde sold it to Pete's youngest brother, Alberto Jauregui, and partner Jose Corta. The deed was recorded at the First National Bank of Winnemucca. Not much is known about their holding, other than that it was short lived, approximately two years. Alberto sold his half interest to Corta on December 16, 1924. In 1925, taxes were paid by Corta and Nick Goicoa (who was not known to have ever owned the Star).

Earlier in the chapter it was mentioned that the Jauregui brothers owned a gold mine. Details are sketchy, but in 1924 Alberto sold his share of the mine in Lee to his brother Pete and he went to live in Gernika with his friend Mariano Aralucea.

Jose Corta managed the Star for seven years. On February 14, 1929, the same day he had become the sole owner, he sold it to G. F. Arrascada and Albert Garamendi. Albert Garamendi sold his half interest to Arrascada for $2,175 and a Hudson sedan on April 1, 1931. Arrascada leased it to Calisto Laucirica for five years in 1937.

When the lease expired on April 2, 1943, Arrascada and his wife, Santa, sold the Star back to Pete Jauregui and Felipe Eizaguirre (Matilde's brother). A little over a year later, on May 5, 1944, the two sold it to Fred and Bibiana Bengoa. They operated it for almost a decade, until October 1, 1953, when they sold it to Marguerite Odiaga Ozamis. The deed was redrawn on November 5, 1955, when Marguerite's husband's name, Domingo Ozamis, was incorporated. They owned the Star until 1959.

The Ozamis and Jose (Joe) Juaristi owned the Star next, until 1962, and Juaristi and Bernardo Yanci owned it after that until 1964, but there is no record that Yanci was a grantee. In 1964 and 1965 The Ozamis paid the taxes. After that, Juaristi took on a new partner, Luis "Luiggi" Esnoz, who died circa 1967 in a car accident with two other Basques. According to one record, the Esnoz Estate had not been settled yet in 1968. The next Star owners were Joe

Sarasua and his wife, Anita, who partnered with John Aldazabal and his wife, Flora Churruca. They ran the hotel from December 1964 until 1989, when Miguel and Teresa Leonis and Severiano Lazcano bought it and ran it until December of 2004.

The frequent ownership change of the Star was not a good sign, Lopategui points out, and during the Depression they lost much of what they owned. Therefore, most of the owners probably did not make a lot of money. Of course, in the economy in general outside the hotel business a similar trend was happening at the time. It was atrocious, and that is why it is known as the Great Depression.

The present owners, Scotty and Tricia Ygoa (now divorced), bought the Star in 2004. Scotty says that he manages the Star pretty much as it has been for a century, and one day he wants to pass it on to the next generation, hopefully the same way as Pete and Matilde Jauregui envisioned it in 1910. That is a beautiful thought, no doubt, but the differences will be striking.

Today, there are no Basque boarders at the Star. The last one died in 2019. This place used to be, Ygoa says, "Home away from home for Basque immigrants . . . but now it is home away from home for people traveling through Elko . . . I realized that's what it is. People come in, regulars that we know for many years now from California, Utah, Idaho . . . they walk in, and they feel comfortable . . . they like the homey atmosphere. . . . I am here to keep it going. . . . There is a lot of history here."

At this point Ygoa becomes a bit sentimental reminiscing about "Old Elko"—the Elko of his father, Alfonso, of ranches, cattlemen, and sheepmen, when Elko was much smaller and everybody knew each other. Then mining came to town, and "Everybody today thinks Elko was always a mining town, because that's all they know," he says.

LONG TABLES, HEAPING PLATTERS

For decades, meals to boarders were served family style on long tables with bench seating, just as in any other traditional Basque hotel. Large pots filled with soups, pinto beans, garbanzos, chorizos, stews, corn, potatoes, chicken, and beef were handed around with the ubiquitous bread and wine. Meals had to be tasty because Basques are hardy eaters and do not put up with mediocrity when it comes to food. Too much salt? They will let you know. You forgot to salt it? They can salt to taste themselves, but just the same they will let you know.

We often hear that the food served at Basque restaurants is sheep camp fare or something close to it. Do not believe it. To begin with, there was little variety at the sheep camp, and if you served the same menu in town day after day your restaurant would close in two weeks. Besides, sheep camps never saw the tender tasty steaks that the Star serves. Steak sandwiches, enhanced with a whitish sauce and served between two slices of French bread, are a popular lunch fare at the Star. Recently I was there, and I ate one; they are totally delicious, and they come with fries.

The Star Hotel may be known for Basque food, but in the 1960s and 1970s they advertised "Italian and Basque Family Style Dinners." So why is it known only for Basque food? Perhaps the "picon" has something to do with it, and the fact that it was also a hotel and that the customers were only or mainly Basques. Today, the Star advertises as Basque Family Style Restaurant and Lounge (www.elkostarhotel.com). In 2011–2015 and in 2016 it was voted the "Readers' Choice," according to the *Elko Daily Free Press*.

A Happy Place

Jess Lopategui arrived in Elko in 1958 and still lives there. He knows a thing or two about Pete Jauregui and his wife, Matilde Eizaguirre, because he is related to them. He recalls that the air inside the Star at and around the bar was smoky and probably unhealthy, especially in winter. It could have been worse earlier on, when almost all the sheepherders smoked, which did not diminish the humor and camaraderie.

Owners Pete and Matilde scheduled dances for the idle sheepherders with music furnished by a local Basque accordion player;

it seems that there was always one in town. It was the place to have weddings as well, or when the need arose it became a hospital for the sick or the expectant mothers. Home away from home, indeed.

Among the vicissitudes that rocked hotels and Basques in general, Prohibition was an uneasy period. It was hard on everyone but especially on people whose culture included wine as part of everyday fare, such as the Basques and Italians. These two populations continued making wine, especially the Italians, and even whiskey sometimes, and there were skirmishes with the police. Prohibition had much to do with women's movements and some with the puritanical traditions of the early Anglo colonists. The local paper thundered from time to time, urging the sheriff to "clean up the town."

During pre-Prohibition years, the following Basques had liquor licenses in town: Pete Jauregui, of the Star; Dan Sabala, of the Overland; William Mariluch, of the Telescope; and a fellow from Etxalar by the surname Marisquirena, who was found guilty of violation and fined. It was common knowledge that many people drank wine regularly and that many establishments broke the law by serving liquor in secret, but the police could not do much about it.

Pete and Matilde started the yearly Gabon Gaba (Christmas Eve) Dinner and celebrations that became the ultimate party among Elko Basques. Drinks were extra, but dinner was free, though it was not just another dinner—ham, clams and rice, rock cod, crab, and a large fish of unknown species that they baked whole with bread and wine; that goes without saying. Mind you, no lamb and beans are mentioned, because those were everyday foods. Chestnuts, *konpota* (apples and plumbs cooked in red wine), cheese, and coffee royal followed dinner. The food ingredients arrived from San Francisco in a great big box packed in ice.

Afterward, all went to midnight Mass at the first Elko Catholic Church, found where the library is today on Court Street. It had been a Protestant church, and it is said that the Basques led by the Jaureguis bought it.

There are accounts that Pete played the accordion, so the Star had its own live music. Whenever the sheepherders cared to dance, Matilde and the maids obliged happily. Most days, however, it was just work. Doing dishes, cleaning, and laundering seemed never-ending chores that fell heavily on the women.

Mecca for Tourists and Miners

Today, most of the Star business comes not from Basques but from local miners and tourists. When Ygoa told me of the many picons they sell every day at $5 each, I reminded him that in the 1960s when I was living in Elko, the picon was not that popular. He agreed and said that the reason was money. Gold miners today make good money, and they have more disposable income than people in the 1960s. Ygoa then added, "But they are broke. They are paying for their trucks, their snowmobiles, motorcycles, houses . . . you name it. At the end of the month, no money left." Without voicing it, he was also saying that it did not jibe with the immigrant mentality he inherited.

Scotty Ygoa, the present-day owner of the Star Hotel.

Ygoa says that now the Star sees considerable traffic of travelers who show up yearly. Some have Basque roots, but others just feel comfortable there enjoying the different atmosphere. Scotty thinks that a DVD or a booklet with the history of the Star would be a good idea if someone undertakes the job.

Tomorrow

Ygoa as the owner would like it to last another century or more. To that end there is talk of modernizing the rooms, and last year the long great balcony in the original hotel, which had been taken down, was rebuilt. In the previous century, the Star had almost twenty owners (counting spouses as one), but it does not appear that trend will continue into the next century. Ygoa did not give any indication of wanting to sell it anytime soon, even though his workdays are many with long hours.

If the Star lives to see 2125, will the Elko Basques still be celebrating their yearly festivals? There are few models for the Star to follow because there are no Basque hotels that have lasted 200 years. But there is always a first time. Even if the Star should change hands and one day be owned by non-Basques, it would not be a big deal if it continued serving semi-Basque food and picons.

The Star has a lot of potential, and if gold mining keeps up it will be in business and do well. Gradually, its American Basque character might fade, just like the Basque culture itself will decline. Yet there is always history to remind us of the heroic times of Pete Jauregui and Matilde Eizaguirre in 1910.

CHAPTER 11

Elko Euzkaldunak Basque Club

As they say, one Basque equals a beret, two Basques equal a handball match, three Basques equal a choir, four Basques equal a festival, and eight Basques (used to be seven) equal a homeland—in Europe or in Elko, Nevada. When you are a small country and when you are few, you have to improvise.

The Basques are gregarious and at the same time individualistic to the point that arguments are settled in absolute terms, 100 to 0. A compromise of 50–50 or 70–30 is not desirable; it is considered a sort of a weakness. I am far from saying that all Basques behaved this way, but you can observe such a trait in immigrants. Some Americanized Basques certainly do, and they provide it as one reason for not participating in the clubs: "There is no way I am going to work with a bunch of Baskos who can never agree on anything." This quote, not just from Elko but from several individuals from other towns and cities, is best left unattributed.

If you look around, you realize that this platitude holds little water. In the US we have the North American Basque Organizations (NABO), which serves as an umbrella for forty-three Basque clubs today. That's forty-three. Furthermore, Euskal Herria in Europe not only boasts of all sorts of associations, fraternities, *txokos* (culinary societies), and clubs, but it is also home to the world's foremost workers' cooperatives of Arrasate/Mondragon. So, the retort of not wanting to waste time with fixed-mindset Baskos may be nothing more than an opinion held by some individuals. In fact, the history of the Elko Basque Club serves as an excellent counterargument.

When the Basques of Elko decided to form a club, most of

the pioneers were Basque Americans, that is, more culturally Basque than American; but they took pains to let their fellow citizens know that they were also proud Americans. Charlene Shobe Dory (related to the Sabalas of Overland) said she was told that at home: They "insisted in us becoming Americans; it was very important." I have heard similar statements from several sources in every town with a Basque community. From the beginning, the Basques of Elko County identified with the ranching culture that predominated in the county. The integration of those living in town was already underway as attested by the businesses they owned, and even by their participation in the local sports. In the Basque Country physical strength and endurance are highly admired, and in the 1950s the group formed their own softball team that, according to Frank Yraguen, "won more games than we lost."

But how did the people of Elko view the Basques? Chris H. Sheering, of the *Elko Daily Free Press*, provides the media's view: "From the Pyrenees has come a hardy race of people, Basques. While they have retained many of their original characteristics, and this is what distinguishes them so sharply, they have blended well in the great American picture. They believe in working and playing hard. The Basque wants to retain his great heritage of the past even as he is a good citizen of the United States."

Earlier on December 27, 1954, the *Elko Daily Free Press* announced a three-part series on the Basques of the county, written by Jean McElrath. The presentation began with "no people have contributed more substantially to the economy of Elko County than the Basques; no people are better liked generally by the people of the county than the Basques. . . . Our purpose here is to salute the Basque people of Elko County as a whole, a hardy fine race of people who have helped make our country great."

On December 29, 1954, the same paper wrote that the Basques were among Elko's first settlers, and that their "instinct for hospitality . . . contributed to their worldwide reputation for friendliness that is part of Nevada's tradition."

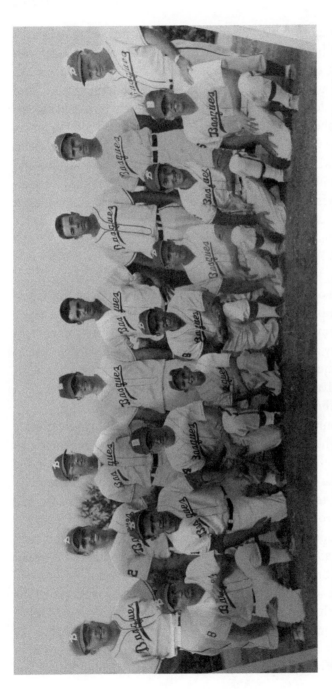

Elko Basques Softball team, 1950s. *Left to right, back row:* Angelo Aguirre, Albert Samper, John Jayo, Martin "Butch" Mariluch, Martin Hachquet, Hank Samper, Albert Aguirre, Domingo Mariluch (coach). *Left to right, front row:* Frank Aguirre, Louie Uriarte, Henry Viscarret, Frank Yraguen, Dan Uriarte, Henry Aguirre, Ray Goicoa, and (unknown). Courtesy Rosie Yraguen.

The majority of Basques in Elko would agree with McElrath's opinion, because, in fact, it is true that the Basques brought with them a deep sense of friendliness and hospitality that helped make Nevada a tourist mecca and the friendly state that it is. Carol Hovey a descendant of Pedro Altube, writes that when her great-grandfather "Palo Alto" met someone, especially on the lonely range, he would pull out a flask of whiskey and offer a drink with a curious invitation: "Hello, you sonofabitch, my friend! Stop and have a drink with me." I don't know why, but it seems like a revealing element of the "Old Elko" that I remember from the 1960s. It was this atmosphere, this civic environment, that made possible the notion and the birth of the Basque Club.

THE STARTING SEED

The idea of a club itself may have been new, but since the beginning the Basques living in this part of the US got together every year during rodeo time. I heard the same story in Winnemucca too. They spent their leisure time in the same way and season as other ranchers. Rodeo get-togethers had a lot of the ingredients that festivals later adopted: the visiting aspects, the swapping of stories, the eating and drinking, the music and dancing.

The only difference was that the Basques tended to congregate among themselves, just like most of the Indigenous people did, among relatives or preferably at Basque hotels, but not out in the street like later. The other distinction from present-day festivals was that few out-of-towners showed up, because each town had its own rodeo days. Of course, eventually at maturity the clubs did introduce some obvious ingredients that rodeos lacked, such as the Catholic Mass, Old World–sport competitions, bertsolari singing, bread making, sheep hooking, and more.

There were other deep-seated desires that gave birth to the Basque club, one being the ethnic propensity to seek each other out. Basques number only a few million in the world, but as the joke goes, a Basque can find a cousin just about anywhere. (Other small ethnic groups, by the way, have comparable stories.) The language, Euskara, encapsulates much of the culture and motivates Basques to travel hundreds of miles to attend summer picnics in the West and to be with compatriots to catch up on community gossip or family news from the Old Country or the New. These exchanges were and still are immensely more rewarding when carried out in the Basque language, though at any Basque picnic you are likely to hear four languages: Euskara, English, Spanish, and French; even though some Euskara dialects can be as dissimilar as Spanish and Portuguese.

Prep Steps

Basque communities in the United States have regularly celebrated their roots with food, drink, singing, music, and dancing. We can go back almost 500 years to find examples of Basque get-togethers in North America during the colonial period; in 1548, for example, near Zacatecas, Mexico, where a group of Basque miners and explorers met. The principles were Cristobal Oñate (aka Cristóbal de Oñate), Miguel Ibarra, Juan Tolosa, and Vicente Zaldibar, and they met at Juan Jasso's roadside inn for a meal and for some camaraderie. It made no difference that Jasso was from Jatsu and spoke a very different dialect from his guests. There were probably a few other Basques but not many during those early years. The documents do not say that after the meal they sang and danced, but do not bet against it. They had reasons for it, in fact, the same reason to celebrate as the miners in Elko: In 1546 they had discovered La Bufa, a mountain of silver near Zacatecas that is still mined today and producing silver, according to Elko's Jesus Salazar, who worked there.

In Elko, social gatherings among the Basques happened in several places. The winter celebrations and dances at the Star Hotel were legendary. The Telescope and the Overland held their own parties and dances when the sheepherders were in town, and we have already referred to the several Fourth of July picnics at the Ramon Lugea and Goicoechea ranches, and we could add Barinaga's, as well.

These events required little organization, and advertising was the old-fashioned way, by word of mouth. Hosts contracted an accordion player, and they made sure there was enough food and drink for a regiment: That was it. The events were viewed mostly as ethnic gathering, always sprinkled with a few non-Basques who were married to Basques or business associates. The outcome of these meetings naturally and logically gave way to more ambitious celebrations, which eventually resulted in a more organized action, that is, a club.

The First Meeting

The Euzkaldunak Basque Club literally means the "club of Basque-speaking people" and functioned a little differently at the start. Elko-born Anita Anacabe Franzoia, the president of the club in 1993, says in her message printed in the festival booklet that the Elko Festival started as a gathering of sheep and cattle ranchers. It was mostly an informal affair for families, relatives, and friends, and for sure most of them were probably Basques. So, back then it may not have been totally open to the public just yet.

But the fact that there were a good number of Basque stock ranchers in the county, who necessarily had commerce with their non-Basque counterparts, may have restrained club members from thinking in a strictly ethnic manner early on.

I have not seen a date, but the first move to start a club was made in 1959. The Western Basque Festival in Sparks, Nevada, also took place in June of that year, and it is a given that some Basques from Elko attended it. This festival has been blown out of proportion: "The Woodstock of the Basque-American Community in the West," according to one internet source. Granted that it was or may have been an eye-opener for some civic-minded Basques, but the main difference was that the old celebrations, once semiprivate, were now taken to the public square. This change encouraged organizers to rethink their festivities and to structure and organize them at another level. Thus, the clubs were born soon after, like the Reno Zazpiak Bat Basque Club, though not incorporated until November 30, 1966. Elko's club was incorporated later, but it was functioning by 1960.

The first dedicated meeting was held in 1959 at the Nevada Dinner House to discuss the idea of a Basque club. There was an agreement to mail letters to as many Basques as they could identify to scout and promote interest. The response was very positive, and at the very next meeting the Elko Euzkaldunak Club was born, with Johnny Aguirre as its first president. According to the *Elko Daily Free Press*, the club started with 42 members in 1959, and by 1968 there were 217. From there the numbers increased fast. A document found in one of the boxes of club materials states they had 225 members by the second year and 301 by 1964.

Under Aguirre, who spoke Basque, some of the early meetings took place in the basement of St. Joseph's Catholic Church or at member homes, as well as at the Stockmen's Motor Hotel. During those years, young blood and energy were in short supply in the community; rather, there was an older generation of Basque townsmen with resources and experience.

All Basque clubs in the West faced the quasi-cultural struggle between the immigrants and the American-born members. Few immigrants could run the club, because of their limited experience and preparation, especially knowledge of English. However, many felt that they were doing all or most of the work, such as setting up the venue, cooking, cleaning, and participating in sports. In Elko the all-important musicians were immigrants too, and they were the backbone of the club's patronage.

However, without American-born Basques, the story of the Elko club early on would have been different. The first eleven presidents were American born; they probably had a limited command of the Basque culture but could navigate American waters. Not only that, but in 1969 the president was Charles "Chuck" Black, an American with a Basque wife. This detail indicates that there was considerable integration already. In the following year, the first immigrant was chosen president, Nicolas Fagoaga, from Navarre.

INCLUSION

The perspectives of an American-born Basque and that of an immigrant ex-sheepherder with a peasant background are oceans apart, which is why since the club's inception there was the fortunate tendency—and necessity—toward integration rather than segregation. And not just integration among the Basques themselves but with the rest of Elkoans as well. Club President Jess Lopategui in his 1971 message printed in the festival-brochure, wrote, "We are immensely grateful to this land. . . . On this Fourth of July 1971 all Basque Americans very proudly will honor the Stars and the Stripes, symbol of this greatest country in the world. The Elko 'Euzkaldunak' Club sincerely thanks the City of Elko, the County of Elko and all the people who supported us to make this National Basque Festival possible."

What more can you ask from someone who five years before was herding sheep in Columbia Basin? Here we perceive total inclusion, and Chuck Black, aka Karlos Baltza, would have agreed. His wife, Florence "Flossie" Erquiaga, was a dance instructor, and Chuck stayed active in the festivals for thirty years. He died in 1996, and in the obituary published in the club's brochure his member colleagues bid him "Agur, Jauna" (Goodbye, Sir).

THE FIRST SETBACK

Elko Basques appeared on the festival scene in August of 1964 with a bang and continued unabated for three years with great enthusiasm, attracting bigger crowds and even a few academic researchers intrigued by the phenomenon. However, with the newcomers' enthusiasm, the club soon lost its balance (bank account balance, that is) and went into debt big time, according to Liz Esparza Moiola, the club's bookkeeper. It took someone who knew money and business, someone like Joe Anacabe, to advise club members. He rented a hall, paid for it, and asked the Basques to show up. At the meeting he told them that it was a disgrace that Basques owed money in town. He said that that's not their way and that they (1) must pay off the debt, (2) should teach their children the old ways, and (3) have to teach children to dance.

It was an incredibly sobering and farsighted message coming from a respected leader of not only the Basque community but also the City of Elko. The club took the recommendations to heart. According to Liz, "In one year, we paid the debt, which was about $7,000" ($54,000 in today's money). That year was 1968, when they organized the first Sheepherder's Ball at the Nevada National Guard Armory. By all accounts, the ball was an unexpected success, and the club made a profit of $3,000. The bartender Julian Jayo secured wine and liquor donations that helped raise part of the money.

Elko Basques learned from the success of Artzainen Dantza (Sheepherders Ball) that had been organized by Winnemucca Basques for some years already (perhaps emulating Boise's earlier model) and was well attended by people from Nevada and Idaho. In jumping on the Sheepherder Ball bandwagon, the club likely started the biggest party in town. Its last edition was celebrated on March 14, 2022.

In the year 1968, there was also a change in the festival's date, from August to the Fourth of July. To make extra money, the club introduced the sale of ads in its festival booklet, held raffles, and cooked their first BBQ. All these activities paid off and its debt was erased that year; in the words of Liz Moiola, "The club has been good ever since." After the splendid success of 1968, one would hope for a repeat in 1969, which indeed happened, despite the snow during the festival on July 4.

A couple of years later the club became a corporation, and the bylaws were approved in January of 1971, according to *Euzkorria*, which at the time was the club's newsletter. It was decided that meetings would be monthly and announced in the local paper. Decisions would be made by majority vote, and the board would consist of eight members led by a president.

THE NORTH AMERICAN BASQUE ORGANIZATIONS (NABO)

The North American Basque Organizations was the brainchild of Jon Bilbao, a historian born in Puerto Rico who had a deep knowledge of the Basque diaspora. Founded in Sparks in 1973, it immediately boosted the morale of many Basque groups. In June of 1974 it published the first newsletter issue, *Alkarte'ko Barriak*, demonstrating that the early push came from the Bizkaians in Idaho as evidenced in the use of the Bizkaian dialect rather than Batua, the unified Basque that is now the standard. The first president was Al Erquiaga of Idaho. As of May 15, 1974, NABO had $2,952.73 in the First Security Bank of Idaho. The second NABO meeting was held in Reno and the third in Elko.

The organization has functioned under the leadership of a mostly American-born Basque men and women with no special preparation for the job, except full dedication. The individual Basque clubs send delegates to the meetings, where proceedings occur in English, though informally Basque may also be used. Although NABO is nonprofit and nonpolitical, the *ikurrina* (Basque flag) and its red-white-green colors that blanket every picnic in the West might give the visitor a false impression of nationalism. In this case, symbolism trumps reality. European Basques attending these festivals get inspiration from the in-your-face monogrammed shirts, colorful T-shirts with Basque emblems, and especially the cute little kids in dancing costumes and red berets. The costumes of Basque dancers in the US tend to be more colorful than the ones in Europe. It is an expression of American culture, where advertising is more developed than in the Basque Country.

The primary task of NABO is to coordinate the effort of individual clubs that are independent as well as nonprofit. Eusko Jaurlaritza (the Basque government of Euskadi, i.e., Alava/Araba, Bizkaia, and Gipuzkoa) awards small grants to clubs submitting project proposals. This funding has helped many to carry the cultural torch and push onward for another year. Some believe that the golden age of Basque organizations is behind us, but not everyone agrees. The main mission of NABO used to be to repair the disconnect between the immigrant generation and the rest of the Basques to keep the ethnic identity alive, but as of 2025 that focus no longer seems crucial, as immigrants are fast disappearing due to old age. In 2020–2021 the Covid pandemic arrived, and NABO advised the canceling of the picnics in most places for a year or two.

Winnemucca-born Bob Echeverria, who moved to Elko in 1972 and was president of NABO for seven years, says that NABO helped the Basques overcome their regional differences, which is an excellent observation. Indeed, the immigrants were very much in need of walking out of their narrow valleys and shaking hands with those in the next. Many came to America without ever having traveled to the next province in the Old Country, let alone crossing the international boundary that divided the Basque Country. Those living near the frontier were an exception because some of them were also engaged in *gau lana* (night work, or smuggling), which was a rich cash cow available to them.

The Club's Pulse Through the Years

After a few years, the Basque club started publishing a booklet for every festival. Although the booklet's pages are filled mostly with ads, they also provide information that allows us to follow the rhythm of the organization. In fact, after oral sources, the brochures (and local paper's coverage) contain primary material on the club's history.

The theme of the festival changed each year, and the brochure reflected that. In 1996, for example, the subject matter was "Our Roots Run Deep," and the cover of the booklet depicted a man facing the Oak Tree of Gernika with its large roots sinking into the ground. The image was copied from the mural painted on the front wall of the handball court the club built.

There was a period roughly after 1970 when the club was dominated by immigrants with limited knowledge of English. They depended on American-born sons and daughters or acquaintances whose knowledge of the Basque culture was less than optimal to produce the brochure. When the presidents were immigrants— that is, native speakers—the message printed in the brochure was often bilingual, or at least it had statements in Basque. We find less Euskara printed in recent years as the baton of leadership passed to American-born children, some of whom, however, went to school to learn the language.

The digital world and computers have changed publishing, and we see evidence of it in festival booklets. In 1970 the festival program was a mere seventeen pages that included little color and cultural content. By 2017, it had grown to forty-eight pages of full-color ads and photographs. It contained summaries of cultural topics beginning with a short history of the club, followed by the Ariñak Dancers, *bertsolaritza* (improvised poetry), dancing, an explanation of the Basque Coat of Arms, *herri kirolak* (Basque Rural Sports, such as woodchopping, stone-lifting, and weight-carrying *txinga*), mus (a card game), and so on.

Typos and misspellings in the Basque language were frequent (and not just in Elko's brochure) because the immigrants could not type and the typist usually did not speak Basque. Plus, there seemed to be no editor in charge. This is not at all to criticize the noble efforts. What would we city people do if one day they sent us into the mountains with 1,500 sheep, a dog, and a burro? Would we turn into expert sheepherders overnight? The same applies to ex-sheepherders when they undertook writing and brochure publication. In later years errors are noticeably fewer, thanks to technology and college-educated volunteers.

The brochure of the fifty-fourth festival in 2017 demonstrates clearly that the organization has come of age and is totally comfortable in the American world. In 1997 the club felt familiar enough with the language to even play word games. The festival's theme for that year was "Basquing in America's Freedom."

Festival publications uncover many nuggets of information about what the club members were doing. For example, in the president's message of 1976, Bob Echeverria tells us that the Basque display case containing slides and photos was now complete and that it would be a permanent exhibit at the Northeastern Nevada Museum of Elko. Today, the club is actively working to document and preserve the culture of the Pyrenees but without rejecting in the least the melting pot of the American experience. That is why it also offers scholarships of $750 for university-bound students: Tim Echeverria, Stephanie Yanci, and Kathy Fagoaga were some of the early recipients.

EUZKORRIA

Euzkorria was the bulletin of the Elko Euzkaldunak Club sent to all the members. The plan was to publish it four times a year: January, April, July, and October starting in 1971. It had a two-column format, English on one side and Euskara on the other. It supplied summaries of the festivals and club business, news from the US and abroad, recipes, and even one bertso by David Aramburu of Elko in the third issue in praise of the festival:

Zoragarrizko Euzkaldun Jaia
Elko'n degu aurten izan
makina bat Euzkaldun lagun
gu antxe alkartu ginan.
Bi milla jende inguru orrek
naikua jan eta edan,
ia berriro urrengo urtian
guztiok alkartzen geran.

A wonderful Basque festival
that we had in Elko this year
extraordinary number of Basques
all of us met there.
About two thousand people
all had enough to eat and to drink,
let us hope that next year
all of us again meet.

Aramburu was in his sixties when in the 1980s he left his name carved on several aspens in Columbia Basin.

Jess Lopategui wrote and published *Euzkorria* four times, and it was mailed abroad, including to China. It started when he was president of the club. The next president was not interested as much, but Lopategui published one more issue anyway. When it first appeared in print, people from all over—Argentina, Italy, England, Germany, and Australia—wanted a copy. *Voice of the Basques* may have been inspired by *Euzkorria*, or so Lopategui thinks because it covered the same topics.

Publicity

By the 1970s, the club was fast increasing in membership and in the quality of its offerings, and in the following decade it continued to mature with more elaborate brochures incorporating glossier photos of the past twenty-six years (1963–1989). The club's civic outlook also matured in recognition of the broad public support. Consequently, many local businesses bought ads that paid for the publication. Miller High Life took out whole-page ads. Starting in 1971 Iberia, the Spanish airline, took out a whole-page ad with the caption in Basque that stated, "*Non Erromeria*, An Iberia (Where there is a festival, there is Iberia)." Franco, the Spanish dictator of the time, probably never found out that Iberia, a state-owned company, ran an ad in Euskara, a language Franco was bent on destroying.

The two biggest Basque banks, the Bank of Vizcaya and the Bank of Bilbao, started providing support in 1972. Bilbao paid $240 for a page in Spanish, and the Bank of Vizcaya printed the message in English. After Franco died in 1975, the Bank of Vizcaya ads were in both Basque and English, but Bilbao continued in Spanish only until 1983, when it switched all to English and nothing in Basque. At that time, these two banks were briefly joined by the French Bank of California (Banque Nationale de Paris). That year, Iberia Airlines stopped submitting ads.

Local businesses took out more and bigger ads to support the club. Basque businesses, of course, were represented, along with mines, car dealers, insurance companies, lawyers, funeral homes, gas and power companies, Sears, and even politicians. Paul Laxalt had a $20 ad in 1974 with just his name (later we will see that local politicians advertised on the *Basque Radio Program*). Five Elko businesses—Red Lion Casino, Stockmen's Hotel, Budweiser Beer, Humboldt Readymix, and Barrick Gold Mine—had whole-page ads each, and a sixth—Carlin Gold Mine—joined them. In 1989, a different full-page message appeared from the Society of Basque Studies (SBS) in America, requesting donations for the National Monument to the Basque Sheepherder in Reno. The project would cost $300,000, and they still needed $100,000 (see the next chapter).

Sports, especially woodchopping and weightlifting, get more exposure than other festival activities. Pilota (handball) is the national Basque sport played in different modalities: barehanded (the most popular), jai alai, *trinkete, joko garbi,* and so forth. It has been played in the West for many decades, and pretty much in every town that had one or two Basque hotels, such as the Winnemucca Hotel in Winnemucca; the Toscano Hotel in Reno; the Brass Rail in Alturas, California; Jordan Valley, Oregon; and Boise, Idaho. Elko had two handball courts since the early 1900s, and today it has one of the newest in the West, built by the club.

CHAPTER 12

Elko Originals

In this chapter we will discuss three subjects that distinguish Elko and its American Basques. First, the SBS of Brooklyn, New York (but born in San Francisco, California, in 1979), promoted the idea that the Basque Sheepherder Monument project was to be erected in Elko. It seems that SBS wanted the monument in Elko, because it was the biggest sheepherding center in Nevada and with a high percentage of Basque population. But first we will consider the Basque Hall of Fame event sponsored by SBS, which led to the conceptualization of the Monument to the Sheepherder. The chapter's third main topic is the *Basque Radio Program.*

BASQUE HALL OF FAME (BHF)

In 1981 the SBS initiated the idea of honoring Basque historical figures who were selected mostly from the US. Its fourth Hall of Fame event took place in Elko, Nevada, on October 13, 1984, when Basque Americans from the West were honored; this was the first such event outside the East Coast. The promoter and president of SBS was Jose Ramon Zengotitabengoa, a Basque industrialist from Durango, Bizkaia, living in Chicago.

According to Lopategui, Zengotitabengoa first called the Laxalts with the idea of a Hall of Fame ceremony, and he was told to talk to Elko people. It is not clear which Laxalt Zengotitabengoa spoke with, but it reflects the high standing of the Basques of Elko to have a prominent Basque make the referral. Representatives of the BHF went to Elko to plan the event, and their first inductee was Pedro Altube, of Independence Valley, and their second Dominique Laxalt, of Carson City, Nevada. The third choice was at the discretion of Elko Basques, and they chose the recently deceased Domingo Ansotegui. Ansotegui played drums in Boise with Jimmy Jausoro and their Oinkari Dancers for many years. Thus, the inductees turned out to be a cattle rancher, a sheepman, and a musician. The selections were also appropriate because the individuals represented three different Basque regions in Europe, although Altube represented only the small independent county of Oñati (today it is part of Gipuzkoa), and Laxalt represented Zuberoa, which was the smallest Basque region and sent relatively few immigrants to the US. Ansotegui, on the other hand, represented Bizkaia, with thousands of its people in Idaho and Nevada. One unanswerable question is why Pedro Altube was chosen and not his brother Bernardo. Why not both owners of the Spanish Ranch?

Present at the unique ceremony, surrounded by Elko Basques, were Carol Covey, an Altube descendant, Domingo Ansotegui's son Daniel, and Robert Laxalt's son Bruce Laxalt. Tenor Valentin Aguirre sang Basque songs, and Josu Gallastegui played the piano. The ceremony took place at the Elko Civic Auditorium in October 1984.

Monument to the Basque Sheepherder

After the BHF event, while waiting for their flight back at the Elko Airport, Emilia Doyaga and her SBS colleagues, in the presence of Lopategui and others, pitched the idea of a Basque sheepherder monument to erect in Elko. There was no mention of other sites at the time. A few months later, Zengotitabengoa arrived in Elko with several prospective sculptors, among them Nestor Basterretxea. They brought with them a huge wooden sculpture, a mock-up of the monument that Lopategui thought was temporarily placed at the library of the GBCC. Lopategui does not know who made the wooden sculpture, and today nobody at the college seems to know what happened to it, but according to Professor Skivington, the college has a photograph of it. In any case, it speaks to the standing of the Elko Basques at the time.

What transpired next is not clear to Elkoans. Some people in Reno approached Zengotitabengoa to suggest to him the idea that Reno would be a better site for such a monument. Or it could also be that at the time Zengotitabengoa's business suffered a downturn, and, as Carmelo Urza suggested to me, the people in Reno were ready and prepared to undertake the project. Some people in Elko were clearly annoyed by the turn of events, though they do not think that the Laxalts had anything to do with it but probably the university did. In hindsight they still think Elko would have been a more suitable location for such a monument, because the county had many more sheep, artzainak, and prominent Basque ranchers than Reno ever did, which was the reason why initially SBS approached the Elko club first.

In the end, Basterretxea's design was approved, and the monument was erected at the Rancho San Rafael Regional Park on a hill at the northern edge of Reno proper. It overlooks the casino skyline and stands exactly where in 1933 Ambrosio Arla spent his first night as a sheepherder and cried himself to sleep. As a footnote, few actual herders liked the sculpture that was promptly dubbed as "Aittitte Mokordo" (untranslatable). Nevertheless, the inauguration of the monument was a success and well attended on August 27, 1989. (Carmelo Urza does not mention Elko in his 1993 book that traces the sculpture's history and symbolism.)

ARTZAINA ZAIN
(THE WATCHFUL SHEEPHERDER)

Eventually, the Elko Basques got their own Sheepherder Monument, a work by sculptor Lowell Svenseid (2000). It stands in the city park a few hundred feet west of the museum, surrounded by a rose garden and facing traffic on Old Highway 40, now Idaho Street. According to Lopategui, the sculpture was fashioned to represent the pioneers passing through or arriving in Elko, but Dr. Morris Gallagher suggested that honoring the Basque sheepherders was more befitting for Elko, and he convinced the museum that it should be located there. The man's headgear in Svenseid's statue already looked like a beret; therefore, hardly any changes were needed to convert this Anglo pioneer into a Basque—just insert a sheep hook within his fingers, and voila, we have *Artz-aina Zain*, the Watchful Sheepherder! The statue was put in place soon after 2000.

Artzaina Zain, the Watchful Sheepherder monument at the Elko City Park.

Basque Radio Program

The third item that distinguishes Elko is the *Basque Radio Program*. The inspiration for radio transmission came, no doubt, from the long-running Espe Alegria's *Basque Program* that originated in Boise in 1952 and was heard in a wide area of the West until its cessation in 1984. There was another program, *The Basque Program* out of Buffalo, Wyoming, that lasted even longer, from 1956 to 1996 on KBBS. In 1997 the SBS inducted it into the Basque Hall of Fame (but somehow overlooked Espe Alegria, with a wider audience).

Few people outside northeast Nevada know that Elko, too, had a Basque radio program. Even fewer people know that Winnemucca had one in 1970–1971. Elko's broadcast began in 1968, when Jess Lopategui and this writer approached the local KELK Radio to promote the idea of having something Basque on the radio. Mr. Gardner, the owner of the station, accepted the proposal rather quickly and added he would do it as community service without charge. The show would start at noon on Sundays and run for ninety minutes. The programming elements were news about local Basques, birthdays, weddings, and so on; news from the Old Country; and a religious message in Basque by the local Catholic priest. But the airtime was mostly filled with ethnic music that the Basques, especially the outlying sheepherders, enjoyed so much.

The Elko program was unique in that, unlike the others in Boise, Buffalo, or Winnemucca, it had paid ads in the Basque language. Prices were set by KELK, $4 for thirty seconds. Lopategui would request the ads in English, and he would then translate and read them in Basque. The advertisers were mostly Basque businesses such the Urriola Bros., Nevada Dinner House, Blue Jay Bar, Star Hotel, Blohm Jewelry, Speedy's Phillips 66 Gas Station, Clifton House, and others.

In addition, the program ran political ads during the campaign season, probably the only time and place such ads were broadcast in the US. Furthermore, they were paid for by American candidates, which speaks to the relevance of the Basque audience in the

The *Basque Radio Program* on Sundays was so popular that trapper Steve Moiola and sheepherder Jose A. Oleaga, in the desert 200 miles away from Elko, rigged an antenna that allowed them reception, so they could sing and dance in the snow. Courtesy of Steve Moiola.

county. For example, when Dutch Stenovich, a local car dealer, ran for mayor, he bought ads on the program selling his agenda to the Basque audience; and he won the election. During the subsequent election four years later, Jim Conner ran against Stenovich. He too wanted ads in Basque, and he won the election. Lopategui became a kingmaker.

Lopategui managed the program for almost ten years, but in the last couple of years there were new faces and voices. Tony Leniz and Joe L. Mallea were two who occasionally relieved Lopategui, until 1979, when Maite Uriagereka Moiola took over. By this time, the program had grown to three full hours, from 9 a.m. to noon on Sundays. She played the guitar, sang songs, and dedicated them to individuals who had a birthday or an anniversary, and continued until the program's closure in 1980.

CHAPTER 13

Early Festivals—Catching the Wind

The beginnings of social gatherings were modest, and the necessary early direction and planning were supplied by a few Nevada-born leaders, among them Johnny Aguirre, Joe Urriola, Louie Uriarte, Ray Goicoa, Joe Mendive, Chuck Black, Ray Jayo, and others. The first picnic was organized with woodchoppers and weightlifting events and happened in 1963. The performers were mostly local, such as Isidro Fagoaga, one of the woodchoppers. Jess Lopategui and Alfonso Ygoa lifted the *kanika* stone, a 225-pound granite ball. Its shape was new to Idaho strongmen Benito Goitiandia and Jose L. Arrieta, who at first balked at lifting it.

By 1964 the festival turned into a two-day affair known as the National Basque Festival, an honor granted to Elko by Nevada Governor Grant Sawyer. Since then, the picnic and the parade have been scheduled during the Fourth of July weekend, a brilliant move. Many civic organizations took part in the parade, and that attracted a large crowd to celebrate the national holiday. The Basque festival and the Fourth of July celebration merged, and this is another reason why Elko Basques were never accused of being unpatriotic. The parade became a vehicle for all Elko citizens to join the Basques and share stories of their own ancestral roots.

In 1968, over 2,000 people attended the festival and 1,470 enjoyed the BBQ dinner, followed by sports and dancing. Benito Goitiandia of Boise won the weightlifting match, and Luis Jayo came in second.

At the 1969 festival, A. Leiza of Craig, Colorado, won the woodchopping contest; Esteban Sarratea was second; and Periko Zubiria came in third. The following year Periko Zubiria came on top. In the txinga-weight-carrying competition, Jose Goicoechea was first, Jess Lopategui second, and Tom Belaustegui of Battle Mountain third. The Olasagasti brothers won the *artzain ogi* (sheepherder bread) contest, and Mitch Moiola won the jota-dancing competition (see chapter 15 for more information on the jota).

By 1969–1970, Nevada politicians began to show up in Elko, such as Senator Alan Bible, Governor Grant Sawyer, and Governor Paul Laxalt, whose father was a sheepherder from Zuberoa. In 1969, foul weather prevented Laxalt from reaching Elko, and his plane had to be grounded in Lovelock, Nevada. (I also read an account that Laxalt handed out trophies that year, so perhaps he made it to Elko, after all.)

The 1971 festival offered a range of presentations, including Basque-song singers and bertsolariak (improvising poets), but their prize money was lower than what other performers were getting. Basques sometimes do not show appreciation of their most important cultural treasure: the language. Without it, the Basques would be just another human group of western Europe, such as the Occitans, Bearnaise, Galicians, Catalans, Andalusians, French, and Castilians: They all speak Latin-derived languages. Only Basques speak their own untraceable isolate tongue, and their neighbors are still wondering and asking, How is it possible?

The Consul of Spain cum Crawdads

The Euzkaldunak of Elko explored avenues that other Basque clubs did not, when in 1964 they invited the consuls of Spain and France to attend the festival. This was the first step in their unlikely relationship with Madrid when they met the Spanish consul stationed in San Francisco. Of course, the Basque sheepherders in America had already played a role in the relations between the US and Spain beginning in the 1940s and culminating in the 1953 Pact of Madrid, sponsored by Nevada Senator Patrick McCarran; that is, the Elko Basques were on Madrid's radar.

But before they could meet the consul, there was a detour in the road that went all the way to New York. Raimundo Blanco, a representative of Bank of Vizcaya in the Big Apple, initiated a crucial contact with the consul, whom he knew. Blanco had attended some of the Elko festival for two reasons: because his bank was a generous donor since 1964, and because he loved to catch and eat crawdads found in the creeks of Elko. He would go to South Fork, catch them, boil them, and prepare a paella (he was from Valencia, after all—the home of paella). He bought all the necessary ingredients and invited people to eat his paella at the park. Following the Bank of Vizcaya's lead, the Bank of Bilbao also jumped into action and became a festival donor.

After preliminary arrangements were met in 1974, San Francisco Consul José A. de Urbina, originally from Donostia/San Sebastian, showed up in Elko wearing a red *txapela* (beret) and marched in the parade behind the ikurrina. For a few years, he would become an unlikely yet ardent supporter of the Basques in Elko. It was then when club members proposed to him the idea of building a handball court. (Pilota is the quintessential Basque sport and the young immigrants very much wanted to play but lacked a location.) Consul Urbina attended the festivals several times and befriended several members, Lopategui becoming the principal link to the club.

Spreading Like Wildfire

Fairly quickly, the Elko Festivals became news and a sensation, and the main ingredient was human: Elko's high-energy Basque population and direction. In 1974, the club paid for and brought bertsolari poets from the Basque Country. These poets were famous in their country, and people wanted to accompany them to Nevada to find out what the fuss was all about. In that year, the club hosted a bike race, which M. Horwitz from Marin, California, won. As an interesting aside, Margaret Shedd, author of *A Silence in Bilbao* (1974) was one of the people who attended the 1974 Elko Festival.

Elko Basques have legitimate bragging rights that their festivals have attracted the largest crowds in Nevada and in Idaho, outperformed only by Jaialdi, which is a quinquennial affair. The Boise Oinkari Dancers, who rank highest in the American Basque pantheon, always travel to Elko. Merry families and their children from far and near spend the national holiday watching dancers in attractive costumes, overcoming the heat or not (Elko weather can change without warning) with cold drinks, visiting old friends and making new ones, and reinvigorating themselves with a culture born 5,000 miles away. The seats at the fairgrounds are usually packed, and only in the last two decades do we see smaller crowds but not by much. Among the Basque community the explanation for this is that the old-timers, those born in the Old Country, are dying off.

In the decades of the '60s and '70s the town of Elko became a celebrity among the Basques here in the US and in Europe. The media sent journalists across the ocean to chronicle Elko and its festivals. *El Correo Español–El Pueblo Vasco* daily from Bilbao published a report by one "S.B.B." in the early 1970s with plenty of platitudes and a few errors: Boise and Elko were the two cities with the largest Basque colonies in the West, which was incorrect. Furthermore, the writer omitted mentioning California and the Iparralde Basques altogether. Perhaps he did not want his readers in Bilbao to know that in the US there are no international borders dividing the Basques like in Europe. At least the writer did look to a future festival when Basques from Europe competed with those in Nevada and Idaho, and that was a correct prediction.

CHAPTER 14

Music and Dancing

WITH MERCEDES MENDIVE

No music, no dancing. No dancing, no festival. It could be as simple as that. Music is a vital part of Basque culture in Europe, but in the US Basque dancing has become the expression of the music, and even more so as the showcase of the entire culture. No wonder that when festival-attending politicians want to be photographed, they always want dancers in costumes surrounding them.

Among the Basques of Europe almost everyone used to sing, especially during Franco's dictatorship, 1939–1975; today, not as much. At the time, singing was the one thing people could do without being arrested. They hiked up to the mountains, sang patriotic songs, and told antiregime jokes. Mountaineering was another face of the resistance to the government's repression. But even before that, all Basque men could whistle, and some women too. It seems that singing and dancing are in the Basque blood. My mother told me she liked men who were good dancers like her. She would take brand-new *abarketak* (espadrilles) to the Sunday afternoon dance and come home needing another pair.

In Basque communities of the West, as in Basque villages in Europe, you could find one or two people who played accordion and perhaps some other instrument, and in this chapter Mercedes Mendive reports on the subject in Elko, her hometown. In rural areas of the Old Country, the accordion was attacked harshly by the priests, who called it *inpernuko auspoa* (bellows from hell). In some towns they would not allow couples to dance together. Many people who landed in Elko can vouch for those days, which today seem so far away. As the *trikitrilariak* (accordionists) Egaña and Kaminazpi used to sing soon after the dictatorship ended:

Gure denboran dena zen bekatua,
guk sinesten genun hainbat tonteria,
orain berriz gazteek dute loteria

In our time, everything was a sin,
we used to believe all sorts of nonsense
today, however, the young people have hit the jackpot

MUSICAL STARS

Among the Basques—especially in Idaho, Oregon, and Nevada—the star musician for half a century was Jimmy Jausoro, who was born in Nampa, Idaho, in 1920. His parents, Tomas Jausoro and Tomasa Mallea, owned an *ostatu* (boardinghouse), and he grew up there watching the sheepherders dance and play their folk music. After serving in the US Navy and returning to Idaho in 1960, he started a dancing group, the Oinkari, which means "people [who do] foot work." Jausoro and Domingo Ansotegui were the main members of the Jimmy Jausoro Basque Band, which for decades spiced up many Basque festivals. They recorded at least one 45 RPM album, *La Jota Vasca*. Jausoro died in 2004. (Joe Mendive, Mercedes Mendive's father and a musical aficionado, had a big music library and he archived most of Jausoro's music.)

On March 13, 2018, I met with Mercedes Mendive, Janet Iribarne, and Amaya Ormaza at Toki Ona Basque Restaurant to talk about music and dancing. All three agreed that growing up with live music was a game changer for them. Bernardo Yanci played accordion, Jean Iribarne (Janet's father) the clarinet, and Juan "Bermeo" Uriaguereca the tambourine. This trio ensemble gave birth to current musicians Mercedes and Janet, who with Anamarie Sarratea Lopategui make up the current Elko musical trio. (Sarratea too hails from Nevada.)

Dance Instructors—the Unsung Heroines

These three musicians enliven the dancing practices of the Elko Arinak, who today number about eighty of all ages. The group boasts about a dozen dancers over twenty-one, and as usual girls outnumber boys sixty-seven to thirteen. Nobody should think teaching music and dancing is all easy and fun. Today's kids have many distractions and other activities they can join, such as sports. According to the trio, the hardest task for instructors is the costumes, which can be expensive and time consuming to make. Their other job is to persuade parents to bring their children to practice. It takes time and commitment. Maite Ugalde, Judy Ugalde, and Jess Lopategui tutored children in other cultural projects (such as typical Basque card games) besides dancing. At the Toki Ona meeting, Mendive, Iribarne, and Ormaza mentioned twenty-six dance teachers they remembered (see their names and others listed in appendix 3).

In 2016, Mercedes Mendive and Janet Iribarne started the Ariñak Project, with the objective to teach not only dancing and music but also Euskara and culture. This was a good move because they themselves are not fluent Basque speakers and wanted to be. So, what better way than to teach others and themselves at the same time? The Ariñak Project ended their first year with great success. The students learned to play tambourine, txistu (three-hole Basque flute), and Basque rhythms, as well as a few phrases in Euskara. In addition, Fernando Lejardi, a former professional jai alai player taught the game at the Elko City Park handball court.

Mendive and Iribarne are committed to influencing and energizing young minds. Members of Ariñak get to dance, speak the language, sing, and learn Basque history. Paraphrasing the two: We must step out of our comfort zone. We do not want them only to dance. We want them to be teachers later, to be passionate about the culture. To accomplish this, we must fight for the dancers in front of the Basque club board.

It is heartwarming listening to the enthusiasm of these women. Luckily, they are not alone; they have friends and colleagues like Maite Uriagereka Moiola and Pilar Fagoaga, who once were young

Dance instructors and big-time supporters Amaya Ormaza and Janet Iribarne.

Mercedes Mendive recorded the CD *Journey to Euskadi*. Courtesy Jon C. Hodgson-BasquePhotos.com.

dancers themselves. Lisa and Enrike Corcostegui, from Reno, are two more who help and have conducted a productive workshop for Elko dancers.

In 2013, Ariñak went through months of stress over some dancers who wanted to leave the group. The splintering of a group, however, is very much part of the Basque culture, especially in politics. Splintering happens when the group has grown too big and there is too much pent-up energy. Or sometimes, the opposite, when all energy is gone. In 2013 about five Arinak Dancers formed another group called Ardi Baltza (The Black Sheep). Their intention was to present traditional dances in a different format, or perhaps they sought to innovate. One performance they offered during the 2018 Cowboy Poetry Event in Elko was interesting to me; their choreography was reminiscent to a degree of the shows of the Olaeta Ballet in the 1960s.

Mercedes Mendive's Story in Her Own Words

A prominent link to Basque culture is Basque dancing and its many faces. They have become the ambassadors for their respective Basque clubs. And although not all Basque organizations in the US have their very own groups of dancers, Elko Euzkaldunak Club is one of those fortunate ones.

To give you a little bit of history on how this all started, we begin with a 1959 organizational meeting at the Nevada Dinner House in Elko. At this meeting, those in attendance were contemplating starting a Basque club. A list was prepared that included the names of local Basques in the community. Subsequently, letters were sent out inviting individuals with possible interest in forming a Basque club to attend the next meeting as well. The responses proved to be tremendously positive. The discussions and efforts of early meetings were pivotal in the formation of the Euzkaldunak Basque Club.

One of the club's priorities was to assemble a troupe of dancers. A key dance instructor was, and still is, Anamari Ozamis Arbillaga. To this day, she teaches every Wednesday evening (during

Anamari Ozamis Arbillaga (*left*), the original dance instructor, with her great-granddaughter Eloisa and granddaughter Madison, Eloisa's mother.

dance season) at the clubhouse, ignoring her advanced age and embracing her gift to teach.

Anamari Ozamis made her way to the US from the Basque County in 1960 at the age of twenty-five. Her mother had passed away and her aunt, who lived in California and happened to be visiting, asked Anamari to come and stay with her. Anamari had two days to decide. On the following day, she made the decision. She went to the Bilbao consulate and obtained her visa and her passport all in one day and made her way to California.

Anamari explains that she spent a year in Santa Rosa. She worked as a seamstress for a couple of women, one of whom was going to Elko to see her brother. She asked Ozamis if she would like to join her and she thought, *why not?* Her first trip to Elko happened in March or April 1961. She recalls seeing so much desert, which she had never seen before. She says she remembers saying to herself, "where in hell am I going?" After her short stay in Elko, she returned to California, deciding within a short time to come back. She took the bus to Elko and began working at the Nevada Dinner House.

Originally from Arteaga, near Gernika, Ozamis explains that she began dancing when she was just a girl. After the bombing of Gernika in April of 1937, her family moved to Natxitua. She remembers that her uncle, who was a priest, taught the *ezpata dantza* (sword dance) to boys, so dancing was in the family. However, the way Anamari really learned was simply by dancing behind older dancers and following their steps. Dance was not taught in a formal setting but consisted of this shadowing experienced dancers, which proved to be crucial instruction.

According to Anamari Ozamis (she married Manuel Arbillaga in 1961), the Elko Basque Dancers (Ariñak) formed in 1968, but instruction had begun in 1967. There were several people who helped her teach Basque dances in Elko. The early instructors included Felicia Basañez (Basanez), Flossie Erquiaga Black, Liz Moiola, Mildred Bilbao, Anita Anacabe, as well as Nicolas Fagoaga (from Lesaka, Navarre) and Jean Iribarne (from Arnegi, Iparralde). She recalls that dance lessons were first held in the basement of Elko's Catholic Church. Charlene Shobe remembers one more instructor, Diane Smith, and she says they also practiced in the basement of the Stampede Motel, owned by Domingo and Marguerite Ozamis.

Fast-forwarding to the mid-1970s, when the Elko Basque Club had not yet built their clubhouse, dance practice was held at the local Girl Scout House, which was located only a block from the downtown city park. Each Saturday morning, the air was filled with live music, which was played by Bernardo Yanci, Jean Iribarne, and "Bermeo." At the time, none of us gave much thought to our Saturday-morning practice, and just how fortunate we were to have live music. Yanci played his red Paolo Soprani accordion with magnificent technique. Iribarne, on his clarinet, could play any jota or traditional dance without missing a beat, and he did so

Jean Iribarne with his clarinet and accordion player Bernardo Yanci, two Elko musicians who for over thirty years provided free music for the dancers. Photograph by Blanton Owen. Courtesy Nevada Arts Council.

for fifty years—they were truly two of the most gifted musicians I have ever had the pleasure of knowing. The accordion and the clarinet together undoubtedly resonate with every Elko Basque dancer who took instruction from the inception of Ariñak until the early 1990s.

Growing up as Ariñak dancers, we were most notable for our jotas. They say that the best jota dancers come from Elko! But those of us who learned from gifted instructors know that it was their input in teaching us that absolutely set us apart from other Basque-dancing groups. And although years have passed since our earliest instruction, the traditions remain largely the same.

Many Ariñak dancers have now taken the reins to teach and to instruct Basque dancing within the Euzkaldunak Club. On any given Wednesday evening the youngest of the dancers learn how to do their one-two-three's and dance the *polka pik*. If the little ones can retain their focus long enough, they get to dance the beginner's jota! The intermediate dancers follow with fandangos and other traditional dances such as the Soka Dantza and Bola Dantza, as well as the more modern choreographed dances. On

Boise Oinkari Dancers in the Elko Festival's parade, 2012.

Sunday afternoons, the older kids come together to collaborate on dancing, learn new footwork, and organize performances, which are ultimately the reward for all their hard work.

In the 1990s, one of Elko's first adult Basque-dance groups who affectionately call themselves Los Vinos Mios formed within Ariñak. The group consisted of retired Ariñak dancers, all over the age of twenty-one. Los Vinos Mios had a great run, traveling to various Basque festivals throughout Nevada, and performing like true Ariñak. In early 2000, the adult Ariñak came together to form Beti Egarri (Always Thirsty) and continued traveling throughout Nevada and California. It was an exciting time in all our lives, and it allowed everyone to hang on to incredible memories a little bit longer. Memories that came by way of dancing and Ariñak.

CHAPTER 15

Festivals on Steroids

The festival reputation that the Elko Basques earned in the 1960s and 1970s hinged mainly on the crowds they attracted and the variety and the level of the sports and entertainment they offered. Sports became spectacles to showcase Old Country Basque culture with an American twist, based on dancing, except that chopping through a log of fifteen-inch circumference in half a minute was more exotic. Many people, especially passing-through tourists, had never seen a woodchopping competition. The fact that Elko had casinos and excellent Basque restaurants was a bonus to entice people to return year after year.

Television and radio crews from Europe, Reno, Salt Lake City, Las Vegas, and even Detroit and the Associated Press would show up in town for the Fourth of July. A magazine dedicated to selecting top summer destinations in the nation reputedly voted Elko Basque Festival at number 7 (but I have not seen it). Euskal Telebista (Basque Television) sent a film crew several times. On May 28, 1980, ABC Sports, Inc. representative Eleanor Riger wrote to Lopategui requesting video footage from the festival; she intended to convince ABC *Wide World of Sports* to include it in their broadcast.

Elko Basques found themselves in the enviable position of having to produce more and newer entertainment for the larger crowds, and most years they delivered without a hitch. Some years, however, were exceptional even by Elko standards. The 1980 and the 1993 National Basque Festivals easily surpassed all earlier festivals, according to Lopategui. To begin with, in 1980 NABO members were in town for their annual convention, which brought traffic from American Basque communities across the nation. Besides the usual kickoff with the parade, breakfast was offered in the city park on Friday, July 4. At noon of the same day the NABO Mus Tournament finals took place at Stockmen's Motor Hotel. Thirteen pairs from thirteen clubs from California, Idaho, and Nevada were present and ready to bluff to win.

In 1980 President Nicolas Fagoaga's message was "Munduko euskaldun guztiak agurtzen ditugu" (We salute all the Basques in the world). In 1993 the president was Anita Anacabe Franzoia, and her message was "Eman ta zabal zazu munduan frutua," part of the *Gernikako Arbola* (Oak Tree of Gernika) anthem by Jose-mari Iparragirre encouraging all Basques to join in spreading good deeds throughout the world. At the same time, the club's motto for that year was "Preserving the old. . . . Cultivating the new," hinting that the Basques were a forward-looking bunch. In 1993 the festival brochure was three times bigger, totaling fifty-seven pages in a larger format. Local businesses took out four-teen full-page ads.

POLITICS AND BBQ

Politicians showed up early at the Elko Festival—we have met the Spanish consul—but in 1993 representatives from all Basque regions in Europe converged. Josu Legarreta represented Euskadi, encompassing the regions of Araba, Bizkaia, and Gipuzkoa. The brochure printed two full pages of his message in Basque and English. Juan Cruz Alli Aranguren represented Nafarroa/Navarre, and his message was in three languages: Basque, Spanish, and English. There was also a rare representative of the Atlantique-Pyrenees, the French government representing the Iparralde Basques. It was a seldom-seen show of unity. To top it off, District Judge Jack B. Ames, married to Francine Shobe Sabala, did his part as well, buying a half-page ad of thanks, "Eskerrik asko to All."

Speaking of politics, in 1976 during the US Bicentennial, Elko Basques scored another first. They were determined to celebrate the bicentennial duly by making at the same time a clear political statement. In the festival brochure of that year, there is a half-page proclamation in the Basque language titled "Askatasuna eta Euzkal Jaia" (Freedom and the Basque Festival) with a rousing eulogy of the United States, its freedoms, and greatness, expressed in the straightforward language of the immigrants. In translation it said, "Thousands of Basques, now and before, have praised the magnificence and the freedoms of America [United States]. It makes no difference that some people, driven by jealousy, want to vilify it. Once you see the United States you must admire it. No, this Fatherland is not without defects—only the heavens are without defects—but in this round planet where we sinners live in, where do we see more prosperity? Where more equality? And [where more] freedom? Don't you think that the last one is the seed for everything else?"

In 1976, Bob Echeverria started as emcee at the festival, something he continues doing. According to him, "In 1976 we bought 2,000 lbs. of chorizos from Boise and we ran out Sunday morning. Many Basques showed up from Europe, and some 3,000 people attended the festival."

But first things first. Let us begin with the incredible annual BBQ, because your belly must be happy before you can enjoy the spectacles. Since 1969, the festival BBQ had taken place at the Elko City Park, under the great shady trees, over cool green lawn that in July felt very pleasant. Families and friends often brought their own tables, drinks, and even food, and despite that the club sold on average 2,500 BBQ dinners. The disposable plates could barely hold the lamb chops, steaks, beans, salad, and bread to the point that you needed an extra hand to carry the wine and dessert. The price of the BBQ feed was $10 per adult in 1993 and $5 for those under twelve.

Life Is Music and Dancing

I wonder how the festivals would survive without the dancers in beautiful costumes. They probably would not. Everybody loves the dancers, who are mostly female teens, young and full of life, who love kicking up their feet. To really understand the passion that dancing generates, suffice to say that the Jota Contest in Elko is divided into five or six categories, including seniors. Jota is a fast dance performed singly or in pairs, which takes a minute or two from start to finish, but whoever wins is considered the best dancer, practically the champion. Children as young as seven years old can earn $100. Not a bad hourly wage.

In 1993 the organizers made sure that if the dancers could help it, nobody would stay in bed too long. For one thing, the Klika of San Francisco with their martial brass instruments would wake you up, even if you were a hibernating bear. The local Arinak Dancers were there, as always, accompanied by Salt Lake City Triskalariak, Boise Oinkari, San Francisco Zazpiak Bat, University of Nevada, Reno, Zenbat Gara? (The name means "How many are we?"), and Kern County, California, Gazteak. It was the biggest smorgasbord of dancing ever seen in Elko.

Each group has its own dances, beyond the regular ones that are most popular, like Godalet Dantza, performed by all. This is a favorite of the crowd and requires the dancer to jump with two feet on a glass of wine without spilling a drop. Ezpata dantza is a martial dance honoring the fallen warrior. The one that all groups practice is aurresku, which is an old dance performed to honor a person; today it is danced at the beginning of many events. There are many other dances, regional, for men only, women only, and mixed that individuals groups proudly exhibit.

Nonstop music, as always, provided by Jimmy Jausoro's Band, accompanied by locals Bernardo Yanci, Jean Iribarne, and Bermeo. They usually perform the evening dance for young and old. Through the years, the Elko Club has contracted many outside groups of musicians to entertain the audience, such as Ordago, Roberto & Kepa, Amuma Says No, Amerikanuak, and so on.

Bertsolari Poets

It was in 1974 when the first poets—Jon Lopategi, Jon Azpilaga, and Joakin Arregi—were contracted from Europe. Since then, many top poets have come, happy to perform in Elko, where they found renewed energy. In 1981, Jon Lopategi and Xabier Amuritza (the champion) returned to play and spar with words and display linguistic contortions, to the delight of Euskaldunak. In the 1990s folk singer Benito Lertxundi and *trikitrilari* (folk musicians playing the diatonic accordion) Martin and Egañazpi traveled with the bertsolari to perform in Elko. These were celebrities who had been entertaining Basques and others in Europe for many years, and now Elko was about to enjoy them. As amazing as it was, they could be fully appreciated only by people with fluency in the Basque language.

Pilota (Handball)

By 1980 Elko had a newly built handball court, and the festival organizers were eager to offer exciting matches with players arriving from several western states. On July 5 and 6, 1980, the Bank of Vizcaya sponsored thirty-six *pilotariak* (barehand handball players) from Basque clubs as far away as Los Angeles. Prize money was $2,000 (worth $7,270 in 2023), and José A. de Urbina, the Spanish consul, awarded the trophies.

In 1993 only California sent players, but the matches on July 3 and 4 were just as hard fought. The sponsor was a local firm, Puccinelli & Puccinelli. Pilota matches waned slowly as the immigrants and their limbs grew older. Younger Basques did not pick up on this tradition; it is not much fun hitting a rock-hard ball with your bare hands.

Harrijaso (Stone-Lifting)

Harrijaso and other rural sports may be as old as farming, or older, but have little historical literary tradition. It was practiced in rural hamlets and villages that attracted little attention from city dwellers inhabited by historians. Other ethnic groups, such as the Scots and the Icelanders, have similar competitive traditions, but they are not as popular as in Euskal Herria. In modern times these rural sports have migrated to the city center, and television has helped to popularize them. There are about four shapes of stones lifted in Basque competition: round, cubic, cylindrical, and rectangular, but naturally the weight is more significant than the shape.

Early festival strongmen were home grown in Elko, and especially in Boise, a city with more Basques than in all of Nevada. We have seen that starting in 1964, Benito Goitiandia and Jose Luis Arrieta, both living in Boise, delighted Elko festivalgoers. A third competitor, Juan Bicandi, also from Boise joined them, but for fewer years. All three were Bizkaians, and their dexterity and strength were evenly matched. People of Elko and tourists passing through were amazed the first time they happened to see them lifting a stone weighing 225 or 250 pounds with ease, and not just once. In 1973, Arrieta lifted the 250-pound stone forty-eight times in two 3-minute periods, that is, 12,000 pounds in six minutes. He was a human backhoe.

The club had a kanika (round stone ball) of 225 pounds fashioned from granite in Salt Lake City, which Goitiandia and Arrieta had never seen before, so Alfonso Ygoa and Jess Lopategui, two local boys, psyched each other into trying to lift it. "If the Boise guys don't want to do it, we will do it ourselves," someone said. Lopategui lifted the kanika at least five times in three minutes, including passing it around the neck, and Ygoa did too. Seeing that, the pros from Boise took courage and they also lifted it, and Goitiandia did so six times. If the strongman still has it in him, he will end his performance by moving the ball around his neck twice. That is "the Basque necktie."

These American stone lifters were local celebrities, but compared to the pros in the European Basqueland, you could say they were weekend sportsmen, which in truth they were. Thus, it was not long before the Elko Club started bringing the European heavyweights over to entertain the American audience. In the Old Country Iñaki Perurena was probably the biggest stone-lifting star; in fact, he was also a TV celebrity, acting in a sitcom that ran for many years. Today, he is still an institution in the Basque Country after coaching many other *harrijasole* (stone lifters).

Inaki Perurena, one of the greatest harrijasole (Basque weightlifters), heaving to the shoulder 485 pounds with one hand. Reprinted from Elko Festival Brochure.

Weightlifting is a battle between gravity and brawn but much more about skill than brute muscle. Being tall is a drawback because you must heave the stone higher. (The Neanderthals had the ideal body shape.) Perurena (six feet tall) never ceased to amaze the Elko audience, as he made it look so easy to pick up a 540-pound stone *with just one hand* and bring it up to his shoulder. Perurena lifted 485 pounds with one hand routinely and more than 700 pounds with both, but these records are broken regularly, it seems.

In 1983 the new weightlifting Basque champion, Jose Unanue "Gonatxo," was in town working with a 575-pound stone, which he lifted several times. In 1993, the new champion, Mikel Saralegi, was in town. *Mon Dieu!* Saralegi beat the records of the great Perurena, something nobody thought possible. By the way, both Hercules Saralegi and Perurena come from the same little town of Leitza, Navarre. Saralegi preferred to lift a rectangle stone, and Jess Lopategui made one for him. He gave an exhibition with a 500-pound cylinder, 250-pound cubic bloc, and 225-pound granite ball. Three months earlier, Saralegi had set a world record with the 329-kilogram cubic stone (725.3 pounds). Perurera's record is 322 kilograms.

WOODCHOPPERS AND WORLD COMPETITIONS

The *aizkolari* (woodchopper) sport has had more coverage than other rural sports, probably because a lot of people used axes for work: lumberjacks, firewood workers, carpenters.... Basque aizkolari matches tend to last hours as they value endurance, while a professional axe man from Oregon goes for speed in cutting smaller logs. Nobody has bested Ramon Latasa's epic 1959 record of chopping a eucalyptus log of 5.15 meters in circumference in three hours and seventeen minutes. Latasa needed a ladder to climb on top of the log to begin his task.

The woodchopping competitions enjoyed by the Elko audiences are another example that the Basque Club blazed new territory. It achieved this by throwing together competitions between American lumberjacks from the East and West Coasts with Basques. It was another way of showing the audience that Basques were more than sheepherders and that they could compete with the likes of Paul Bunyan. The log cutting, however, is done a little differently: In America, logs usually are placed upright, while the Basques position them flat on the ground with the woodchopper standing on them. Cutting is done between their two feet, just inches away, and non-Basques might think that is sheer madness.

American lumberjacks were first invited to the 1976 festival. Two teams of three men each came from the East and West Coasts and competed against three local axe men—Agustin Garde, Manuel Choperena, and Sebastian Larralde—all ex-sheepherder immigrants from Navarre. The Basques came in last by a wide margin, but they could have done a little better with more training. After all, these guys had regular jobs that had nothing to do with woodchopping. However, this first woodchopper meeting was the seed, and Elko became a liaison between other top world axe men and the Basques, resulting in world championships being organized in the Basque Country.

Some of the actors and organizers of these world championships were Rafael Aguirre, of Donostia/San Sebastian; José A. de Urbina, the Spanish consul, in San Francisco; and Jess Lopategui, of Elko. On January 18, 1976, three woodchoppers from Australia met in Donostia/San Sebastian for a match contest against three Basques. The expectation was high, and 7,000 people attended the event. The local axe men were Jose Orbegozo Arria II, Miguel Mindeguia, and Francisco Astibia. The Australians were Frank Whiteside, Ken Jackson, and Col Shaferrius. The Aussies won by teams, but individually Miguel Mindeguia, from Ezkurra, Navarre, was the fastest.

The Basques did not take very well to losing to the Aussies, until they figured out why it had happened: Australian axes cut the wood differently, and faster. So, rather quickly they organized a rematch for November 1976 in Donostia between American, Australian, Canadian, and Basque aizkolari. This time, the Basques using Australian axes won the world championship, and this happened because of the Elko initiative.

In 1978 and 1979, the Elko festivals featured world champions Arria II and Mindeguia. Their task was to challenge each other by cutting seven logs of fifty-four-to-seventy-inch circumference. It was going to be a rematch for Arria II and Mindeguia because earlier Arria II was the winner. This time Mindeguia took fifteen minutes twenty-nine seconds to complete the job, and Arria II took just two seconds more. In this sport, two seconds is a razor-thin win, and you should have heard the audience screaming. Basque words came out the loudest: "Hori, emon, jo, eman, hor, beste bat!!!" Loosely translated, "That's it, hit it, strike it, there, one more!!!" (The words *emon* and *eman* are dialectal variations.) The next day, Sunday, they held an exhibition cutting through two large logs, and Arria II was the winner.

In the 1980 festival, Arria and Mindeguia were back in Elko, pitted against three Americans: Russ Gates, Robin Eslinger, and Melvin Lentz. Gates was from Lincoln, Montana; Eslinger from Mccloud, California; and Lentz from Creswell, Oregon. The third Basque was Agustin Garde of Elko. The match was to take place in stages with a two-day elimination process. The first day contest ended without any clear winner, so everyone was waiting for the next day final! The task was to cut fifteen logs in a relay race. Some of the logs were standing in the American tradition, and some laying down flat, the Basque way. It turned out to be very competitive, and the people were yelling and standing in their seats, cheering on their teams, and in the end the Basques won.

In 1991, the club brought from Euskadi the Saralegi brothers, Esteban and Narciso, the champion woodchoppers then. In Euskadi people bet considerable money during a major aizkolari event, including whole farmsteads, but in the US, sports betting is a little different. However, in 1969 David W. Toll wrote that in Elko as much as $5,000 might change hands during a woodchopping match. The article contains enough errors that the statement can be taken with at least a grain of salt.

Oregon and Wisconsin

After the 1980 festival, Arria and Mindeguia went to Albany, Oregon, to take part in two other competitions with the Americans and Canadians. Our Elko man Lopategui became instrumental in helping to organize these events.

The format of the Wisconsin show was totally new to the Basques: The logs were in water and numbered. Each axe man had to find his log, bring it to the cutting platform, set it up, and

cut it. All this was foreign. Of thirty participants only twelve qual-
ified for the next day. Mindeguia was eliminated, and Arria barely
made the cut, but at the end of the day, he won. On the third day
everyone had to cut bigger logs—an endurance competition, a
nod to the Basques—and Arria and Mindeguia won easily. At
one point, the two competed against three other axe men—the
job being to cut five large logs—and won.

Basque Relay

This competition combined woodchopping and stone-lifting plus
other fast-moving tasks. In 1993, for example, work consisted in
lifting a 175-pound stone twenty times, chopping three logs, picking and placing thirty cans (that were scattered on the ground) in
the basket, and walking 500 feet with txingas. The money prize
was $600, and the winners were Jose Tellechea, Jon Legarza, and
Steve Goicoechea. In second place were Frank Zaga, Mark Etcheberry, and Aitor Narvaiza (the future sheriff of Elko County), and
they got $300.

Txinga

There were txinga carriers of all ages. In 1993 Amuchastegui's
record of 1,200 feet was broken by Jerry Englebert, who walked
1,700 feet holding 208 pounds in his hands. The junior txinga contest for those sixteen and under amounted to carrying seventy-
five pounds in each hand.

Irrintzi Contest

It is believed that ancient Basques used to communicate from
mountaintop to mountaintop with the *irrintzi*, which has been
loosely translated as the "Basque war cry" but surely was used
for other purposes as well. Today it is used mostly in public celebrations as a display of high-spirited euphoria. It sounds like
the neighing of a horse and the cry of a pig when in trouble, like
when it is being butchered. Men's and women's irrintzi, naturally,
sound very different, but both make you shudder. Most people

who attempt to mimic the irrintzi for the first time usually run out of breath and fall short.

In 1993 Ana Marie Manzisidor won the irrintzi contest on July 4, and second place went to Lisa Aguirre Pirtle. As with dancing, usually more women compete in irrintzi than men do.

Ardi Txakurra (Sheepdog Exhibition)

The scores of ex-sheepherders in the audience greatly appreciated the Sheepdog Exhibition by Rig Griffin from Dixon, California. In 1980 the exhibition was presented by Danny and his wife, Jackie Prichard. It was sponsored by Biltoki Basque American Dinner House; Anacabe's Elko General Merchandise; Brico Inc.; Quinn Dufurrena, DDS; and Read & Powell.

In 1983, there was a sheepdog exhibition, and another in 1993 presented by Kurt and Wanda Beebe, father and daughter, each with their own dog. It would have been interesting to compare a working sheepdog from an Elko ranch with these exhibition dogs, but it probably would not be fair to either canine.

Evening Dance

There is an evening dance at every festival, and, as mentioned in chapter 14, for decades Jimmy Jausoro and his Basque Idaho Band provided the music. In 1990, as in many other years, Elko's accordionist, Bernardo Yanci, accompanied Jausoro. Furthermore, the wildly popular trikitrilariak from Euskadi, Martin and Egañazpi, were on hand.

125th Nevada Anniversary

This was another special occasion for Elko Basques to reaffirm their roots in town and in Nevada. The 125th anniversary of the State of Nevada in 1990 was the occasion for a special festival message by club President Ramon Zugazaga. It coincided with NABO's Udaleku (Music Camp), which took place in Elko, and at its conclusion on July 6 there was a talent show at the Elko Convention Center. Udaleku lasts two weeks and is designed for boys and girls ages ten to fifteen to learn about Basque music, songs, dance, and culture. For the finale, the kids are cajoled to show off what they learned at the camp. It is heartening for the older generation to watch youngsters being initiated in aspects of the ancient culture, albeit Americanized, that they will take back to their hometowns in California, Nevada, Oregon, Idaho, Utah, Wyoming, and beyond.

CHAPTER 16

The Handball Court

For a couple of years from 1974 to 1976, club members tap danced delicately as they debated the merits of asking the Spanish government for funds. This initiative pointed to a new direction in the management of the club, and there was surprisingly little opposition from the membership. The need to build a handball court was paramount, and the rationale for raising funds was quite simple: *If they want to give us money, we will take it.* The club approached Consul José A. de Urbina sometime in 1974 through the agency of Raimundo Blanco, who ran the Bank of Vizcaya in New York. Lucky for Elko, Urbina was Basque and a fan of pilota.

However, even before that, the club had developed a preliminary plan to build the handball court. When they heard that the City of Elko had announced grant money for improving the park, Jess Lopategui and Nicolas Fagoaga went to a meeting and applied for a grant to build the handball court. The city promised them $19,000, so they got busy planning and preparing the blueprints. By the time they returned to the city several months later to reclaim the money, they received news that it had all been spent. Despite the disappointment, they asked the city whether it would grant permission to build the court if the Basque club came up with the funding. Mayor Dutch Stenovich said, sure, no problem.

This development was during the unpredictable period of the waning of Franco's tenure as Spain's dictator. The old fascist general had a long record of hostility toward the Basques, and ETA (Euskadi Ta Askatasuna, or Basque Country and Freedom) was not helping. In the Basque Country, just criticizing Franco or displaying the Basque flag was severely punished, but the Basques

José A. de Urbina, the consul general of Spain in San Francisco, provided funds to build the handball court in 1975. Here he hands the trophy to champion Benat Iribarne. Reprinted from Elko Festival Brochure.

of Elko were 5,000 miles away enjoying American liberties. The ikurrina was exhibited freely at the festivals since the beginning (though none appears in the photographs of the 1959 festival in Sparks).

A letter from Consul Urbina to Lopategui dated March 21, 1975, announced that the Spanish Institute of Emigration had awarded the Elko Club $25,000 to build the handball court (in today's money, it amounted to about $138,500). He added, "as a Consul General of Spain and as a Basque it gives me special satisfaction to be able to obtain, after many petitions, this important contribution." The check was made out to Lopategui, though at the time he held no office in the club. The president was John Aldaya, the vice president was Marguerite Odiaga Ozamis, and the secretary was Robert Goicoechea.

With funds in hand, club representatives returned to the city with the blueprints for approval. The city manager objected that the height of the court walls was excessive, so the project's participants had to settle for walls four feet lower than in the original plans. In a letter dated April 4, 1975, club President Aldaya informed the City of Elko that Jess Lopategui and Robert Goicoechea would take charge of the construction of the new handball court at the city park. It was helpful that at the time Aldaya worked for the city.

Court's Inauguration

General contractors Pete Ormaza Sr. and Nick Fagoaga bid on the project, and Fagoaga's was the lowest and accepted by the club's board. The *pilotoki*, or handball court (also called *frontoie* in Bizkaian dialect), was to be thirty meters long and ten meters wide. Normal ball courts in the Basque Country measure forty to fifty-two meters long (especially jai alai courts) and ten meters high, so the Elko court is a reduced replica of conventional ones. Several years later, however, the club was allowed to raise the walls. Construction began in March, and the handball court was finished in a couple of months, ready for the 1975 festival.

Consul Urbina wrote Aldaya on May 5, 1975, thanking the club for having made him an honorary member, which Urbina says will extend to other consuls after him. In June 1975 he announced his intention to attend the Elko Festival, to which he was bringing six trophies for the pilota champions. Three of them donated by the governments of Bizkaia, Araba/Alava, and Navarre. He donated the other three himself as consul general of Spain. Urbina also brought a dedication plaque, which read in English, Basque, and Spanish: "Fronton Euzkaldunak, Built by Spain," and he asked that it be affixed to the court wall. The Basque version was misspelled, with "Estaniak" instead of "Espainiak."

Upon completion of the handball court, Lopategui, as tournament director for the first couple of years, called and wrote letters to Basque clubs in Bakersfield, San Francisco, Boise, and New York inquiring about players desiring to take part in the tournaments

Basque Handball Court located in the Elko City Park. For years the Bank of Vizcaya was a major sponsor of pilotariak (handball players). Courtesy Jon Bilbao Basque Library, University of Nevada, Reno Libraries.

to be held at the Elko Festival. Twenty-eight handball players from various Basque communities in the West showed up, challenging each other singly and in pairs in the brand-new handball court. Benat Iribarne of San Francisco won the singles match, earning the $300 prize money awarded to the *txapeldun* (champion). He was a cook, and his boss would not give him time off, so he flew to Elko on Friday to play a match and flew back to San Francisco to cook on Saturday morning. After putting his time in the kitchen, on Sunday morning he flew back to Elko to play in the championship match that he won. Such dedication! Alas, the prize money won on the court may not have paid for the flights.

Consul Urbina awarded trophies to the winners, and Raimundo Blanco handed out $500 to the double's champions on behalf of the Bank of Vizcaya and $300 for second place. The same bank donated $300 to Iribarne and $200 for the runner-up. Those

Robert "Bob" Echeverria, NABO president, six-time
club president, and festival announcer for decades.

amounts were considerable at the time, as $500 today would be
worth about $2,760.

After the obvious success of the handball court grant, the
Basque Club kept asking for more funds from Consul Urbina, and
he delivered. In a letter of April 5, 1976, he announced another
$3,000 from the same source as before: the Institute of Emigra-
tion. In that same year, President Bob Echeverria informed the
city that the construction of the handball court was complete and
that the Basque Club had deeded it to the City of Elko.

Players from Bakersfield and San Francisco came again the
following year, lured by the considerable dollar awards. In addition to the $500 put up by Bank of Vizcaya, in 1976 the $300 for
second place came from the Ormaza and Fagoaga Construction Companies. In 1977 Consul Urbina and Raimundo Blanco
were at hand to take photos with the winning pilota players. The

club has many photographs of the event, but the names of the people in them are unfortunately lacking. In 1981–1982, Urbina was again in Elko, handing out trophies. With that kind of support, handball games were played feverishly at every festival for a couple of decades.

Around 1978, Tony Jauregui of Elko took over the pilota part of club activities that he coordinated with NABO, which by this time oversaw organizing the pilota championships in the West. Jauregui was Elko-born but grew up in Gernika and then returned. He and his *pilotari* friends from Elko traveled together to Basque festivals in Chino, San Francisco, Boise, and so on for more than five years. These are their names: Jose Martiartu, Isidro Fagoaga, Jose Telleria, and Juan Leniz—and they were later joined by other local players. Ramon Zugazaga and Miguel Leonis, for example, started competing a little afterward, and in 1991 they took the Class A NABO Championship. Jose Arbillaga was another local player.

Unfortunately, a complete record of the names of many players who traveled long distances is missing. In a fortunate conversation I had with some ex-handball players at the Iparreko Ibarra Festival in 2018 in Lincoln, California, I learned the names of the following California players: Marcel Etcheverry, Emil Goyenech, Felipe Elizagaray, Noel Goyenetch, Noel Nigueloa, and Jean B. Echeverria. They told me that they not only traveled to Elko festivals for about ten years but also went to Vitoria/Gasteiz (Basque Country), Mexico City, Biarritz, Bolivia, and Iruñea/Pamplona—always as pilotari.

Thus, the pilota program continued for years, but in the 1990s competitions declined. The sport did not agree so much with the legs of American Basques, who in the 1960s and 1970s were young men. We should also mention here that while attending and assisting with the World Woodchopping Championships in Donostia, Lopategui had befriended Gipuzkoa Secretary of Tourism Rafael Aguirre, who reciprocated by sending to the 1980 Elko Festival all the top pilotari in the Basque Country. That exchange speaks eloquently to Elko's ranking.

CHAPTER 17

Euskal Etxea—The Clubhouse

After the club formed, it was only natural for the Basques to think about a permanent meeting place of their own. Already in the late 1960s, some club members were floating the idea of an Euskal Etxea (Basque Clubhouse) that would serve their needs. The idea kept burning hot for some years in the minds of at least a few people. The recently built handball court surely served as the catalyst when the club members realized that they could dream big, and the dream became a reality in 1978.

In 1976 the City of Elko sold the club 1.5 acres for $4,500. The transaction occurred without any advertising and on the condition that the Basques would not sell it for profit or use it for any commercial purpose. As soon as the transaction occurred in 1977, club members were anxious to start the construction of the *home* they had dreamed about for more than fifteen years. No more delaying, some of them were saying. But what about financing it? Had they put the proverbial cart before the donkey?

BETIKO (LIFETIME) MEMBERSHIP

Once before the club had been in the red some $7,000, but eight years later according to another document they had $36,000 in the bank, of which $20,000 were earmarked for the building of the clubhouse. But more resources were needed, and one day, according to Lopategui, the club had a great idea. It consisted in offering the club members a chance to buy a lifetime membership. If the idea worked, the club could end up with enough capital to start construction of the clubhouse.

At the time membership cost $8. The fees for the Betiko (Lifetime) membership were estimated at $125 per single person and

at $175 per couple. Their children would become members auto-
matically until they turned eighteen. Immediately, club officers
and others set about selling the idea, and seventy people quickly
said *bai* (yes), which was the response they hoped for. Bob Echeverria shared that they raised $40,000 with Betiko memberships.
The capital helped secure the funding to begin construction, and,
in addition, interested individuals could buy memorial plaques
to hang on the building's walls (see appendix 6 for the list of lifetime members).

Nick Fagoaga and Pete Ormaza Sr. bid on the project, and Fagoaga's was the lowest, $75,000 (worth $342,600 today). On May 7,
1978, the club officers—Joe L. Mallea was president—and some
twenty other members took part in the groundbreaking ceremony of the Euskal Etxea.

THE BUILDING

If the cost of the building seems low (especially today), you are
right. That amount was just for a barebones building. Later, other
expenditures for fencing and landscaping were added, but never-
the-less costs to the club were much reduced because members
donated many hours of free labor. The following year, the City of
Elko assessor valued the property at $21,020. A photo of the brand-
new Euskal Etxea graced the cover of the 1979 festival brochure.

Initially, the building's name was to be Danon Etxea (Everyone's Home), but later project organizers decided on Euskal Etxea.
Blueprints were drawn purposely to resemble a baserri (farmstead)
measuring 3,200 square feet, and it was built rather quickly, before
the year was out. The site of the 1.5-acre property is below the
I-80 freeway, near the fairgrounds and overlooking it. A humongous American flag very visible to freeway motorists flies a few
hundred yards from the clubhouse. The address is, suitably, 1601
Flagview Drive, Elko, NV 89803.

Throughout the years many clubhouse improvements have
enhanced the original building. Lopategui co-owned a blacksmith
shop, and installing an iron door at its entrance seemed like an
easy decision, one that gave the building that classic look. The

Euskal Etxea, the Basque Clubhouse, built in 1978 to resemble a Basque farmstead.

paved-tile entry was installed by the free labor of Jose Martiartu, Nicolas Fagoaga, Esteban Elexpuru, Joe Juaristi, Lopategui, Juan Uriaguereca, and Jose Telleria (and there may have been others.)

Today, the grounds surrounding the clubhouse are made attractive, with copious mature trees that provide much-needed shade from the July sun in the high desert. Circa 2015, more landscaping and tree planting were done around the clubhouse perimeter by a landscaper from Boise, who donated some of the trees as well. Several thousand added dollars were spent on sand and cement work on the outside of the building.

RENOVATIONS

Further upgrades took place inside. The original bathrooms were small and inadequate, and they were expanded with funds secured from the government of Euskadi. The original kitchen served the needs of small-scale affairs, but when events exceeded 100–200 people, there was no remedy but to rethink and redo it. Funds from Euskadi, once again, came through and made possible the installation of a commercial kitchen. (I must add here that in the old days money traveled from America to Euskadi, but at some point in time it reversed course.)

As proud as the members were of their accomplishment, they soon realized that the building itself was too small. In 2019 I heard people talk about ideas or plans to expand it soon. No one is more aware of the building's limitations than the regulars who spend time there, such as Bartolo Echebarria, who is the caretaker of the grounds, and those who do the cooking: Choch Zaga, Ramon Zugazaga, Zach Arbillaga, Frank Zaga, and Wes Walker. Echebarria also helps in the kitchen.

The kitchen and the bar being the nuclei of the building were first remodeled, and when everything, or almost everything, was completed, considerable money had been spent. According to Ramon Zugazaga, and in approximate dollars, the expenses were as follows:

Kitchen, $60,000
Laminate floor, $12,000
Bar, $3,000
Bathrooms, $3,000
Landscaping (fence, etc.), $12,000

The Basque government's funding, and the income from the many ads (fourteen pages) in festival brochures, plus the ongoing Lifetime Membership program, helped pay for these expenses.

Before the proposed expansion of the building can begin, funds will have to be secured, because today the original amount of $75,000 would not pay for much. The club gets donations when the premise is reserved for parties, weddings, and other events. Mexican Americans are some of the club's best clients. Rental donations are negotiable, but there are a $350 security deposit and a $100,000 liability insurance requirement.

So, life is good in Elko, and the Euskal Etxea really gathers the Basques and their friends like a mother hen would. It truly serves the purpose for which it was built. The newcomers, the miners, have no connection to the ranching world of Old Elko, therefore, none to the sheep and the Basques. It will be interesting to see if down the road mining culture wins over ranching culture—not likely—or how the two fuse together.

Labe (Oven)

On the clubhouse grounds, there sits a relic of Elko's sheepherding history in the form of a unique *artzain labe* (sheepherder's oven), which for decades was used on the range to bake the acclaimed sheepherders' bread. It was originally in the Columbia Basin, seventy-five miles north of Elko at the main camp of the Allied Sheep Company. It was brought into town in 1999, and in the brochure of that year's festival the following people were acknowledged: Dan Landa, Pat Laughlin, Bob Aguirre, Dan Bledsoe, Jason Bledsoe, Dusty Allen, and others. Fagoaga Construction built the base on which the oven stands, and the Elko Blacksmith Shop built the bbq grill. Jess Lopategui handwrote the following history of the oven:

> It was built in the early 1950s by Manuel Arbillaga, the Allied foreman, and camp tenders Jean Iribarne Sr., Pete Ampo, and Fernando Sorhondo. It is brick-built, and later to protect it from the weather two Elko construction workers, Genaro Zarrabeitia and Jose Azurmendi, covered it with cement on a weekend in exchange for a lamb. In 1964, the year of the First Basque National Festival, foreman Antonio Mindeguia and the camp tenders Luis Viscarrondo, Santiago, and Jess Lopategui baked eighteen big loaves in the oven for the festival. The oven holds nine no. 10 Dutch ovens for baking. It was used until Allied sold the sheep in the 1970s.

As far as the oven goes it looks rather common, a round, cement-covered construct, which is not as traditional-looking like brick. In California and in other parts of Nevada, there are more conventional brick-built ovens. However, this oven is still in operation to bake bread; during the festivals one of the contests is baking sheepherder bread, which takes place on-site.

CHAPTER 18

Food and Service Businesses

Bob Rosevear says, "Any man with Basque blood in him knows he can cook. I cook at home." In fact, he is such an accomplished chef that Roger Izoco told him he should open a txoko in town (txoko used to be a culinary "man cave" found in most Basque towns, but today women are also members). Bob's son Joe was also a cook, and with a diploma. This example should help us understand why food is a Basque cultural norm that has found a home not only in Elko but in Northern Nevada, and beyond.

Male cooks appear to be a Nevada phenomenon and mostly where Bizkaians congregate for two reasons: First, naturally, cooking skills and ambition come from the hills. All sheepherders had to cook for themselves, and if you want your food to taste good, well, you better learn how to. Second, a considerable portion of Bizkaians who ended up sheepherding had been cooks before in merchant marine vessels.

Though Basques are not born with a big toque and a wooden spoon in their hand, Basque cuisine in Europe today boasts of luminaries and star-studded restaurants, many in Donostia, such as Arzak, Karlos Arguiñano, and Martin Berasategi. Victor Arginzoniz in Bizkaia is another, just to name a few. Their trade has spread widely over the Iberian Peninsula as well, where Basque dishes such as cod fish *pil pil* (also known as Bizkaian style) are available in many Spanish cities; Madrid has several. Cooking may not be in the Basque DNA, but the fact is that proportionally more Basque males seem to cook in the US than in Euskal Herria, the Basque Country.

So, it is no wonder that after ranches the earliest Basque businesses in the county were a combination of hotel restaurants, the

Overland, for example. It is not known if the Saval-Ballarena-Telescope offered food, but chances are that it did. Food and drink stood out because they are an integral part of lodging. These Basques knew more about the value of food and drink than about accommodations. They could put food on a table fit for a king, but they knew less about putting together a royal chamber or even a bedroom. A half a century later and more, Elko could still take pride with its number of Basque restaurants: the Star, the Nevada Dinner House, Biltoki, and Toki Ona. In 2020, there were three remaining: the Star, Toki Ona, and Ogi.

In this chapter I try to list as many Basque-owned businesses as possible, but I do not pretend that the list is exhaustive, any more than this research has covered every inch of Basque history in the county. There remains plenty more investigative work available for an interested student.

Jauregui-Eizaguirre—The Power Couple

The couple that built the Star Hotel in 1910 deserve further attention because they stayed in Elko and continued in business even after selling their hotel several times. But let us backtrack and explain how the most celebrated Basque business couple found each other. Matilde Eizaguirre came to Elko to work at the Sabala-owned Overland Hotel, but her train was late, and the Overland representative at the station went home. When the train finally arrived Pete Jauregui happened to be there, and after the quick initial exchanges, he took her to the Saval-Ballarena Hotel, where he was the manager. Jeronima Echeverria tells a slightly different version of how they met, but Matilde's own daughters vouch that it was their father who took her to his hotel. She immediately started working as a maid, but barely, because within a few months Pete proposed and she accepted, and they were married, becoming the parents of two daughters.

Pete and Matilde themselves had little formal education, but they valued it exceedingly and sent their daughters to college. After selling the hotel in 1922, the Jaureguis did not go to California to retire, nothing like that. After selling the Star for the second time in 1942, they owned or built half a dozen other businesses in town, because Matilde, in the words of her daughters, was not ready to retire and be a housewife.

There is a lesson here: Women can be business oriented, entrepreneurs, and successful as much as men when the situation arises, but often we forget to credit them. When it comes to the success of the Star Hotel, Matilde certainly deserves as much recognition as Pete, or more, according to their daughters. The fact is that Pete and Matilde merged beautifully, and they are the prototype of Elko's Power Couple.

Eventually, the Jaureguis did retire and stayed at home. Pete liked beans and makailu (salted cod fish), and Matilde was happy to cook for him. He had a big barn on the property and a basement where he made wine (he had a permit) and sold it. Pete and Matilde loved fishing and cooking their catch. Pete was one of the earliest Basques naturalized in Elko. He died in 1975.

Elko General Merchandise Store

This establishment is almost as well known as the Star Hotel. The name is long, and just about everyone, especially Basques, calls it the Anacabe Store or simply Anacabe's. It is the second oldest Basque-owned business still in operation in the city of Elko. Jose Mari "Joe" Anacabe was born in an ancient baserri of Astarrika, a hamlet near Berriatua in Bizkaia in 1888. He came to the US circa 1901–1902 and landed in Paradise Valley, Nevada. Joe worked at several jobs. He did buckaroo work for the Altubes, drove a ten-horse team, and later had a small ranch in McDermitt. In 1924 he opened a store with Fabiana Guenaga, his first wife, at the Basque-owned Commercial Hotel in McDermitt, Nevada. The two had a son, Frank. He sold the store in 1929 so that Frank could go study in Vitoria/Gasteiz in the Basque Country.

The Great Depression apparently did not affect the Anacabes as much as others, because Joe was able to open a haberdashery in Berkeley, California, while Frank studied there at the University

Joe Anacabe with wife Fabiana Guenaga and their son Frank in front of the Anacabe General Merchandise store on Idaho Street. Courtesy of Anita Anacabe Franzoia.

of California. Frank received a degree in aeronautical engineering and was employed by Lockheed and at Curtis-Vega.

The clothing business in Berkeley was short-lived, and Joe kept several fixtures that he eventually used at the General Merchandise Store in Elko, which he managed from 1936 until his death in 1971 at eighty-two. The premises had earlier been Gaiety Theater, which showed silent movies. The building had had Basque connections since 1907, when Dan Sabala owned the Overland Hotel, adjacent to the theater. In 1918 Eulogio Onaindia sold his half interest in the Overland to Jose Bengoechea, and in 1919 he and Sabala bought the theater.

Anita Anacabe Franzoia at her Anacabe General Merchandise store, which opened its doors in 1936 and still in business in 2025.

In 1923, there is a recorded deed that Ramon and Segunda Iriondo of Boise paid Dan Sabala $5,000 for the Gaiety Theater. By December 1936, Joe Anacabe was running the business, which may have been the result of a deal with Sabala. In 1937, John J. Hunter and his son Jack bought the Overland at an auction, which included the Elko General Merchandise Store. The *Elko Daily Press* reported that it was an L-shaped building, with the hotel's entrance on Fourth Street and the Anacabe store facing Idaho Street. The Overland's handball court abutted with the store. It is in this rear area of the store that one can find some Basque names even today, such as Eulogio Onaindia's, written on the old wall. Joe Anacabe took proper ownership of his store circa 1938.

Fabiana and Joe operated the Elko store from 1936 to 1950. In 1950, Joe offered his son Frank 50 percent of the business. Fabiana passed away in 1952, prompting Joe to return to his homeland to find a new spouse, Margaret Olave, born in 1917 in Iruzubieta, Bizkaia. They were married in 1953, and after returning to Elko Joe tried to teach Margaret a minimum of one new word of English every day. It was not long before they had a daughter, Anna Teresa, affectionately called "Anita."

Joe was a member of the Elko Chamber of Commerce and the Basque Club. His son Frank passed away unexpectedly five years later (1958) while playing tennis. Anita completed college in Boise while running the store in Elko with her mother.

During the thirty-five years that Joe ran the store, he achieved prominence in Elko as a businessman. When new Basque herders arrived, they all went to Anacabe's to buy work clothes, boots, jackets, bedrolls, hats—you name it and he had it. Without missing a step, Joe gifted each of his customers a knife with the reminder, "Hau ondo etorko jatsu mendien" (This will be useful to you in the mountains). For decades, the store has been supplying Elkoans—sheepherders and cowboys—with work clothes of the finest quality at fair prices, which explains the store's longevity.

In 2025, the Anacabe Store is still at the same location as in 1936, open for business. Anita Anacabe Franzoia has been running it for some forty years, with the assistance of her trusted employee of thirty some years, Maria Gonzalez. Anita married Mike Franzoia, who was mayor of Elko for fourteen years, and they have four children (Teresa, Andrea, Mateo, and Kristina), all of whom speak Basque.

French Bakery

The Mendives owned the French Bakery located behind the Star. It was an old-fashioned bakery with brick ovens. According to the locals, nobody has ever made bread like they did, or custard, pastries, flan, and rice pudding. Antonio Mendive (Mercedes Mendive's grandfather) was from Markina, Bizkaia, and operated the place until 1944 when the bakery was sold to the Armuths, who renamed it Home Bakery.

Blue Jay

The Blue Jay Bar, which Henry Samper acquired in 1930 with Frank Arregui, was first a coffee shop. Esteban Azpiri also owned it until 1932, when it was sold to Fred Zaga, John "Kiputxe" Mugarza, and others. In 1965, Pierre/Pete Amestoy sold it to Joe Juaristi. In 1977, Juaristi sold it to his countryman Jose Antonio Leniz, who had it until he opened Toki Ona Restaurant near the east end of town in 1990.

Nevada Dinner House (NDH)

Anastasio Vicarret built the Nevada Hotel in 1927, and Calisto Laucirica moved it across the railroad tracks. Laucirica's daughter Mary married Johnny Aguirre, and they assumed control of the Nevada Hotel around 1960, at which time they renamed it Nevada Dinner House, and added five feet to the dining area. Nicolas Fagoaga built the expansion. According to Steve Urriola, Mary created the salad dressing with egg and mayonnaise that all the Basque restaurants adopted. The Aguirres separated in 1980 or so, and Mary owned it for a while. She sold the NDH to Leone Elizagoyen and Leo Morandi, who operated the Marquis Motor Inn. They expanded the NDH another ten feet or so. They had it for about ten years, after which Franzoia and Anacabe bought it and expanded it another four feet. They in turn sold it to Luke Gerber and Erin, and now it is called Luciano's, an Italian restaurant.

Bastida Store

Manuel and Teresa Bastida of Mountain Home, Idaho, built the Bastida Store in Mountain City, Nevada, in 1931. At the time, Manuel was working at Goicoechea's Ranch. Imagine constructing a store during the Great Depression! The couple had the audacity to open a store in an isolated mining town that lacked services, eighty-five miles north of Elko. The initial supplies to the store came from Jarbidge, of all places. The Bastidas dug a well that benefited many in town. They also installed a gasoline pump—an essential service in the age of automobiles. Furthermore, they extended credit to customers, even to some who could not pay. After some years the store was expanded to accommodate the increased business.

The Tremewans, Oliver and Anna Sabala, were the next owners, followed in 1974 by their daughter Louise Tremewan and Louise's husband, Melvin Basanez. The Native Americans from the nearby Duckwater Reservation were frequent customers, and Melvin said that he spoke better Paiute than Basque. He and Louise ran the store for forty years until 2002.

STOCKMEN'S MOTOR HOTEL CASINO

Red Ellis owned the Stockmen's from 1940s until 1952, when Dan Bilbao Sr. and partners bought it. Bilbao was born in Errigoiti, Bizkaia, and he came to Mountain Home, Idaho, in 1918 at age sixteen. He operated a gambling establishment in Sun Valley, Idaho. Ernest Hemingway was living in town, and he and Dan used to go fishing together. Then one day in 1952 Idaho banned gambling, and the Bilbaos packed their basement-gaming tables and headed out of town to Winnemucca, Nevada, where they built the Sonoma Inn. Bilbao's daughter Lina says, "We had our own gasoline pump, two Cadillacs, one black, one gray, and a Jeep. We were living well in Idaho, but it was not an enlightening enterprise precisely. It was grit and a pride in being American. Citizenship was very important for my father. He had to study hard to pass the test. They spoke Basque when they were too upset, or when they did not want us to know what they were saying."

Soon after moving to Winnemucca, Bilbao and his partners bought the Stockmen's in Elko. Eventually, Bilbao bought out his two partners, but in 1957 the casino burned down completely. Luckily, it reopened in the following year bigger and better than before. By 1974, Dan had passed the business to his son Dan Jr. and retired to Boise, where he lived to be ninety-two. Dan Jr. was elected Elko City councilman in 1981. He joked that he was the first person with a gaming license elected to public office.

Lawrence Moiola remembers that in Elko the Basques used to patronize Basque establishments (mostly on weekends), and one, naturally, was the Stockmen's. It had a desk in front where Basques would sit and talk, and Louie Uriarte used to call it, "The Basko Stockage Exchange."

BILTOKI

Biltoki in Basque means "Gathering Place," and Ramon Zugazaga operated it for thirty years, from 1983 until 2013. Zugazaga came

Ramon Zugazaga, a man of many talents—sheepherder, restauranteur, soccer coach, and club president eight times.

to Elko in the 1960s to herd sheep for Jess Goicoechea for $300 a month plus room (a tent) and board. In Beaver Creek, north of Elko, Goicoechea gave him a band of sheep, traced a map on the dirt for him to follow the next ten days, and told him off you go. Goicoechea was a native speaker of Basque, so Zugazaga replied, "Ze ein biot oin? Lurrezko mapie eskun erun?" (What am I supposed to do now, pick up the earthen map and carry it in my hands?)

Zugazaga's family in Gernika was in the restaurant business, so it was a natural move for him to go from the sheep to the kitchen business. He first went to Gooding, Idaho, where he operated a restaurant—called Biltoki—but only for a couple of years. He soon returned to Elko.

His days seemed to have forty-eight hours, because he not only found time to run the restaurant but also to organize and coach girls' soccer teams and be the president of the Basque club eight times. In addition, from the restaurant he ran a catering business. Biltoki is another immigrant success story. When you walked in, the place was dark but a picon and the food would quickly take care of the gloom. The food was characteristic of Basque restaurants, though with very generous portions and several sides.

Zugazaga was president when the festivals were moved from the city park to the Basque clubhouse. He said, "I like to listen to people. I took a lot of heat when I moved the picnic, but I let people talk and say their piece. After the move a lot of people came to me and apologized. They realized that the move was the right one." Today, Zugazaga is retired, that is, busier than ever.

TOKI ONA

Jose Antonio "Tony" Leniz was born in Gizaburuaga, Bizkaia, and arrived in Elko to herd sheep in 1961. He and his wife, Ruth Salvi, opened Toki Ona, which in Basque means "the Good Place," in

Salazar brothers, Jose L., the cook, and Jesus,
the manager, owners of Toki Ona Restaurant.

1990 after they sold the Blue Jay Bar. The business was previously named Casa de Colores when it was owned by Kay Goodnight.

Toki Ona is a restaurant with a bar, but it is not set up as a typical Basque-family-style eatery with long tables. After Tony passed away in 2005, his wife and son operated it for a year or two. It was then purchased by a real estate agency, which leased it to Jose L. and Jesus Salazar, two Mexican brothers from Zacatecas, who subsequently purchased it. Jose said that he had worked fourteen years for Severiano Lazcano at the Star Hotel and learned Basque cooking there.

The Salazars kept not only the name (after all their surname, Salazar, is Basque, too), but also the Basque-American menu. People agree that they do a fine job of serving Basque food. My favorite is the spicy-red, grilled cod, which comes as an unusually large piece.

OGI AND MACHI'S

When Biltoki closed, at its heels, fifty feet away, came Ogi (which means "bread" in Basque). It opened around 2014 by Anamarie Sarratea and her husband, Mikel Lopategui. They served great

Ogi Deli came to life soon after the Biltoki Basque Restaurant—fifty feet away—closed in 2013. It closed in 2022 and was sold to Choch Goicoechea and Carolyn Walther. Machi's, though not a Basque business today, is a shortened version of Amatxi's (Grandmother's) once owned by the Josephine Saval family of Battle Mountain.

sandwiches and soups, and an absolute favorite was the unique red pepper puree soup that you seldom find anywhere else. They offered Basque sagardo (apple cider) and chorizos, and so much more.

Next door to Ogi is Machi's (short for Amatxi's, or "Grandmother's"), whose roots go back to the Josephine Saval family of Battle Mountain, but today it is not considered a Basque-food restaurant.

THE PINE LODGE

The Marisquirena brothers, from Navarre, who already owned two bars and a hotel in Elko, built the Pine Lodge Bar/Restaurant in Lamoille, at the foot of the Rubies. They operated the business in partnership with the daughter. The grand opening was something else. As the area's prominent Basque personalities, Celso Madarieta and Pete Elia were the chefs attired with tall white hats. Unfortunately, the lodge burned down soon after its opening, but it was rebuilt. In 2009, it changed hands and the Elko paper stated, "Hope it is for the better."

MUDD HUTT COFFEE

Today, another visible Basque sign in town is the Mudd Hutt Coffee, a kiosk serving coffee in many variations. Located on Idaho Street in the Sunrise Shopping Center near the east end of Elko, it is owned by the Aguirre sisters, Alisa and Valerie, who by profession are retired teachers. They also own a second Mudd Hutt in Spring Creek, south of Elko. The kiosk is embellished with *lauburus* (Basque symbol of the sun).

TRANSPORT BUSINESSES

Albert Garamendi (originally Garamendia) came from the town of Ispaster, Bizkaia. He was kin of Celestino Garamendi, who herded sheep in the Jarbidge area, where he carved several aspens from 1943 to 1945. Celestino was interested in prospecting, and in his tree carvings he always added the figures of hammers and chisels. His descendants still live in Elko. John Garamendi, the ex–lieutenant governor of California and now US congressman for California's Third District, is a relative.

Albert Garamendi Jr. owned the Silver State Trucking business in Elko, which he then sold to Pedro Olabarria. The third owners of this trucking business were the Urriola Bros. Garamendi and Olabarria hauled mostly livestock.

GAS STATIONS

Jacinto "Jay" Garteiz, born in the coastal city of Bermeo, and his Utah-born wife, Lucile, owned a couple of gas stations, the first one on Fifth and Idaho Streets since 1925. At the time, it was the best that Elko had to offer. Garteiz was an early promoter of post-cards to advertise his business to the motoring traveler. Later he widened horizons to the east end of town, where he owned both sides of Highway 40. There in the 1940s he built an upscale air-conditioned lodging called Jay's Cottages Motor Hotel with 140 rooms. Later a restaurant was added as well.

In the 1960s, Elko had at least two gas stations owned by Basques. The Urriola brothers, John and Jose, owned one of them, located across from the Commercial Casino on Idaho Street. The Urriolas also owned a fuel delivery business. Their father and uncle leased a ranch in Jack Creek near Tuscarora, Nevada, around 1920. Steve Urriola, born in Jack Creek on April 14, 1922, said that on that day there were three feet snow on the ground, and somebody had to go get the doctor. It was Calisto Laucirica who saved the day but by damaging his best team while trying. The second gas station was Speedy's Phillips 66, run by Robert Urrizaga. It was also a garage for car repairs on Idaho Street.

LOSTRA BROTHERS

John and George Lostra owned and managed a tow truck and a "wreck recovery" business. It started in 1949 and operated for over fifty years on the south side of Elko. Their specialty was handling big wrecks such as semitrucks, on twenty-four-hour call. There was no one else around with such capabilities, so it was a vital service between Salt Lake City, Boise, and Winnemucca. In 1985 the Lostra brothers sold to another Basque, John Palacio, the current owner, who relocated to Idaho Street.

LAWYERS AND CPAS

The historian's job is never finished and complete, and it is fairly possible that more business should be added here, but information is lacking. I will close the chapter by mentioning two professional businesses that I know about: Robert B. Goicoechea is a lawyer with a centrally located office on Idaho Street that includes the firm of Goicoechea, DiGrazia, Coyle, & Stanton. Goicoechea has practiced law in Elko since 1970 specializing in wills, estates, and trusts. The other is Robert (Bob) Heguy, an accountant and a partner with Kafoury Armstrong & Co., with an office on Fifth Street, Elko. He retired in 2020 after thirty-eight years of service. He is also the treasurer of the Euzkaldunak Basque Club.

CHAPTER 19

Construction, Manufacturing, and Mining

When mining steamrolled into town, it was a powerful shot in the arm for local businesses, including Basque-owned ones. You did not expect immigrants arriving in the US to herd sheep forever, but with immigrants having no command of the English language, politics, teaching, and lawyering were out of range. But there were other activities where mastery of the language was not critical, one being construction. Miners made good wages and tended to buy homes rather than rent. To cater to them, four Basques construction companies—Fagoaga, Elizagoyen, Ormaza, and Achurra—came to life. As of 2023, the first two are no longer in business, but the others are.

Sauveur Elizagoyen (Salbat Elizagoien in Basque) started and owned the Elizagoyen Construction Company. He was born in Heleta, Iparralde, in 1930 and arrived in the US in 1950 to herd sheep in California and Nevada. Within eight years he had gotten a general contractor's license in Elko, where he did most of the work. He built houses, mobile homes, businesses, motels such as the Marquis on Idaho Street in partnership with Pete Jauregui, and so on. In 1960 he married Norma Macari, and they had three daughters. He retired in 2004 to spend time flying (his passion— the family established a flying scholarship), hunting, and fishing. Salbat Elizagoyen died in Elko in 2010.

Nicolas Fagoaga was born in Lesaka, Navarre, in 1926 and learned carpentry as a young man, but his passion was cycling, and he won several races in the Basque Country. He came to the

US to herd sheep in 1951, first in the Rubies, where he carved several trees with his name, date, and comments on his early observations of life in Elko. We are told that he hated herding and the mountains. He moved to California ranches but returned to Elko in 1959 to work for Elizagoyen Construction as a carpenter.

In 1961 he married Betty White and the two had three children, Philip, Casey, and Catalina. In 1963 he left Elizagoyen to start his own construction company, which he managed for thirty-six years. During this time, Fagoaga, like the dedicated Basque that he was, led the club for seven terms (he was its first immigrant president) and built the two prominent Basque structures associated with the club: the handball court and the clubhouse. He strove to pass on his heritage to his children, and he no doubt succeeded. His daughter Catalina, an architect, became active in the Basque community and was president of the club in 2002

Nick Fagoaga, originally from Lesaka, Navarre, owned a general contractor business and built the handball court and the clubhouse. Yet he made time to serve seven times as club president. Reprinted from Elko Festival Brochure.

and 2003. Fagoaga died in Elko on September 30, 2015. His wife, Betty, lived in Elko in 2023.

Pete Ormaza Sr. was born in 1930 in the seaside resort town of Bakio, Bizkaia, and learned the trade of carpentry by age fourteen. He served in the Spanish Navy and was later employed on an oil tanker that arrived in Philadelphia in 1955. From the ship he made a beeline to the sheep camps of Elko County, but his stint at sheepherding was cut short because he caught tick fever (Rocky-Mountain Spotted Fever) and was taken to the Star Hotel to recuperate. There he met the young waitress Dawn Miller; they fell in love, got married in 1958, and had four children, Paula, Begoña, Pete, and Amaya.

Pete Ormaza, born in Bakio, Bizkaia, started his construction company in the 1960s, and today it is run by his son Pete Jr. (pictured) standing on Ormaza Alley, site of the old train depot, which he owns.

Like Fagoaga, Ormaza started working for Elizagoyen Construction as a carpenter, until he became more settled and ready to start his own company that engaged in building home dwellings and commercial and business properties. Ormaza hired Basques, who sought work and ran his company for forty years. He died in 2006 and his son Pete Jr. still runs the company that he took over in 1995.

Ormaza Construction today owns quite a bit of property, with acquisition beginning in earnest in 1973–1983, when the railroad tracks were being moved from the center of town. When the train depot was auctioned, Ormaza Sr. was interested in it, but the price was steep. Pete Jr. told me that during the auction Dan Bilbao Jr., owner of the Stockmen's Casino, told his father in Basque to go ahead and buy it: "Neuk emongotsut dirue" (I will give you the money), and we will be partners. Today, Ormaza Jr. also owns what used to be Puccinelli's Market across the street. He cleaned up the old trashy area and now the street is called *Ormaza* Alley, written on the pavement with steel rebar.

Ed Achurra started the Achurra Construction in the 1980s. His father, Tom Achurra, was American-born and had a ranch in Jiggs. Achurra did mostly excavation jobs, earth moving, foundations, and mining work. Ed retired and lives in Elko, but the company continues.

ELKO BLACKSMITH SHOP

Blacksmithing and iron manufacturing have a long tradition among the Basques. Historical accounts mention iron mines during the Roman Empire, and in the Middle Ages Basque *olak* (smith shops) supplied much of the war hardware to the Castilian kings. Shakespeare himself mentions *bilboes* (named after the city of Bilbao in Bizkaia), which were heavy iron bars to hold prisoners on ships. Many Basque farmsteads and surnames have the root *ola* in them, such as Olazar, Olagoiti, Urola, and Egurrola, which shows that, at one point, they engaged in iron works.

I wonder who is responsible for the not-so-upright reputation blacksmith workers seem to have in the Basque Country. Many

Basque children know the story of "Patxi Errementari" (Patxi the Blacksmith); reportedly, he was so bad that when the Chief Devil heard about his deeds, he could not wait—he sent one of his minions to bring him to hell. Axut the little devil showed up at the shop and informed Patxi the reason for his visit. Patxi amazingly agreed to go with him but tricked him, and two others as well—Zart and Gatz—sent later from hell for the same purpose (obviously, the little devils were not very smart). Finally, one day Patxi died and went to hell, but when the devils heard his name, they quickly locked the door. So, he went to heaven and knocked on Saint Peter's door, but after hearing his name St. Peter told him to go away. Just then, a lady happened to show up and she told Saint Peter, "Patxi is a good man, he helped a lot of people." Thus, Patxi was admitted into heaven (another example of veiled female power in Basque popular culture).

It is not surprising that Basques owned blacksmith shops in Elko, Winnemucca, and Gardnerville, Nevada, and Alturas, California, and those are the ones I know in this area. Such industries used to be a necessity in every town, as well as on large ranches. Partially discussed in chapter 3, the Altubes and the Garats hired Basque blacksmiths, Ramon Lugea and Gregorio Aldaya, the latter who set up his own blacksmith business in Elko in 1915. His son served as president of the Basque club.

Aldaya had competition across the street: the Elko Blacksmith Shop that advertises, "Since the early Elko years, 'from horse and wagon days' to the present gold mining boom." In 1939 Sam Etcheverry and Jack Etcheverry, both from Iparralde, bought and operated it until Jack returned to Europe in 1950 and Frank Arregui bought his share.

Recently, much of their blacksmith business relates less to fabrication than to providing supplies to the mines. The shop has served "virtually every mine in the area," Lopategui said. He started working with his father-in-law, Arregui, in the 1960s and had been a partner since 1971. In 1981–1982, the State of Nevada built a bridge on Fifth Street and appropriated part of the shop, which was extended in the opposite direction. The shop expansion

Basque blacksmithing in Elko goes back to 1915. The Elko Blacksmith Shop has been owned by Basques since 1939.

was built by Ormaza. The Elko Blacksmith Shop is big, 250 by 100 feet and over 30 feet high in parts.

Elkoans, and Lopategui himself, got caught up in a modern Sagebrush Rebellion of western politics, the Shovel Brigade controversy, which started in 2000 between Elko County and the US Forest Service. Lopategui manufactured a gigantic thirty-foot-high shovel, which stood driven into the lawn in front of the Elko County Courthouse facing the traffic on Idaho Street. In honor of the soldiers in Iraq, he also built a 13.5-foot-tall candle, which is still burning with fuel donated by Suburban Propane. And he was not done yet. He built a huge bucket for the Klamath Falls farmers in southwest Oregon who were protesting water rationing by the federal government. As a recognition of these creative contributions, the county commissioners presented Lopategui with a plaque.

The services of the Elko Blacksmith Shop were in constant demand by the surging mines that needed welding work, or just a new part made of iron such as tubing, pipes, structural steel of all types, pumps, chains, and steel parts made from scratch. The sales department was more lucrative than the welding one. The shop hired several Basques, including Inazio Torrealday, of Busturi, Bizkaia, origin, who worked for twenty years alongside Lopategui.

Frank Arregui worked at the shop, at least part time, even at ninety years of age. He and Lopategui sold the business to John Mentaberry, another Basque from Winnemucca, in 2006, and both retired.

MINING

We can say that the immigrant Basques migrated easily from the sheep camp to the mines of Elko. At times, the mines came to them, unexpectedly into areas used by sheep for a century, for example, at the entrance of the North Fork Canyon, north of Elko. One day a mining operation arrived and set up barriers and fences. As you approach the fence, you see three warning signs in three languages, clearly addressed to the sheepherders:

Danger, Authorized Entry Only, Keep Out
Arriskue, Legebako jendea ezdago sartzerik
Peligro, Gente no autorizada, no hay entrada

This is Jerritt Canyon Mine, located where Vicente Bilbao discovered the special rocks as he was trapping in the Independence Mountains. Bilbao held the Lost Mine antimony claims since the

Warning signs in three languages posted at the Jerritt Gold Mine in northern Elko County, mostly directed at the sheepherders, 1990.

1940s. He was born in Bizkaia in 1897 and came to Oregon as a sheepherder in 1914. Shortly afterward, he arrived in Elko on horseback and never left.

By 1928, he settled near Jack Creek, married, and started trapping, which continued until 1969. By 1951, Bilbao had his son Tom manage his mining claims. In 1972, geologists recognized that the sites had similar characteristics as the already famous Carlin Gold Mine, yielding three-tenths of an ounce of gold per ton of ore. The Bilbaos leased their claims to Freeport and two other mining companies. The Jerritt Gold Mine is operating in the same place today, and it has produced so far more than 8 million ounces of gold. Tom Bilbao says his friends used make fun of him for holding "worthless" claims, but he was having the last laugh.

Several ex-sheepherders were employed at the Newmont Gold Mine, where the chief surveyor was Elko-born Domingo Calzacorta Jr., who worked for twenty-two years. He and Dick Emensh, whose Basque wife was Berrueta, were some of the earliest Newmont hires in Carlin. Others joined soon after, among them: Santos Areitio and Manuel Basabe worked the leach fields; Javier Urquidi was a truck driver; Joe Goyeneche was a driller; Carlos Arceniaga worked with explosives and at the lab; "Giputxe" Echegoyen was a mechanic; Esteban Urriola was a foundry boss (he retrieved the gold); Juan Martin Erro worked for a few years before retirement; Julian Ybarzabal was a shovel operator; and Joe L. Mallea was a senior shovel operator. At the nearby Barrick Goldstrike Mine at least two Basques were employed: Steve Goicoechea and Scotty Ygoa. We can say that many more Basques were sheepherders than miners, which was a decision they made in the Old Country. They could have gone to work in the mines and steel mills of Bilbao, but they preferred to emigrate to the open spaces of Elko.

To end this segment on mining, I will provide some quick numbers and facts for those of us who have never been in a modern gold mine. Some of the biggest pieces of machinery ever made are found there, shovels, loaders, trucks . . . most of us have no

Operator Joe L. Mallea with the German-made monster shovel Demag at the Newmont Gold Mine in Carlin, Nevada. It had 1,800 horsepower and a scoop of twenty-five tons. Courtesy of Joe L. Mallea.

idea how big they are, so I am going to let Joe L. Mallea give us the rundown, because he was a shovel operator at Newmont Gold Mine in Carlin for thirty-five years. Paraphrasing Mallea:

> I started in 1970 as a grease monkey in the cabin next to the operator when these big shovels needed a man dedicated to just keep them greased. The newer ones grease themselves. I operated several shovels, and one was the Demag H285 which was German made. It was shipped to San Francisco and 50 semi-trucks were needed to bring

it—in pieces—to Elko, where a group of German techni-
cians assembled it. This shovel had 1,800 hp and it had a
scoop of 25 tons. Later I operated a Hitachi 5500 shovel,
which had two 16-cylinder diesel motors of 1,800 hp each;
so, it was twice as powerful as the Demag, able to scoop
50 tons at once. It sold for millions of dollars, of course,
and a rental cost $2,500 an hour. Shovels ran 24 hours,
except for some short intervals, and the Hitachi burned
3 gallons of diesel every minute and 2,400 gallons in a
day. The shovel operator works 12-hour shifts and with a
Hitachi I was loading 180 trucks of 250 tons each. That's
45,000 tons per shift.

Because of his seniority, Mallea test-drove eleven new shovels that Newmont brought to the mine. He relished feeling the
awesome power of the monster machines that obeyed the slight-
est touch of his hands. "They have that new smell," Mallea said.
To him, it was as exhilarating as test-driving a Ferrari. Finally,
he was more than a shovel operator, because for twenty years he
trained more than 100 shovel and loader operators hired at the
mine. Newmont used between four and eight giant forty-yard
loaders and four shovels that required careful handling to avoid
accidents, therefore training the operators was a critical task with
which Mallea was charged.

CHAPTER 20

Elko People and Places

By Anita Anacabe Franzoia

Elkoan Anita Anacabe Franzoia tells us in this chapter about her recollections of growing up in Elko. The reader will notice that she mentions some of the places and people already cited in the narrative, but here she provides her own twists and angles as only an eyewitness can.

Lehen Kontua (The First Story)

Margaret Olabe Anacabe enjoyed having colored water in interesting bottles and placing them high on a ledge so that the light from the skylights created a serene atmosphere in the home above the busy dry goods store that operated below. In the early 1970s, I found a bottle in the crawl space near those colorful bottles. The bottle was old and empty, but it had a Sabala label on it. I was ready to rush it down to the museum, but when I showed it to my mother, she said I could not take it like that. I assumed she was going to put it in a bag. Out she comes from the back of the store with a shiny clean bottle with no label. That canceled my trip to the museum! I am sure it did not make it to the ledge either—it was too plain.

Downtown Idaho Street and East

On one of the main blocks in downtown Elko in the 1950s and 1960s there were three pharmacies, two banks, a men's clothing store, a shoe store, and a five-and-dime next to the Western Auto. Before my time there was a market across the street, and one on our block that gave way to a modern business supply store, an ice-cream fountain, a veterinarian, a boardinghouse converted savings and loan, three bars, and the general store that became a dry goods after World War II and that was originally a part of the Overland boardinghouse. At one time, the Sabala family lived where I grew up. They even labeled *booze* with the Sabala name! As I said, I found one such Sabala bottle. Ghosts of neither the midwife, Gregoria, nor any deaths that may have occurred there have haunted me. They are all good ghosts of the history of Elko and of Basque people also.

In the basement of the old First National Bank there were ovens where the Alberro and Mendive families used to create wonderful loaves of bread like they were accustomed to eating in the "old" country. Both North and South, French and Spanish Basques maintained their unique language, Euskara or Eskuara depending on where you were from. By gathering at the bars and boarding-houses that were in the area, these people ensured that their language and their customs kept them together. The Overland was just one of several boardinghouses in the downtown area, with the others located in between and on the other side of two sets of train tracks south of Idaho Street.

Next to the world-famous Capriola's western store, which has Basque ties, you had the Clifton Hotel, now the Duncan Little Creek Gallery, where the Errecart family keeps alive Basque roots. Barbara Errecart, a bright political woman who was not Basque, made her mark on Elko. When I was growing up, we would head over there in the evenings to visit with the Plaza family and later attended potlucks with the Errecarts. Mrs. Concepcion Plaza swore that giving her children a couple of fingers of beer each day was essential for their well-being. Beer served as our present-day pro-biotic, and her children grew to be much taller than their mom and dad! Maybe we should go back to that!

The next block on Silver Street heading west is Ogi Deli, which was previously owned by the Lopategui-Sarratea union, a welcome addition to Elko; it used to be a hotbed of Basque pool halls and clubs. Goitia, Leniz, and Elia were the owners. Machi's was founded later by Dorothy and her mother, Josephine Saval Bartorelli. With similar traditions, many Basque women married Italians, some of which are the Bartorelli, Barone, Franzoia, Moiola, Puccinelli, and Salvi.

The Itcaina/Ytzaina family, followed by the Fagoagas, managed the Silver Dollar for many years. Both families helped many other families and friends become citizens. More bars and casinos lay around both corners.

There were the Bilbaos with the old and new Stockmen's, after the original ones went up in flames in 1957. Other businesses included those of the Brust, the Leniz, Juaristi, Amestoy, and Leniz at the Blue Jay Bar. But that is not all—there were the Jauregui, Yanci, Ozamis, Sarasua, Aldazabal, Leonis, and more at the Star across the next set of tracks. The spouses were of Basque descent, either born in the States or emigrants from the various provinces.

There is a long list of women who helped the Arinak Dancers and could be found at downtown functions, either working or dancing, such as Ozamis-Arbillaga, Basanez, Esparza-Moiola, Erquiaga-Black, Echeverria, Ugalde, Alberdi, Alberro, Martiartu, Franzoia-Anacabe, Chabot, and Van Derdussen, who is a member of one of the Mendive families.

A must mention is Mercedes Mendive, who returned to Elko with her jai alai athlete spouse Fernando to continue in the tradition of her teacher and mentor, Bernardo Yanci. Janet Iribarne, who in 2020 was named Elko County assessor, continues in her father's footsteps, accompanying Mercedes on various instruments as does Mikel Lopategui and his wife, Anamarie, on accordion.

From the Bilbao family you have Mildred Menchaca Bilbao, who eventually married a Bartorelli and who helped teach Basque dancing in the late 1960s. Her daughter Lina Bilbao married Ted Blohm and, with help from the next generation, continues a successful jewelry store in downtown Elko. Several started their businesses in other cities and states and eventually settled in Elko, as did the Bilbaos and Anacabes.

Many Basques came to herd sheep but not all. The high school English teacher Miss Grise became Mrs. Amestoy, and Miss Campbell became Mrs. Ardans. The days of the "Black" Basques had made a turn, and they were doing well and had establishments to which everyone wanted to go. Crossing over the second set of tracks you had the Corner Bar, which one of the Jauregui family transitioned from a bar to a pizza joint managed by Anna Urrizaga Alberdi (an artist and dancer instructor with her daughters), and later it became the Biltoki with the Zugazagas.

Going west, across the street was the Telescope, a hotel with restaurant and handball court converted into one of the popular bowling allies in town. Matilde Eizaguirre Jauregui hired many women to work at the Star Hotel. The Samper family acquired the Telescope and produced a variety of women by marrying into the Goicoechea family from North Fork, the Aguirre family from Ryndon, the Mariluch family of Ely, and some nice non-Basques as well.

Eventually, next door to the Telescope would be the Nevada Dinner House, where after the 1940s the Hachquet family from Carson City, good friends with the Laxalts, established roots in Elko. Adele married into the Brust family and Marge into the Wunderlichs. At that time, the building was behind the Stockmen's until the next owner, Calisto Laucirica, moved it next to the Telescope. The bar never closed, as it was lifted over the tracks, rotated, and relocated on its new foundation. Eventually his daughter Mary owned and ran the restaurant, and the Aguirres called the Nevada their home.

After a successful motel business, Leone Elizagoyen with her Italian husband, Leo Morandi, owned and operated the Nevada. Some women come to mind as working there and being a part of the lives of those who settled with patrons becoming a part of their extended families, such as Anamari Ozamis-Arbillaga, Menchu Fagoaga, Dominica Arostegui, and Dolores Goicoechea Samper.

Over at the Star, owner Bernardo Yanci, of accordion fame, set his eye on Estefania, who had made her way down from a boardinghouse in Mountain Home, Idaho, to Nevada, and for many of us in Elko, the rest is history and a part of the Arinak Dancers musical group. Jean Ardans played the spoons until "Bermeo" Uriaguereca started playing tambourine with Yanci. Bermeo's daughter, Maite, came to visit her father and stayed, marrying Steve Moiola, and continues to stay involved musically with her daughter.

Jean Iribarne, a clarinet player and an artful Basque dancer, found his future wife, Shirley White, at the Star. That is where Norma became Mrs. Lara and where Dawn Miller was working when she met her beau Pedro (Pete) Ormaza Sr., who made his family name in the construction business that is continued by their son. The fruit never fell far from the tree when Basques named Samper, Ormaza, Iribarne, Yanci, Zugazaga, Fagoaga, Leniz, Lostra, Alzugaray, Ygoa, Aguirre, and the Barone-Aguirre cousins were the young people working at Toki Ona, Biltoki, Telescope, and at the Star up until present day.

A boardinghouse called the Amistad was next to the Star. The Marisquirena family went on to build and to operate the Pine Lodge in Lamoille. Even O'Carroll's (Bar & Grill) has a Basque connection! A Calzacorta cousin married another Italian and was involved in Puccinelli's Market across the alley from the Depot. Another cousin, Marguerite Calzacorta, operated an insurance company where Basque herders could find someone to translate papers and handle transactions for them.

Shorty's Bar first off was owned by "Shorty" Miglioretto, who married Juanita Ansotegui. Later, another "Shorty," a "Txapo," from the Leniz family, owned it straight across the parking lot where the tracks had been before and his brother had a club. Over the years, the heart of downtown Elko has been a mixture of cultures, events, and places for everyone!

Behind the Star Hotel and by Southside School, boardinghouses were strategically placed right by both sets of railroad tracks and close to the "white" houses, as some of the Basque women called the five houses of ill repute that continue until the writing of this book. The Basques were good neighbors to the ladies who were generous donors when kids went asking for donations. The Aldazabal, Lostra, Jayo, Samper, Mendive, Shultz-Bilbao, and as of late, Telleria, Basabe, and Erro families have made that area home.

As time went on, Basques started to marry or partner with more nationalities. Italians gave way to Native Americans, Filipinos, Mexicans, and other Caucasians. Others were married briefly. Few found other Basques. Dominica Orbe, married to Julio Arostegui, the barber, worked at the Telescope, Nevada, and the Star. It was a quick walk from her home behind the barbershop, across from the Star Hotel on the same block as the other two restaurants. Mrs. Lostra, who lived behind the Star and raised two sons, made homemade ravioli for the restaurant. She probably learned how to make it from the Italians living behind the Star too. The people and the raviolis were wonderful!

Dominica Arostegui oversaw getting eggs for many friends and relatives in the Jiggs area for any large event. A friend from Sacramento went to make the deliveries in the summer heat. The friend asked if the car had air-conditioning, and Dominica said, "Sure does, roll down the window!"

The newest addition to this area has been the renaming of a street by the downtown post office to Ormaza Alley. The Ormazas allowed many functions to take place there, including Elko Jaietan, also known as the National Basque Festival. By the way, during the festival, a group including the Ormaza, Heguy, Zaga, Arbillaga, and Zugazaga families are renowned for making paella and for having the largest pan in the USA.

The area around the Garcia rodeo grounds, south of the Humboldt River, provides plenty of room for Southside School and several trailer courts including Palacio's. Some families living by Southside School were the Lespade, Yraguen, Basanez, Eguilior, and Martiartu families. A Bilbao who returned to the Basque Country also lived down there. The Lostra brothers found space for their successful towing and mechanical business. You can still see the Quonset Hut that they used up Fifth Street. Closer back

Bob Heguy, a retired CPA and club treasurer, working the gigantic paella pan imported from Spain.

to downtown and the train tracks, on the west side of Fifth Street, lives the Ugalde family.

Headed out Bullion Road, the Echeverria-Ispisua and related Zubietas found their place to live closer to the Errecart Bridge. Out on Lamoille Highway, after selling the Blue Jay Bar to a cousin of the Leniz family, Joe and Rosie Juaristi bought a small ranch so their entrepreneurial family could learn old family values, raise animals and crops, and study hard to be outstanding students like the ones they now support with their scholarship fund for both Elko and Ely high schools. Later, Txapo Leniz bought it when the Juaristi family, sans raised children, moved.

IDAHO STREET—EAST AND WEST

After a time at the Star Hotel, the Ozamis family built the brand-new Stampede Motel on the west end of Idaho. Going east from there but not far, the Urriola brothers raised their families in a beautiful Spanish-style home from the Bing Crosby era, which was next to the motel their parents had and that was next to the gas station the brothers owned and worked. Down past the busy intersection of Fifth Street, Hermengilda Achabal lived in a nice brick fourplex on the 800 block of Idaho Street in Elko. It was by the Basque-dominated Arctic Circle fast-food chain where the Alacano and Ernaut families started very successful entre-preneurial lives.

The Achabal building and later another large brick home were moved high into the tree-lined streets to make way for Elizagoyen Morandi motels on Idaho Street. The modern Marquis Motor Inn was the latter's endeavor.

Sheep owners and business and engineering professionals, the Calzacortas lived close to the Laucirica-owned Starlight Motel. On the 1000 block, Mari "Erreketa" Ispizua Jayo raised her family and boarded her husband's stepfather, J. M. Capriola, then Harry Landa, and finally married "Sam" Etcheverry famed for the Elko Blacksmith, which he owned along with the Arreguis and Lopate-guis. Before coming to this country, Mari was a young teacher who helped refugee Basque children escape the Spanish Civil War via France.

Getting closer to the city park, the Travelers Motel was yet another boarding place of Jauregui, just as his relatives had in the past. Starting in the 1920s, the Garteiz family operated gas stations starting with one at 5th and Idaho, and later a gas and service station, hotel, and motor court complex. Not only was it at the east end of Idaho but also on both sides of Idaho Street by the Main Municipal Park. By the mid-1960s, the Garteiz complex became a popular place for Basques, including visiting dance groups from San Francisco and Boise to stay during the early years of the National Basque Festival.

On the opposite side of the street from the popular award-winning keeper of all area history, the Northeastern Nevada Museum, is Toki Ona. Ruth Salvi Leniz, another of many folks who moved from Ely, helped her husband, "Tony," run the restaurant and worked as a bookkeeper around town before eventually closing it. Toki Ona reopened by the men who learned family-style cooking at the Star. Pretty much out where Idaho Street ended back in the day until the Moiola, Leniz, Ygoa, Jayo, Alacano, Ormaza, Goyeneche, Barone-Aguirre, Goicoa families moved into the area behind the Red Lion before it existed, those homes replaced a gravel pit converted into fishing hole and now lie North of Interstate 80 that replaced Highway 40, "the Victory Highway" as the road from coast-to-coast USA.

Across Idaho Street, and tucked away on Manzanita, lived the Holbert-Sabala family. All three of its females, starting with Lenora, are fantastically witty and bright. Gretchen Skivington received her mother's wonderful writing talent and is a modern author. Closer to the turn of the twentieth-first century, Elko City expansions saw the Fagoaga-Guttry family operating a beautiful furniture store clear out on Thirtieth Street! Interestingly enough, the Fagoaga family in Lesaka, Navarre, were involved in the furniture business also.

CHAPTER 21

Notable People and Murals

In this narrative, I have tried to mention many individuals, many of them sheepherders. In literature and the media, they do not stack up very high today, but . . . for thousands of years sheep-herding was an elite profession. The word for *rich* in Basque is *aberats*, which means "(owner) of many animals." We should not forget the value the sheepherder was entrusted with, 1,500 ewes and their lambs, worth a lot of money. We could have compared the sheepherder to a stockbroker or to a financial manager, but you will not find him in the telephone directory.

So let us talk now about the people you might find in town, as you walk down Idaho Street. These are better-known Basques with jobs, sometimes in the role of elected officials. Some of them may be carrying books. Basques did not seem to be par-ticularly active in politics, though Henry Etchemendy was city manager in the 1960s, Dan Bilbao Jr. served as a councilman in the 1980s, and in 2005 Jay Elquist (whose mother is Basque) was elected to the City Council at the same time he was Basque Club president.

Writers

Elko is the proud birthplace of several published writers of Basque descent. The distance from the sheep range to an office with a typewriter or computer, if we could measure in miles, would be astronomical—that is why the story needs to be told. Let us not forget that Elko is a relatively small town, set in the high desert, and isolated by hundreds of miles from the nearest cities in all four directions. It was the first campus of the University of Nevada, and since 1967 Elko has been home to the Great Basin Community College (GBCC), with more than 3,800 students.

Gretchen Skivington, a language and humanities professor at the GBCC, is probably the Basque pioneer writer in Elko going back to her publication on the Overland Hotel in 1975. She speaks Basque (her mother was a Zabala/Sabala) and is involved in collecting data—Memoria Bizia and Oroitzapenak—from Basques in the county. The many interviews she has conducted on video and otherwise are curated at the Northeastern Nevada Museum. Skivington is involved in the GBCC Virtual Humanities Center and other professional pursuits. She published her novel *Echevarria* in 2019 at the University of Nevada, Reno, Center for Basque Studies. *Echevarria* is a fictionalized account of historical characters in the old Overland Hotel—Basques, Native Americans, Chinese, Mexicans, and others—who parade through the novel. She retired from teaching in 2020 to pursue her fiction writing.

Gregory Martin grew up in the small mining town of Mountain City. His Basque connection there is the Bastida Store, which operated since the Great Depression. His book *Mountain City* (2000) deals with the characters who came to the store and whom he knew in town. According to his aunt Louise Tremewan, who was from Mountain City and who ran the store, Martin identifies himself as Basque. He is a professor of English at the University of New Mexico.

Shawna Legarza was born in 1970 on a cattle ranch near Elko, and after college she became a firefighter in 1989. She took part in the 9/11 recovery work, and after considerable experience and years fighting fires in California, in July of 2016 she was appointed National Fire and Aviation director for the US Forest Service. In 2009 she published *No Grass*, which deals with firefighting and firefighters and contains some personal stories. In 2020 Legarza moved to Durango, Colorado, after retiring from the Forest Service.

Vince J. Juaristi was born in the late 1960s in Elko to Basque parents. His father, Joe Juaristi—already mentioned (chapter 18, following local paper and online in Medium.com)—was an immigrant who owned several businesses in town. Vince earned a degree from Harvard University, and today he lives in Alexandria, Virginia, where he owns and manages Arbola, a consulting company. In his first book, *Back to Bizkaia: A Basque-American Memoir*, he dwells on the visit of his father, and himself, to his father's birthplace in Gizaburuaga. I described earlier (chapter 1) his second book, *Basque Firsts: People Who Changed the World*, where Juaristi revisits consequential Basque historical figures. In addition, Juaristi has written several articles in the local paper.

Others

Aitor Narvaiza—Elko County Sheriff

The *Elko Daily Free Press* of March 13, 2018, ran its main story on the front page, "Narvaiza Running for Sheriff." Aitor Narvaiza, a deputy sheriff at the time, filed to run for Elko County sheriff, and in November the voters elected him by some 1,500 votes. He took over the sheriff's office in January 2019.

Narvaiza (written Narbaitza in Europe) was born in 1975 in Urko, a tiny hamlet high above the town of Ermua in Bizkaia. His father was a sheepherder in northern Humboldt County, Nevada, and Aitor came to the US as an eight-year-old boy. His family settled in Battle Mountain and worked in the mines. He came to Elko and has been in law enforcement for twenty-five years. Earlier in his career, when he was not helping people abide by the law, Narvaiza used to be harrijasole (weightlifter). He is burley and physically strong, as he must be to tackle stones weighing hundreds of pounds that Narvaiza has been lifting at Basque festivals and other events.

His wife, Crissy Garamendi, has deep roots in Elko, taking after her grandfather Albert, who owned a trucking business. Her dad was a parole and probation officer for the State of Nevada. The Narvaizas have two children: daughter, Saioa, a dancer, and son, Gaizka, who lifts stones like his dad.

The sheriff of Elko may be physically intimidating, but he is also jovial and warm. When he must travel to some outlying ranches,

Aitor Narvaiza, the popular Elko County sheriff elected
in November 2018, son of a sheepherder, in his office.

say, seventy to eighty miles, he is known to call ahead the people
he knows, especially elderly folks with reduced mobility, to ask
them if they need anything from town, such as groceries or a trac-
tor part. Narvaiza says that you can be sheriff and a good neighbor at the same time.

He has a huge territory to patrol. Wendover is over 100 miles
east on I-80 with a sheriff's office. Jackpot up north on the Idaho
border is another hundred miles from the town of Elko; Narvaiza
has six deputies there. Going north eighty-five miles is Mountain City, some fifteen miles from the Idaho border. Fortunately
for the sheriff, the more prominent inhabitants of the immense
expanse in the northern half of the county are mostly cattle, sheep,
elk, and deer.

Narvaiza is an avid cyclist. He favors Specialized bikes and is known to ride to Carlin for a forty-mile round trip. He loves biking as well to Angel Lake, situated high up in the east end of the Rubies. The sheriff enjoys a good story. He jokes that all the Garamendis (his wife's family) in Ely were Republicans until John Garamendi, the congressman from California, came along and suddenly all became Democrats.

Elias Goicoechea

Elko-born Elias "Choch" Goicoechea is the grandson of Elias Goicoechea, of the Goicoechea's Ranch. He was elected justice of the peace of Elko County in November 2016 and started working

Elko Judge Elias Goicoechea, elected in 2016.

on January 4, 2017, at the Department B of the County Justice System. Prior to becoming a candidate, he was a Highway Patrol officer for seventeen years.

Goicoechea is a great jota dancer and in the 2019 festival, he took part in the jota contest. "I probably danced with my daughter," he says. He has a son who carries weights during the festivals.

As a judge, his day in court was spent mostly with paperwork, dealing with warrants, evictions, harassments, small claims, traffic arrests, protections orders, and so on. As Sheriff Narvaiza stated, and Goicoechea agreed, Elko's growing pains were keeping both very busy. Goicoechea's tenure as judge ended in 2023. And, finally, we might add another name here, Justin Barainca, who is one of the five deputy district attorneys working with Goicoechea in the legal system of Elko County.

MURALS

When you are a celebrity, you never know when you might be walking in the streets of Elko and suddenly come face to face with your own portrait painted on a wall. In September 2019, Sebas Velasco showed up in town with an assistant and in a matter of days covered many of its bare walls with murals. Velasco was born in Burgos (Castile, Spain), moved to Bilbao, and now lives in Donostia. He has been painting most of his life, earning awards and painting hundreds of murals in many cities.

In Elko he painted several dancing boys in costume and red berets on one wall, mythological beings on another, a horse smoking, a cowboy, a woman, and others.

The length of the outside east wall of the Ogi Deli, which must be about thirty feet long, displays an array of Basque motifs coming out of Velasco's brush: beginning on the left is Bernardo Yanci, the famed Elko accordion player; a sheep wagon; IGO (Ogi backward) in large yellow letters on black; a scene from a *sagardotegi* (Basque cider house), where a man is performing *txotx* (that is, holding four glasses on his left hand while grabbing a bottle of

A mural depicting a forest of fifteen carved aspen trunks painted by Sebas Velasco. Arborglyphs represent a self-published sheepherder history in a nutshell, which the Basques have come to appreciate. The mural is located on the eastern outside wall of Ogi Deli.

cider and pouring from about three feet up) without spilling a drop; in the next scene we see fifteen aspen tree trunks carved with the names of many Elko Basques; and finally a dancing girl in costume. It is an impressive mural capturing a part of Elko's past.

The most impressive painting in my view are the aspens, which take me back to the 1980s and early 1990s when I went to Elko to record arborglyphs. The ex-herders I talked to about the trees they carved in the forest wondered why I was doing it. They were not important, they told me. One of the Leniz brothers said, "You won't

Mural masterpiece painted by Sebas Velasco on the southside wall of Vogue Laundry on Silver Street. The mural represents a group of Elkoans who were photographed in front of the Star Hotel, and Velasco painted them from the photograph. *Back row, left to right:* Anita Anacabe Franzoia, Denise Arregui Lopategui, Esteban Elespuru, Mary Bajoneta Ygoa, Jose Martiartu, Dawn Ormaza, Pete Ormaza Jr், and Scotty Ygoa. *Front row:* Anita's dog Coco, Jess Lopategui, Alfonso Ygoa, and Agustin Ugalde. Courtesy of Sebas Velasco.

find them," but then advised me, "Don't look at them!" Apparently, those opinions are no longer valid today, and Basques have learned to appreciate the carvings. It is the children of the sheepherders who value them more than the carvers themselves. However, this mural seems to refute that, because Velasco was told by some Elkoan that the carvings captured a significant aspect of the history of the Basques.

The masterpiece mural for the purpose of this research is on the south wall of the Vogue Laundry on Silver Street, facing a gravel parking lot. The painting surprised even the people portrayed. One day, they were photographed in front of the Star Hotel, and a couple of days later they were on the back wall of Vogue Laundry. They could not believe it.

"Gaur eta Bihar"
(Today and Tomorrow)

March 8, 2019, may have been just another day for most Elkoans but not for those with Basque roots and their friends. An impromptu noisy party organized at the Ogi Deli Restaurant was not only well attended but also well "orchestrated" with five accordion players. There were food and drink, and some sagardo (hard apple cider) straight out of the Basque coast in Europe. Some of these musicians were in town for the following day's event. In short, it was a mini-festival, and a prelude to what was to come.

On March 9, 2019, the Basque Club was hosting the annual Artzainen Dantza (the Sheepherders Ball), an event with a century-old tradition going back to the early years of the Star Hotel and other such establishments, though as previously mentioned, its second edition dates to March 1968. Around 200 people, young and old, showed up to enjoy the buffet of delicious Old and New Country dishes, the music, the dancing, and the camaraderie, which always happen together. It turned out to be another great and enjoyable gathering, with female teenagers dancing together, parents dancing with their children, friends with friends, and, at least in one case, a grandmother taking to the floor and dancing the slow jota with her great grandchild. She was Anamari Ozamis Arbillaga, the doyenne of dance instructors. But the celebrations did not end there.

The following day there was more to do, for the NABO Mus Tournament took place at the Euskal Etxea, where twenty-two pairs showed up. This is one type of recreation that Old Country

Mus champions in Elko, 2018. *Left to right*: Anamari Garijo Smith, Nekane Gabica Etcheverry, Choch Zaga—president of the club—with the runners-up Agustin Ugalde and Esteban Elespuru.

Partial view of the crowd inside the clubhouse on Sheepherders Ball celebration, March 9, 2019.

Presiding over the Elko Mus tournament. *Left to right*: Mary Bajoneta Ygoa and Judy Ugalde, March 9, 2019.

Basques look forward to because it affords them another opportunity to get together, eat, drink, visit, and communicate in their ancient language. (All players must know some Basque words to play this game, but in fact most of the people who show up for the card game are immigrants who are fluent in Euskara.) Though the old-timers are dwindling, there are no signs of the mus game disappearing any time soon. At the 2019 meeting, some of the players came from as far as Gooding, Idaho, and from Gardnerville, Nevada, distant 540 miles.

Mike Franzoia, an Italian German married to a Basque was one of the mus players, and he said, "When you put together an event that includes food, drink, entertainment, dancing, visiting among old and new friends, you cannot go wrong. It will continue and endure."

It takes a few skills to keep track of the mus games played by forty-four people: how many games, how many points, and so on, and in the end declaring the winners. Judy Ugalde and Mary Ygoa were there at the big table to take care of business with a smile.

From all this, we may rightly conclude that the state of the American Basque community in Elko County today is strong, which in turn makes the town and the county even more exceptional.

The Ending of an Era

The immigrants brought the culture and the festivals, and they continued to be the backbone for many decades. Nevertheless, we saw that in Elko many of the club's early leaders were Nevada born. Without trying to diminish the work of other outstanding leaders, such as Bob Echeverria and Jess Lopategui, I think many Elkoans would agree that Ramon Zugazaga and Nick Fagoaga deserve a special *eskerrik asko* (thank you). Both originally came to herd sheep, but they transitioned from the sheep camp to the thick of urban life (restaurant and construction business, respectively). Together they still logged fifteen years at the head of the Elko Euzkaldunak Club. Only commitment can explain that.

For starters, Fagoaga was more than a builder: He was a dance instructor as well. Zugazaga, a tireless worker, made the controversial decision in 2013–2014 to move the festival from the city park to the clubhouse, thus breaking a forty-nine-year-old tradition. At first, many people did not understand the benefit of leaving the shady trees and the green grass of the park, but later they did. On the club's property there was more control of the event, and the all-important revenue went up.

The current president, Choch Zaga, is a second-generation American Basque, and in 2019, he said he would stay on one more year, but as of 2025, he is still serving as the longest elected president. Kudos to him! Most members and helpers today are American born, and a few of them are not even Basques; Wes Walker and Brad Martin, for instance, are not Basques but club officers. There are many others, of course, and right here I am giving every one of them due credit.

What we see in Elko is the end of an era, and the situation is no different in other towns with Basque clubs. In Winnemucca today, you can count the immigrants on one hand. In Battle Mountain, you may need two. Surprisingly, in the small town of Burns, Oregon, there are still eighteen Basque immigrants (counted by Pedrotxu Zabala of Burns in September 2019).

Elko has a few more. As of June 13, 2018, we identified the following: Julian Ybarzabal, from Markina; Jesus Escandon, from Camijanes, Cantabria (but honorary Basque); Anamari Ozamis Arbillaga, from Arteaga; Fermin Arbillaga, from Gernika; Maite Uriagereka Moiola, from Bermeo; Fernando Lejardi, from Bolibar; Bartolo Echebarria, from Ea; Jess Lopategui, from Muxika; Alfonso Ygoa, from Lesaka; Ignacio Iriondo, from Larruskain; Eustaquio Mutuberria, from Leitza; Ramon Zugazaga, from Lumo; Agustin Ugalde, from Zeberio; Tony Fagoaga, from Arantza, Baztan; Jose A. Oleaga, from Gernika; Ignacio Esquibel, from Busturi; Inazio Torrealday, from Busturi; Esteban Elespuru, from Lekoiz/Aulesti; Jose Martiartu, from Kortezubi; Jose Telleria, from Urduia (also known as Urduña); Manuel Basabe, from Lumo; Juan Martin Erro, from Erro Valley; Jose M. Susparregui, from Lesaka; Fermin Alzugaray (who died in 2020), from Lesaka; Miguel Yrurueta, from Irurita; Jean Iribarne, from Arnegi, Iparralde; Santiago Lopez, from Asturias (but honorary Basque); and Aitor Narvaiza, the sheriff of Elko County, from Ermua. And they came from the following regions:

Bizkaia, 18
Nafarroa/Navarre, 7
Iparralde, 1
Cantabria, 1
Asturias, 1
Total: 27

Some Elkoans moved out recently: Agustin Garcia, from Lesaka (to Reno); Santos Areitio, from Ermua (to Boise); and Javier Urquidi, from Markina (to Boise). Finally, Jose Antonio Telleria and Ramon Lastiri died in 2018, and Josemari Fagoaga, from Arantza, Baztan died in 2019.

Basques who came to herd sheep are all senior citizens now in their seventies and eighties, and beyond. Some of them are still in good physical condition, while others are not. The group reminds me of the aspen carvings they left in the mountains: Most of the glyphs have disappeared, and the remaining ones are fast deteriorating. But the sequel of their legacy—their children—will endure and the festivals will go on, just like many of the carvings have been saved for posterity.

Of those herders who came in the 1950s and 1960s, half wanted to return home, Lopategui says, to start a business or buy an apartment to get married. But they were ambivalent: Most of them still wanted to come to visit the US. Why? According to Lopategui, many sheepherders like the Nevada lifestyle, because here nobody bothers you too much; you can do as you please most of the time. If you want to go fishing, you go fishing. If you want to hop on the bus and go to California, you can do that too. In the Basque Country, the way of living is more routine based, more controlled by neighbors, by family, or by friends. They want to know everything you do, Lopategui says, with a chuckle. What he means, I think, is that once you have been a sheepherder and tasted isolation to the point that you feel like you are alone in the world, there is no going back. You want your space, the bigger the better, and Elko provides that abundantly.

Transforming the Festivals—1990s to 2021

Toward the end of the last century, the Euzkaldunak Club had matured enough to slowly hand over the reins of leadership back again to Nevada-born Americans with Basques roots. In 1996 the president was Steve Goicoechea, whose great-grandfather came from Bizkaia in the early 1900s. In his message published in the festival booklet, he said that four generations later the Goicoechea roots run deep and that he is not about to forget where they come from.

To energize and keep the cultural flame alive, the club keeps offering those sports and events that are most popular and unusual to Americans at large, one being the lifting of humongous slabs of stone or iron approaching 700 pounds. Just by looking at them makes one weak at the knees. No one in Nevada or the West can handle them; only titans from Europe have the skills to grab and raise them to the shoulder.

There are other developments in the festival's sport world. The moment of women has been knocking for some time, and the door now is open. They may not be as flashy or powerful as the great aizkolari Latasa, but today we have female woodchoppers, such as Stephanie Braña, the Nevada-Basque woodchopper from Reno. Her father, Juan Braña, the festival champion for years, taught her how to cut logs. As a student, she won several top university woodchopping competitions in the West. She was cutting logs in Elko in 2019 and said she planned to retire in five to seven years. Christina Saralegi came from Europe to Elko in 1996 to cut logs as well. Women cannot compete with men, but she is another outstanding female athlete showing skill and endurance in her own league.

When it comes to sports, the Basque club gladly extends itself to the community. In 1999 there was the usual *soka-tira* (tug of war), but this time it was between two teams from two high school football players, the Elko Indians and Spring Creek Spartans. The contest involved six people per team, not to weigh more than 1,300 pounds altogether and no cleats allowed. It was an exciting variation, and the club knew they had to continue down the path of innovation to keep the festival relevant.

By 1999, you could tell that immigrants were not showing up at the festival in the same numbers as they used to. Nobody gets younger, and the old folks were making room for the young. This is something the old-timers dreaded. Can the club survive? Can the next generation pick up the slack? Bob Echeverria should know what he is talking about when he says, "The Basque future in Elko is bright and shiny because we have these young leaders [in the club]."

Therefore, we must surmise that the National Basque Festival of Elko is not showing any signs of fading; on the contrary, it is still maturing. The children of immigrants are more educated, and it shows as you peruse through the annual brochures, which are becoming more sophisticated. The 1999 publication had seventy-five pages. (Compare that to Los Banos 2001 NABO Convention brochure with 184 pages but 80 percent ads.)

The 1999 festival ran for three days, July 2–4, and the theme was "Amerikanuak! Basques in the High Desert. Preserving the Culture." It alluded to an exhibit at the Northeastern Nevada Museum of Elko, produced by the High Desert Museum of Bend, Oregon. The club and the museum collaborated by reprinting a black-and-white copy of the original booklet from Oregon with funds provided by the Nevada Arts Council, Elko Recreation Board, Basque government, and NABO.

Choch Zaga, president of the club since 2015, is also one of the chefs in the kitchen and always busy.

The floats taking part in the parade give you an idea of how well integrated the Basque Festival is in Elko. The participants in 1999—and most years—were the following: several groups of Basque dancers, Newmont Gold, Cortez Gold, Red Lion, Humboldt Ready Mix, Western Nevada Supply, Scoreboard, Commercial, the showy Filipino Group, the US Forest Service, the Bureau of Land Management, the fire fighters, and, necessarily, the police force.

Another noteworthy ingredient since 1999 is that in memory of the old camp tenders, someone fires the brick oven outside the clubhouse and bakes sheepherder bread. Big, round, golden loaves come out of the oven and are auctioned during the festival.

Despite the additional ingredients, the festivals today are nothing like the ones in the 1960s and 1970s, when Elko could count on hundreds of immigrants, ex-sheepherders thirsty for not only picons but hungry to meet fellow compatriots and find out what America was all about because at the time their knowledge of the civic culture was tenuous. The Western Range Association had about 1,200 Basque herders under contract in the 1960s, compared to zero today. Peruvians have taken over the few remaining sheepherding jobs.

Elko's Ethnic Melting Pot

Valerie Olabarria Rodgers and Charlene Shobe Sabala Dory agree on what being Basque in Elko is: "It was no big deal being Basque when I was young; there were so many of us . . . I didn't think anything special about being Basque because everybody was." That was then. Today, Elko is a different town; new arrivals from points West have swollen the population, and made Elko County number one in gold production among all US counties. Today's miners are the cowboys of old; they get most of the attention but they do not present a homogeneous group.

Along with Mexicans, Basques and Italians are probably today Elko's other notable ethnic group, but like the rest, they are mostly Americans now. Period. Martin Hachquet Sr. did not want to talk about the Old Country. He was a proud American, his son Martin says. When pressed, he would say, "Basque values are American values, patriotism, hard work, honor."

Having said that, I have met six to ten people who told me they wished their parents had taught them Euskara. They really feel that void, like being deprived of something that belongs to them. They hate not being able to understand what some of their immigrant friends are talking about. I might venture to console them: "You can take classes and study the language; how do you think I learned English?" In the end, a few—very few—do study and learn to speak a little Basque. The most recent example is Etienne Lekumberry, a young man from Gardnerville; he spent a month in a *barnetegi* (live-in language school) in Gipuzkoa and returned to Nevada being able to hold a conversation. It was exhilarating for him and for this writer too. Now we can text in Euskara.

The Basque community of Elko is visible enough that in 2000, the Spring Creek High School Music Department went to the Basque Country for spring break. Once there, they took Basque-culture classes, and did sightseeing. It was like reverse culture. The students returned with a very positive outlook of the country. "Loved the people," one said.

Perhaps a bigger story is that of the Elko Indar Girls traveling to the Basque Country to play soccer. They are not necessarily Basque, but the idea and the push behind the effort started with and still belongs to Ramon Zugazaga. It all started in 2007, when Zugazaga took Elko teenage girls and their parents, about eighty to ninety people altogether, to Donostia/San Sebastian to play with other 582 teams from all over the world.

They made four trips in total and, during each tournament, organized by the City of Donostia, they played five to six other girl teams. They were very successful too. The first three times the Elkoans stayed on the university campus in Donostia. The fourth time they stayed in Zarautz, another coastal town of Gipuzkoa. Zugazaga hoped to take his Indar team back to the Basque Country in 2021, but the pandemic iced the trip. The Elko Indar Girls regularly play other teams here in the US.

Another cultural development is the new athletes we see and enjoy at the festivals. These days several non-Basques compete regularly in them. The veteran is Tom Davison, from Salt Lake City, originally from Sparks. He has been lifting round stones and carrying *txingak* for years in Northern Nevada towns. Recently, he was joined by a young woman, no less. Stephanie Herr, who in 2020 was working at the Sheriff's Department and started lifting stones with the encouragement of Sheriff Narvaiza. Cole Lavelle is another young local axe man who started to chop wood several years ago and has a brother who is learning as well.

And yet, Jose Tellechea of Baztan, Navarre, origin, and living in the Bay Area, usually wins the aizkolari contests. At these developments, young Frank Zaga may catch up with him one day. Among other Elkoans who toyed with big stones, father-and-son duo Aitor and Gaizka Narvaiza have lifted them, as well as Choch Zaga and Patxi Amuchastegui. As these outcomes show, festivals are no longer viewed in Elko as exotic or ethnic, and we will not be surprised if tomorrow people with names like John Smith may take over the Basque rural sports born 5,000 miles away.

Cowboy Poetry Gathering and Bertsolariak—2018

Elko is blessed with more than just the Ruby Mountains, the Star Hotel, or gold in the ground. The National Cowboy Poetry Gathering was born here in 1984, and in 2018 participants celebrated their thirty-fourth annual event. But this one was unique because in attendance were not only singing cowboys and ranchers but also Basque sheepherders, who were finally invited to the party. After all, they both represented life on the Elko Outback and sang and played music. Moreover, they can improvise rhymed poetry on any topic given to them and sing it, all at the same time. Sound impossible? A bertsolari can do this while sparring with another poet, conducting an argument, or simply telling a story jointly. A Canadian rancher happened to be attending one presentation in 2018, and at one point he turned around and asked, "Why are the Basques part of the Cowboy Poetry?"

The 2018 event was mostly dedicated to women, and three bertsolari women from the Basque Country were on hand to sing with two male colleagues from the US. The women were Ohiana Iguaran, Miren Artetxe, and the two-time, world champion Maialen Lujanbio. The American poets were Martin Goicoechea, from Rock Springs, Wyoming, and Jess Goñi, from Reno, Nevada—both ex-sheepherders and well known in these parts.

The poetry singing (with English translations provided by the author) went on for almost the whole week, and as part of the festivities Basque dancers visited the Spring Creek Elementary School, where hundreds of children enjoyed the singing and dancing. You should have seen their faces! They were totally mesmerized by the performances. Some first and second graders in the audience, sitting on the floor, could not keep still; they were trying to imitate the moves of the girl dancers as they watched them.

There were several other Basque cultural presentations during the poetry gathering, one led by Vince Juaristi and another by Gretchen Skivington. We heard that the crowds attending the 2018 events were some of the largest seen in Elko. In my estimation, the 2018 Poetry Week was a signal event in the history of Elko County, when cowboys and sheepherders gathered like never before. Not to work or shoot the breeze about the conditions on the range, as they had done for a century, but to simply elevate themselves and sing and tell stories of their past and present lives as fellow Americans.

Suggestions for Tomorrow

The 1987 festival brochure called attention to the future of the community by headlining "Gure etorkizuna, Gure aurrak" (Our future, our children). Children are the focus of Basque culture, and the club does a good job attracting them early on with music and dance. This is the gateway for Elko youngsters to immerse themselves in the oldest culture of Atlantic Europe. If the children are engaged, it seems that the future is assured.

Some club members say that they would enjoy getting together more often. Currently, the club offers monthly dinners and meetings of the officers. Several people think that the club could do more to promote singing along with dance, and as we explained earlier, there are instructors working on that. When it comes to singing, the Iparralde Basques used to be far superior to the rest, but that is all in the past. Those fortunate enough, who in their younger years heard their parents sing old songs, could now take the lead and start a choir. It would be an immediate success because singing is in the Basque DNA. And there are so many beautiful and haunting old songs out there, most of them from Iparralde, especially Zuberoa. You can find many of them on YouTube.

Another initiative could be the formation of a txoko right on the site of the clubhouse, which is equipped with a professional kitchen. People could learn Basque cooking and experiment with the added ingredients "Made in Nevada." With so many visiting tourists, our state could use creative new chefs, and a few could emerge from right here in Elko. As Gretchen Skivington said recently, any event can be a success if you advertise that chorizo

Four Elko Arinak youngsters who know how to dance around you. *Left to right*: Kristina Franzoia, Jake Jaureguy, Christian Indaburu, and Christine Idiart.

and rioja wine are part of it. And if you added codfish pil pil or paella, it could truly be a new experience for many.

Elko County's sheep companies, sheep numbers, and sheepherders excelled in Nevada. We are talking about 150 years of history, but what remains? What is left of it? There are still some sheep and a few sheepherders, but they are a shadow of the past, and I have this idea about remembering and preserving history. There should be some physical evidence of the sheepherding culture for future children to see and touch. In the Reno area, adjacent to the eastern Sierra of California and Nevada, there are several restored and preserved sheep camps and bread ovens, which are now protected by the US Forest Service. Outdoor loving people go there in the summer months to picnic, to cook in the oven, eat and drink.

Elko should come together to restore and preserve a sheep camp the way it used to be, at least one of them. Bob Heguy thinks that the Sun Creek Sheep Camp would be ideal for this purpose. It has two cabins, an oven, water, and trees; is accessible; and is not a wilderness area. I think the US Forest Service would be receptive to the idea, and a preserved sheep camp would enrich the county's cultural stock.

Sheepherders sometimes built *harri mutilak* (cairns) wherever they had rocks and leisure time. They served to guide the new herder and to indicate boundaries of allotments. Their situation in prominent places allows a new herder to spot them easily. There are several of them in the Jarbidge area, and an imposing one on top of Copper Mountain that roughly divides the Goicoechea and the Elisson/Spanish Ranch sheep areas. In the 1960s, a leader of the Lee, Nevada, Indian Reservation told me that he destroyed the cairns in the Rubies because to him they signified the power of other gods over "our gods." I tried to explain that the cairns had nothing to do with gods, but I wonder if he believed me. In any case, it would be good if we had an inventory of all Basque cairns in the county.

Aspen carvings (arborglyphs) are another part of sheepherder heritage that is fast disappearing, but there is still time to record some of them and save them for posterity. The fewest recorded ones are in the Rubies, which are hard to access. Hunters wandering through a stand of aspens could take a few seconds to snap a photo when they see a carving, then send it to the Northeastern Nevada Museum. That simple action could save history. Several people I know—such as Cody Krenka, Lee Raine, and Mike Laughlin—have in fact taken photos of the carvings in the Rubies, and there could be others I do not know about, but we should do more of it.

I recorded several thousand arborglyphs in the county, in Jarbidge, the Rubies, the Independence Mountains, Columbia Basin, and the Tuscarora areas. There are videos and photos available, where people in Elko could see the names and the dates of their father or grandfather, uncle, or cousin.

Today, most Elko Basques look back at a not-so-distant past with longing. They realize that they have lost a considerable cultural legacy since the early sheepherders came to Elko. Historians do their share to preserve the record, but it is not enough. John Goicoechea, who grew up in a sheep-owning family, says that his mother, Mariana, "would save everything . . . she kept a diary." "I wish I had listened more" to the stories she told, he says. We need more people like Mariana, and who knows? There may be a few more out there, but we just do not know. We need to find and preserve those family archives.

How Nevada has changed! Retired teacher Bob Echeverria has been very visible in the local community, but he grew up in Winnemucca, where, he says, in his younger years, "you could walk anywhere [in town]. I used to walk down Bridge Street to Winnemucca Mountain with my dog and my .22 rifle. Today I would be arrested." Indeed, Nevada has changed, and we cannot go back to Bob's days.

But some people are trying. Basques are rediscovering the sheepherder's history in their own terms, not waiting for writers to bring it to them. One such attempt entails the trips to Elko's Outback organized by Bob Heguy. In 2016, he started taking a few friends and family members to faraway sheep places and trails to camp out for a few days. Bringing loads of good food and wine helped, but in such remote regions you quickly learn that you cannot fool around. You must prepare for anything: vehicle breakdowns, getting stuck in the mud, flat tires, downed trees across the road, or whatever. You are on your own, you cannot dial 911, and no tow truck will come to rescue you. Out there in the wilderness, you get a close-up picture of what the sheepherder must have been dealing with. It is a crash course history lesson far away from the classroom. And this is but one way of experiencing today the brave, lonely, lost world of the sheepherders. They were the ancestors and pioneers of the present-day American Basques of Elko County, Nevada.

In this research I make a point to recognize the achievements of as many people as possible in Elko's Basque community, and, in particular, I mention history's neglect of Basque women. Thus, it is befitting to acknowledge the current movements among the Basques to restore women to their rightful place in history. In October 2023 the Basque Educational Organization of San Francisco, California, published the first edition of The Impact of Women in Basque Communities, followed by a second in November 2024. We want to recognize Florence Larrañaga Frye's yearly luncheons, beginning in Reno in 2015, to pay tribute to the contributions of Basque women. Florence gives credit to Nina Laxalt's initial idea and push for championing the cause. Florence and her associates have been carrying the torch ever since. The organization boasts a membership of some 240 women.

Acknowledgments

I am grateful to Tony Mendive and the good people at the Northeastern Nevada Museum and the Elko County Courthouse. In no order, I owe thanks to Jess Lopategui, Anita Anacabe Franzoia, Mercedes Mendive, Anamari Ozamis Arbillaga, Ramon Zugazaga, Choch Zaga, Janet Iribarne, Gretchen Zabala Skivington, Fred Zaga, Simone Young Zaga, Jean Iribarne, Jess Goicoechea, Mariana Lugea Goicoechea, Joe Mendive, Pete Ormaza Sr., Alfonso Ygoa, Scotty Ygoa, Joe Madariaga, Louise Basanez, Denise Arregui Lopategui, Valery Olabarria Rodgers, Toni Mendive, Joe L. Mallea, Begoña Cenarruza Mallea, Robert Echeverria, Jan Petersen, Mikel Lopategui, Bartolo Echebarria, Mike Franzoia, Steve Moiola, Maite Uriagereka Moiola, Jess Goñi, Elias Goicoechea, Dawn Ormaza, Bob Rosevear, Esteban Elexpuru, Jesusa Mallea Yzaguirre, Joe Rosevear, Pete Ormaza Jr., Mikel Lopategui, Bob Heguy, Aitor Narvaiza, Veronica Mendive, Joe Anacabe, Jose "Txapo" Leniz, Inazio Torrealday, Agustin Ugalde, Miguel Leonis, Bernardo Yanci, Nicolas Fagoaga, Jim Ithurralde, Jose Recondo, Liz Esparza Moiola, Cassandra Torrealday Stahlke, Mitch Moiola, Jean Flesher, Frank and Rosie Yraguen, Juanita Ansotegui Miglioretto, Larry Goicoechea, Marilyn Sustacha, John Sustacha, Erremon Jayo, Koldo San Sebastian, and, last but not least, Meg Glaser.

I may be forgetting conversations I have had with many other Elkoans since 1967. To them I apologize.

I am appreciative of Margaret F. Dalrymple, who had great interest in this book, and despite her poor health pursued it during the early stages of my writing. Margaret died in August 2022, leaving Nevada with an editorial legacy that will not be forgotten. I am also grateful for the manuscript's readers, and in particular Professor Gretchen Skivington's review and meticulous editorial comments in support of its publication.

I am not forgetting the University of Nevada Press staff—Director JoAnne Banducci; Editor Curtis B. Vickers; Editorial, Design, and Production Manager Ryan Masteller; Marketing Manager Caddie Dufurrena; Editorial and Marketing Assistant Caroline Dickens; Designer/Typesetter Michele Quinn; Indexer Cindy Coan; Copyeditor Sonya Manes; and Cartographer Bill Nelson. When Margaret died, my wife, Sara Vélez, took over her editorial role and further shaped the manuscript in the spirit of her expressed vision for the book. Thank you all for collaborating with me. The writing of the manuscript for this book took place in 2021. We recognize that since then changes have occurred in Elko among the Basque people and associated establishments. We tried to update the facts as much as possible. No book is perfect, and I acknowledge that any remaining errors are mine.

Appendix 1

Key Festival Ingredients

For those interested in the details of the Elko Festivals, the following are the elements that were part of the festivities year on year:

- Parade through the town of Elko on the first day to celebrate the Fourth of July, a joint celebration of American history and Basque culture. It is presided by a chosen grand marshal.

- Anthem singing, American and Basque.

- Dancing by several dance groups, highlighted by the Arinak of Elko, and assisted often by the Oinkari of Boise and the Triskalariak of Salt Lake City.

- Jota Contest, fast-Basque dance, singly or by couples.

- *Irrintzi*, Basque war cry contest.

- *Harrijaso*, weightlifting contest, as an exhibition or at times as a championship. Some of the greatest performers in the world have paraded through the streets of Elko.

- *Aizkolari*, woodchopping contest, as an exhibition or a competition. Top Basques and American woodchoppers from California, Oregon, and Montana have competed in Elko, matching strength, endurance, and skills against each other.

- *Txinga*, weight-carrying contest. The irons weigh 104 pounds and are to be carried one in each hand for as long as possible. Younger contestants carry lighter txingas.

- *Soka-Tira*, tug-of-war contest.

- Bota, contest of drinking from a wine bag; children get grape juice or similar but no spilling allowed!

- *Artzain ogi*, sheepherder bread contest. In 1975, sheepman Jess Goicoechea donated the trophies.

- *Bertsolari* performance, singing poetry that is rhymed and improvised. In 1974, the club submitted for publication in the local paper *Elko Daily Free Press* the following: "Elko'ko Jaiari asiera emateko, Lopategi, Azpillaga, eta Arregi Bertsolariak egingo dute saioa . . . Txapelketan bezela gaiak edo temak emanda izango da. Etorri Euzkaldun guztiak." (In order to start the Elko Festival, the Improvising and Singing Poets Lopategi, Azpillaga, and Arregi will offer a performance . . . [that] will be done just like in the [Old Country] Championship with topics provided. All you Basque people, come.) Back then, unlike today, such performances were not translated, so many people did not understand what was being said.

- Catholic Mass on Sunday, in Basque and English, whenever a priest was available.

- Basque BBQ meal on the second day, which in 1970 cost $3.00 and $18.00 in 2017. For years, Txapo Leniz was the BBQ chef and chief. The lambs were usually donated, and in 1997 the following were the donors: Silver Creek Ranch, of Austin, Nevada; Eureka Livestock, of Eureka, Nevada; El Tejon Sheep Co., of Bakersfield, California; Ellison Ranching Company, of Tuscarora, Nevada; and Dr. Quinn Dufurrena, of Elko, Nevada.

- Evening Dance, Jimmy Jausoro's Band of Idaho,

accompanied by local talent Bernardo Yanci and Jean Iribarne who provided music for decades. More recently,
many groups have performed, such as Ordago, Gaupasa,
and soloists Louis Michel Irigaray and Benito Lertxundi.
The group Amerikanuak has been a regular music maker in
recent years with Jean Flesher and Jean-Pierre Etchechuri.

In addition, from time to time the Elko Euzkaldunak Club
offered special spectacles and games, for example, when NABO
comes to town to hold its convention. North American Basque
Organizations brings increased traffic to every festival, so the club
may offer added amenities:

- *Pilota*-handball matches and championships, starting in
  1975 with players from the US or Euskal Herria. Recently,
  fewer such games have taken place because of lack of
  players.

- Bicycle races (on occasions).

- *Ardi Txakurra*, Sheepdog Exhibition.

- *Ardi gantxo*, sheep hooking; in 1970 Alfonso Ygoa was
  the champion. Jose "Txapo" Leniz was also the winner
  another year.

- Basque-beans cooking contest.

- *Gizon proba*, a hauling contest, in which one man pulls a
  chunk of concrete weighing 1,600 pounds as far as he can.
  Juan Vicandi won a few times dragging the "little piece"
  forty feet in a period of five minutes.

- Golf tournaments, starting in 1997 and costing $35 per
  entry.

- "Running from the Bulls" was presented for three years,
  from about 2000 to 2003. Sections of the streets were cor-
  ralled off to confine the bulls inside for safety reasons. All
  the brave souls who jumped into the bullpen had to be over

eighteen and sign a waiver beforehand. Elko Basques tried to emulate the Running of the Bulls in Iruñea/Pamplona, the ancient capital city of Navarre. Elko received national attention and publicity, but the success was short lived because of high insurance premiums and local criticism.

Appendix 2

By the seventh annual festival the club was fully organized and staged by committees:

Programs: Jim Ithurralde and Paul Rogers

Advertisement: Barbara Errecart and Flossie Black

Parade: Fred Zaga and Simone Zaga

Tickets: Mary Goicoechea

Basque float: Jim Wright (a local car dealer)

Bar: Guy Aguirre

Picnic: Speed Urrizaga, "Txapo" Leniz, and Winona Ispisua

Decorations: Wendy Ispisua

Txorizos: Juanita Ansotegui Miglioretto

Catholic Mass: Earl Shobe

Master of Ceremonies: Jess Lopategui

Admission to the fairgrounds was $1.50, students 75 cents, and children under twelve free. The spectacles included sheepherder-bread baking, jota dancing, stone-lifting, and weight-carrying contests. A notable absence was that of the full-blown Elko Arinak Dancers, which was undergoing development.

In the festival brochure, there are sixty-one ads in two-by

three-inch blocks, and forty-four ads half as big, which indicate support by local Basque and non-Basque (most of them) businesses. Iberia Airlines and Miller Beer were the biggest early sponsors, with each having an entire page. The BBQ lamb was donated by eight Nevada sheep companies and seven from California:

Cadet Mendiburu, Bakersfield, California

El Tejon Cattle, Bakersfield, California

Elias Goicoechea, Elko

Ferrera Meat Co., San Jose, California

Fred Harris, Elko

John Basabe, Grandview, Idaho

John Carpenter, Elko

John Lasgoity, Madera, California

Paul Inchauspe, Austin, Nevada

Philbert Etcheverry, Eureka, Nevada

Roaring Springs Association, Elko

Roy Schurtz, Elko

Sorensen Livestock, Wells, Nevada

Talbott Livestock, Los Banos, California

Western Range Association, Los Angeles, California

Two local distributors donated the wine and brandy, and the cooking utensils came from the Arctic Circle Franchise owned by the Alacano brothers. All this generosity is a clear sign of the dedicated support the festival enjoyed in town and beyond. Barbecue meals cost $2.50 for adults and $1.50 for those under twelve. By then, the club had 282 members and was growing fast and dreaming big. This was the first year when "all functions pertaining to the festival [were] performed by members" of the club, according to the festival brochure.

Appendix 3

DANCING INSTRUCTORS AS OF 2018

Alisa Aguirre	Janet Iribarne
Ausa Aguirre	Jean Iribarne
Valerie Aguirre	Kaia
Ana Urrizaga Alberdi	Mercedes Mendive
Malaina Alberdi	Liz Moiola
Yusanka Alberdi	Brandi Oroz
Cassie Alberro Sinotek	Val Ratliff
Anita Anacabe Franzoia	Kiaya Sabala
Anamari Ozamis Arbillaga	Marquitta Samper
Tabitha Arrillaga	Diane Smith
Felicia Basanez	"Bermeo" Uriaguereca
Mildred Bilbao	Anna Urrizaga
Lisa, Michelle Carter	Alicia Westmorland
Christi Chabot	Amaya Ormaza Winer
Sara Connor	Holly Wines
Flossie Erquiaga Black	Denise Zaga
Nicolas Fagoaga	Kassidy Zaga
Kristina Franzoia	Shaela Zaga

Appendix 4

Printing: Kassidy Zaga Arbillaga, *Elko Daily Free Press*

Program: Cassandra Torrealday Stahlke

Artwork: Lissa Overlie

Program Photos: Anita Anacabe Franzoia, Wes Walker, Mercedes Mendive, Sweet Light Photography

Dance Instructors: Anamari Arbillaga, Tabitha Arbillaga, Sara Connor

Music: Fast Times and Mercedes Mendive

Parade: Sara Connor

Emcee: Bob Echeverria, John Ysursa

Tickets: Adriene Urdaneta and Stephanie Aguirre

Bar: Zach Arbillaga, Raymond Basanez, Tony Fagoaga

Chorizos: Stacie Guenin

5K Race: Cody Krenka

Games: Aitor Narvaiza, Bartolo Echebarria, Joe Martiartu

Sheepherder's Bread: Dawn Ormaza and Veronica Mendive

Mass: Shaela Zaga

Meal Line: Denise Zaga

Picnic food: Ramon Zugazaga, Choch Zaga, Wes Walker, Brad Martin, Zach Arbillaga

Picnic Desserts: Begoña Ormaza Hull, Anamari Arbillaga

National Anthem: Summer Nielsen

Basque Anthem: Mercedes Mendive

Advertising donors: Elko Broadcasting–KELK/Jack FM, KENV-TV

Event Sponsors: Elko Federal Credit Union and Blach Distributing

Logs: Tom Barnes

Beef and Lamb Donations: Roseann Carpenter/Cimarron West RV & Mobil Home, Ellison Ranching Co., El Tejon Sheep Company/Melchor Gragirena, Glaser Land & Livestock, Goicoechea Ranches in Eureka, Rich Grant and Sons Ranching in Ogden, George Gund, Goicoechea's Ranch, Maggie Creek Ranch, Paris Livestock, Pete & Rama, Silver Creek Ranch/Ynchauspe, Squaw T/T Ranch, Jess Sustacha Ranches, Thomas J and Patsy Tomera

Appendix 5

The premise for this research has been that when it comes to history, everybody counts. Thus, whenever possible we have tried to identify the individuals by their names, though we know that some (or many) probably fell through the cracks.

History has always recognized gods, kings, queens, religion, and wars before everything else, therefore, it seems fair that we salute the Euzkaldunak Club president (or Lehendakariak). Being president is a tough job, and the individuals deserve extra attention. It takes certain skills of leadership and dedication to head a large club such as Elko Euzkaldunak. Some tried and after the experience of one year called it quits or were not reelected. It does not necessarily mean that they were lazy or not up to the task. They probably were not temperamentally suited. Others endured longer.

The club had twenty-seven different presidents during sixty-six years (1959–2025), though properly the club became an official entity in 1963–1964. Three presidents had non-Basque surnames. Some served one year, while others were elected multiple times, for example: Ray Goicoa, five times; Fred Beitia Jr., five times; Nicolas Fagoaga, five times; Bob Echeverria, six times (he was also NABO president for seven years); and Ramon Zugazaga, eight times. The president as of 2025, Choch Zaga, has been serving eleven times so far, which makes him the longest-lasting president. He is a third-generation member of the well-known Zugazaga (Zaga) family. "Zorionak" (Congratulations), Choch, and best of success to you.

All the following presidents are listed in chronological order, with the current spelling of their surnames in the Basque Country (in parenthesis):

1959 Johnny Aguirre (Agirre)

1960 Johnny Aguirre (1921–2008)

1961 Joe Urriola (1918–2011)

1962 Ray Goicoa (Goikoa) (1928–1971)

1963 Louie Uriarte (1930–2004)

1964 Ray Goicoa

1965 Ray Goicoa

1966 Ray Goicoa

1967 Ray Goicoa

1968 Ray Jayo (Jaio) (1943–1982)

1968 Charles "Chuck" Black (1930–1996)

1970 Nicolas Fagoaga (1926–2015)

1971 Jess Lopategui (Lopategi) (1938–)

1972 Jim Ithurralde (Iturralde) (1941–)

1973 Pedro "Pete" Ormaza (Ormatza) (1930–2006)

1974 Bob Goicoechea (Goikoetxea)

1975 John Aldaya (Aldaia) (1916–2005)

1976 Bob Echeverria (Etxeberria) (1942–)

1977 Bob Echeverria

1978 Jose/Joe L. Mallea (1943–)

1979 Anita Anacabe (Anakabe) (1954–)

1980 Nicolas Fagoaga (1926–2015)

1981 Johnny Aguirre

1982 Bob Rosevear (1937–)

1983 Bob Rosevear

1984 Bob Echeverria

1985 Bob Echeverria

1986 Ramon Zugazaga (Zugatzaga) (1946–)

1987 Ramon Zugazaga

1988 Anita Anacabe Franzoia

1989 Ramon Zugazaga

1990 Ramon Zugazaga

1991 Bob Echeverria

1992 Bob Echeverria

1993 Anita Anacabe Franzoia

1994 Jack Lusar/Judy Ugalde

1995 Nicolas Fagoaga

1996 Steve Goicoechea (1961–)

1997 Ramon Zugazaga

1998 Nicolas Fagoaga

1999 Nicolas Fagoaga

2000 Ramon Zugazaga

2001 Fermin Arbillaga (Arbilaga) (1963–)

2002 Catalina Fagoaga Laughlin (1968–)

2003 Catalina Fagoaga Laughlin

2004 Jay Elquist (1968–)

2005 Jay Elquist

2006 Chris Walther

2007 Ashley Rose Arbillaga

2008 Fred Beitia Jr. (the original family name was Gerrikabeitia)

2009 Fred Beitia Jr.

2010 Fred Beitia Jr.

2011 Fred Beitia Jr.

2012 Fred Beitia Jr.

2013 Ramon Zugazaga

2014 Ramon Zugazaga

2015 Choch Zaga (today written Txotx)

2016 Choch Zaga

2017 Choch Zaga

2018 Choch Zaga

2019 Choch Zaga

2020 Choch Zaga

2021 Choch Zaga

2022 Choch Zaga

2023 Choch Zaga

2024 Choch Zaga

2025 Choch Zaga

Appendix 6

Fred Acaiturri

Johnny and Mary Aguirre

Juan and Flora Aldazabal

Pete and Pauline Amestoy

Anita Anacabe Franzoia

Manuel and Ana Marie [Anamari] Arbillaga

Carlos and Maria Arceniaga

Carlos F. Arceniaga

Jean and Eleanora Ardans

Frank and Elena Arregui

Julia Arregui

Leon and Velma Belaustegui

Manuel and Cathy Birch

Ted and Lina Blohm

Pete and Adele Brust

D. A. Calzacorta

Teresa Comish

Joe Echegaray

Bob and Cheryl Echeverria

Samson and Marie Etcheberry

Mr. and Mrs. Mike Etcheverry

Nick and Betty Fagoaga

Ysidoro and Menchu Fagoaga

Ralph and Clarice Gamboa

Albert and Margarite Garamendi Sr.

Al and Kathy Garamendi Jr.

Agustin and Letty Garcia

Jess and Mariana Goicoechea

Robert and Genie Goicoechea

Marcial and Glenna Goitia

Emily Heguy

Hayden and Jean Henderson Jr.

Leonard and Rita Holdren

Antoine Igoa

Jean and Shirley Iribarne

Dee Dee Jauregui

Mrs. Maria Jauregui

Mrs. Pete Jauregui

Tony Jauregui

James and Linda Jayo

Marilyn Jayo

Antoine Lascaray

Calisto and Pilar Laucirica

Pete Laucirica

Jose Antonio and Ruth Leniz

Richard and Barbara Lespade

Jess and Denise Lopategui

John and Mercedes Lostra

Jean Luciaga

Jose Luis [Joe] and Begoña Mallea

Candido and Sally Mendive

Mary Lou Mendive

Steve Mendive

John and Francisca Mendive

Jose Menaca

Georgina Moiola

Larry and Liz Moiola

Leo and Leonie Morandi

Domingo and Marguerite Ozamis

Lester and Renae Preader

Joe and Anita Sarasua

Roy and Lisa Shurtz

Jim and Elaine Starr

Bruce and Delfina Swackhamer

Jose Telleria

Alex and Marguerite Tourreuil

Agustin and Judy Ugalde

Glen and Evelyn Waither

Bernardo and Estefani Yanci

Fred and Livia Zaga

Glossary

ARDI: sheep

ARTZAIN: sheepherder, artzainak, plural

AIZKOLARI: woodchopper

AUZOLAN: traditional communal-work program

BASERRI: Basque farmstead

BERTSO, BERTSU: verse

BERTSOLARI, BERTSULARI: improvising and singing poet

EUZKALDUN, EUSKALDUN, EUSKELDUN, ESKUALDUN: Basque speaker (the native name for Basque; adding -ak makes it plural); Euzkaldunak is the old spelling

EUSKAL, ESKUAL: Basque (used like an adjective in compound words)

EUSKAL HERRIA, ESKUAL HERRIA: Basque Country, but literally "Basque-Speaking Country"

EUSKARA, EUSKERA, ESKUARA: Basque language

EUSKADI: Basque Autonomy of Araba/Alava, Bizkaia, and Gipuzkoa

ETXE: house

ETXEA: the house (adding -a to the noun denotes the article)

HARRI: stone

HARRIJASOLE: stone-lifting person, as in a contest

HEGOALDE: the four regions of Araba, Bizkaia, Gipuzkoa, and Navarre (Nafarroa) on the south side of the Pyrenees

IPARRALDE: the three regions of Behe Nafarroa, Lapurdi, and Zuberoa on the north side of the Pyrenees, on the French side

IRRINTZI: Basque war cry

ITZAIN: cowherder, cowboy

MUS: a card game of bluffing (as in poker)

NABO: acronym for North American Basque Organizations

NAFARROA: the Community of Navarre on the south side of the Pyrenees, on the Spanish side

OSTATU: boardinghouse, ostatuak, plural

PICON: an aperitif

PILOTA: handball game played with a hard ball

PILOTARI: handball player, pilotariak, plural

TXINGA: weight of 104 lbs., txingak, plural

TXISTU: flute with three holes

TXOKOS: culinary societies

Source Notes

Key phrases in boldface italics refer to quotations. Many of the cited interviews and videos are curated at the Northeastern Nevada Museum, Elko, Nevada. Others are the author's own. NNM refers to Northeastern Nevada Museum and FA refers to Family Archives.

Introduction—The Eye of the Study

4 In 2016, Newmont produced 1.6 million ounces of gold: https://www.newmont.com/home/default.aspx.

4 *"In 2018 Nevada produced 5,581,160 troy ounces"*: https://en.wikipedia.org/wiki/Gold_mining_in_Nevada.

4 Output is down to 4.63 million ounces: *Elko Daily Free Press*, October 14, 2021.

6 Sol Silen . . . mentions only twenty-six Basques (only for Elko): *La historia*, 312–321.

Chapter 1: Better Representatives of Western Tradition

7 How do you explain so many toponyms: Theo Vennemann, *Europa Vasconica*.

9 Adapted from "Cave Art History," Royal Society of Chemistry. Accessed via https://edu.rsc.org/resources/cave-art-history/1528.article.

12 Luigi Luca Cavalli-Sforza contends that Basque carry unique gene mutations: *Genes, People, and Languages*.

12 David Reich seems to mostly disagree: *Genes, People, and Languages*.

Chapter 2: Accounting Everyone

16 The average number of children was two: Marie-Pierre Arrizabalaga, "A Statistical Study," 72, 80.

17 In the 1970s, the club had a list of 650 adult individuals: *Euzkorria*, Elko Euzkaldunak Club Newsletter (Elko, Nevada, 1971–1972).

20 Through contacts, he arrived in New York City: Joxe Mallea-Olaetxe, *The Power of Nothing*.

Chapter 3: The Pioneers—Altube Brothers and the Garats

24 But Urdiñola was not only a cattleman . . . he also built cloth and hat factories: Vito Alessio Robles, *Francisco de Urdiñola*.

25 The point here is that the Basques were in the West/Southwest long before Altube and Garat: Donald T. Garate, *Juan Bautista de Anza*.

25 (Carol W. Hovey—Altube's great-great granddaughter—says twelve, from two marriages): "Pedro and Bernardo Altube," 58.

27 Carol W. Hovey states that the Altubes founded the Spanish Ranch: "Pedro and Bernardo Altube," 57–79.

28 Altube's Tuscarora Meat Company products sold at most butcher shops: *Northeastern Nevada Museum* papers, Elko, NV, hereafter NNM.

28 The two were "charitable." . . . Pedro was "irascible and quick tempered." . . . Bernardo was just the opposite: Theo Dierks, NNM-FA.

28 *"I ride my horse all day and I do not leave my ranch."* Funny that this immense ranch had no house: Janet Petersen and Cyd McMullen, "From Gupuzkoa," 2, 7.

29 According to sheepman Jess Goicoechea, the county tax collector: personal communication, August 6, 1990.

29 Theo Dierks tells us that . . . cattle sold for $39.50: NNM-FA.

20–30 According to *The Reno Journal*, the ranch was sold to a syndicate: NNM.

30 According to the same Reno paper, the Altubes had first arrived: *The Reno Journal*, NNM.

30 A few days later, *The Elko Independent* reported . . . sales figures . . . were *"50 percent lie"*: NNM.

30 The property came with 42,000 acres (Hovey says 74,000): Carol W. Hovey, "Pedro and Bernardo Altube," 78.

30 The paper reported that these figures are more believable: NNM-FA.

30 Freddie Francisco claims that the town of Palo Alto was a land grant: *San Francisco Examiner*, January 2, 1947, NNM-FA.

31 Roger Butterfield wrote in *Life Magazine* that the Altubes paid the Mexican vaqueros in yellow gold: April 18, 1949, NNM-FA.

32 It is not known if Lugea . . . answered any of them: NNM-FA.

32 The *Daily Independent* of Elko reported on June 10, 1907, that two young Basques . . . had left Altube's ranch: NNM.

34 The Garats trailed approximately 1,000 cattle . . . they purchased about 320 acres from the estate of Captain Stiles: Edna Patterson et al., *Nevada's Northeastern Frontier*, 419.

35 She vividly remembers that *"one cold winter Mrs. Garat died"*: Mary Urriola Smith, "Memories of Jack Creek," 39.

36–37 Mike Laughlin of Elko says, *"the Basque stockmen were cattlemen . . . . could well have been the start of the buckaroo tradition in Nevada, as we know it today"*: "Basque Ranching Culture," 39.

Chapter 4: Counting Ranches

38–39 In 1906 R. B. Wilson of the US National Forest wrote a report on the Bruneau, Jarbidge, and Mountain City areas. . . . The names of seven more companies. . . . *"nearly all the small owners (are) nomadic 'Bascos' with no ranches of their own and paying no taxes."* . . . their only aim, he says, is *"to live here until they have made enough money to go back home"*: "Favorable Report on the Proposed Addition to Independence National Forest, Nevada," https://www.fs.usda.gov/Internet/FSE_DOCUMENTS/stelprdb5422500.pdf.

42 No carvings by the Altubes have ever been found, but I recorded one in the Copper Basin by Ramon Garat, dated 1901: J. Mallea-Olaetxe, *Speaking*, 52.

43 Sol Silen says they arrived in 1892: *La historia*, 313.

44 Shearing the sheep began in Buffalo Meadows: Josephine Saval Bartorelli, interview by Jan Petersen, Family research Files, 1998, NNM.

45 Pauline Mendive stated that Pete was one of the Basque pioneers: interview by Gretchen Skivington, NNM audio tapes.

46 In 1912, Francisco and his brother Pedro homesteaded: Larry Goicoechea, personal interview, December 20, 2019.

46–47 Edna Patterson says that Pete Goicoechea, Frank Hoye, and others started buying parts of the ranch: Edna Patterson et al., *Nevada's Northeastern Frontier*, 488.

48 He soon bought Hereford cattle . . . but his widow, Marilyn Kane, says it was at the University: personal communication, December 20, 2019.

50 Finally, . . . the Sustachas and the Aguirre tribe of Elko are related: Family Research Files, NNM-FA, 1998.

50 These were the languages spoken in the neighborhood: Frank Yraguen, interview by Gretchen Skivington, NNM.

51 *". . . if I had money to buy a ticket"*: *Elko Daily Free Press*.

53 Pete Corta was the first rancher in the county to sell his 1920–1921 wool: Edna Patterson et al., *Nevada's Northeastern Frontier*, 309.

54 When it was Livia's turn, you were assured a gourmet feast: Simone Young Zaga, interview by Gretchen Skivington, NNM.

55–56 *"We used to fear them . . . A lot has changed from the Rubies to the Idaho border. . . . When I was young, we had deer. . . . When dozens of deer were eating . . . my dad used to complain to the Fish and Game . . . "* Fred misses the people he knew. . . . He remembers Pete Ytcaina's big outfit: Fred Beitia, interview by Gretchen Skivington, 2018, NNM.

57 Edna Patterson says that Martin Elgora (?), Martin Segura, and Gracian Bidaurreta were associates of Heguy: Edna Patterson et al., *Nevada's Northeastern Frontier*, 301.

57 Bob says his father was *"tough as nails"*; . . . being Basque is being responsible. . . . *"I trust Basques . . . they will come"*: Bob Heguy, personal communication, 2018.

58 During the Depression . . . his wool sold for . . . 20 cents/pound: Edna Patterson et al., *Nevada's Northeastern Frontier*, 301.

58 He owned thousands of acres that were sold at more than $1 million: Enda Patterson, et al., *Nevada's Northeastern Frontier*, 312.

60 Historical photo of Pete Ytcaina: Sol Silen, *La historia*.

61 After the sheep industry slump . . . Juaristi was the first in the county to sell his 50,000 pounds of wool: Edna Patterson et. al., *Nevada's Northeastern Frontier*, 310.

62 A photo of Vicente is found in Sol Silen's book (no page): *La historia*.

63–64 In the same year, Bernard Yribarne . . . sold his ranch to the Alzolas: Arsen V. Alzola, "History of the JP Country."

64 Lamoille had a flour mill: Sustacha, NNM-FA.

65 The Lugeas sold the ranch during the Depression. . . . Ramon died in 1958: Elena and Mariana Lugea, interview by Begoña Pecharroman, 1998, NNM.

65 This first ranch was lost during the Depression, . . . Calisto bought another ranch: Mary Laucirica Aguirre, interview by Begoña Pecharroman, 1998, NNM.

68 A 1906 Forest Report of northern Elko County indicates: https://www.fs.usda.gov/Internet/FSE_DOCUMENTS/stelprdb5422500.pdf.

68 In 1909 . . . Elko County received grazing applications for 560,000 sheep: Edna Patterson et al., *Nevada's Northeastern Frontier*, 293.

Chapter 5: Sheepherders' Happy Hour

72 *"Hotel Suddenly, still open three days a year"*: J. Mallea-Olaetxe, *Speaking*, 103.

72 *"Len neskatan (Before I used to chase girls). . . . / Beti amesetan (I am always dreaming)"*: J. Mallea-Olaetxe, *Speaking*, 49.

73 With the help of his two daughters, he published the story of his life: Sallaberry, *I Achieved the American Dream.*

73 Joe Mattin Etchamendy of Bakersfield, California . . . published his story in the Basque dialect of his hometown Ezterentzubi: *Urruneko Mendebalean Artzain.*

76 As soon as you land in town, they will invite you to a drink. . . . after losing all your wages: J. Mallea-Olaetxe, *Shooting*, 56–59 (translation of a verse).

Chapter 6: Life on a Remote Ranch

79 These are the thoughts and words of Bob Heguy: personal interview, 2018.

79 *"You were snowbound most years from November to April"*: as told to Gretchen Skivington, NNM.

81 A *"large tub [was placed] on the kitchen stove"* . . . , and *"[t]he final rinse was [done] in the creek"*: Mary Urriola Smith, "Memories," 39.

82 *"Ranch food consisted in killing a heifer. . . . We also ate non-laying chickens"*: Steve Urriola, 2002, NNM-FM.

83 Even children of well-off ranchers had chores to do: NNM-FM.

83–84 We have enough such accounts . . . but the inventory that Grace van Dalfsen Erskine provides is a little different. . . . She wrote that Griswold had a Portuguese cook: "Tom Eager, Sheepman."

Chapter 7: The Forgotten Basque Woman?

86 As Sara Sabala Ghrist said, *"Basques love to get together, swap stories, and find out we are all related"*: interview by Gretchen Skivington, March 2016, NNM.

88 From their account, we can understand, too, why the sheets were changed. . . . The Star had twenty-two rooms . . . so chamber pots were de rigueur. . . . Emptying them three times every day: Jauregui sisters, interview by Begoña Pecharroman, 1998, NNM.

90–91 She raised eight children . . . in 1958 the judge asked her to *"Sign here, Republican"*; thereafter she always voted Republican: interview by Bill Price, October 5, 1993, NNM.

92 *"My name is Georgina A. M., and I was born in a mining camp. . . . I met my husband, . . . in Fallon. He was fifty-two when he died; I have been a widow for forty-four years"*: interview by Begoña Pecharroman,1998, NNM.

93 *"There wasn't much to choose from. We both dated Martin Gastanaga. . . . Our parents had a big gathering at the Elko Hotel. . . . We had an uncle, Philip Echegaray. . . . He was a popular bachelor"*: Teresa and Anita Jauregui, interview by Begoña Pecharroman, 1998, NNM.

93 One day she pointed at a nicely dressed woman . . . *"That is the kind of girl you want"*: NNM-FM.

93 *"I agreed, and married one"*: NNM-FM.

95 *"So, our parents sold El Dorado and built a motel, The Travelers, . . . Leone . . . the Marquis Motor Inn"*: Teresa and Anita Jauregui, interview by Begoña Pecharroman, 1998, NNM.

96 *"We thought Mom was the boss, but we found out Dad was"*: Sabala, interview by Gretchen Skivington.

97 The daughters went to school with delicious ham and bean sandwiches: Elena and Mariana Lugea, interview by Begoña Pecharroman, 1998, NNM.

97 More than once the Barrencheas chose to go hungry: personal communication.

Chapter 8: Government Trappers

101 In fact, trapper Steve Moiola not only looks back. . . . Authenticity counts, he says—lamb, big round loaves of bread: personal communication, 2019.

102 According to Grace van Dalfsen Erskine, Bena was *"a fine Basque gentleman . . . much respected"*: "Tom Eager, Sheepman."

103 Zaga always dreamed of owning a ranch. . . . someone stole all the pelts. . . . he tracked the thieves and recovered all of them. With that

money he and Livia bought the Zaga Ranch. . . . Fred Zaga died in Elko in 1987: Fred Zaga, interview by Gretchen Skivington, NNM.

104 Iribarne plays the clarinet . . . with his friend and accordion player Bernardo Yanci. . . . Jean also baked the sheepherders' bread. . . . In 2023 Iribarne was living in Elko: Gretchen Skivington tapes, NNM.

104 According to Alfonso Ygoa, . . . the coyotes took an average of 250 lambs: personal communication, 2018.

106 In the winter of 1974 to 1975, Steve recalls, *"Mitch and I were in Wendover, Nevada, . . . we found ourselves facing the Nevada Highway Patrol. . . . but it all ended amicably."* The aerial program grew . . . the Moiolas left . . . and the Moiolas retained the memories: Steve Moiola, interview by Gretchen Skivington, 2016, NNM.

109 According to the US Department of Agriculture . . . coyotes killed or injured: *Reno Gazette-Journal*, November 7, 2021, 3A.

Chapter 9: Basque Hotels in Elko

110 By then the hotel was built and it included a *pilota* (handball) court, . . . a famous match took place: the first handball championship in Elko: Koldo San Sebastian, *Basques in the United States*, 233.

111 Jeronima Echeverria wrote that Saval and Pete Jauregui owned and opened the hotel in 1907: *Home Away from Home*, 151.

111 Goicoechea bought the Saval Hotel with his partners . . . and they renamed it the Telescope Hotel: Jeronima Echeverria, *Home Away from Home*, 151.

Chapter 10: The Star Hotel

118 Jeronima Echeverria says that Pete Jauregui's financial backer was Emilio Dotta: *Home Away from Home*, 151.

119 Historical photo of Star Hotel, ca. 1920: Sol Silen, *La historia*.

119 The year is disputed, but according to Silen he had arrived by 1905: Sol Silen, *La historia*, 313.

120 Historical photo of Pete Jauregui and wife, Matilde Eizaguirre: Sol Silen, *La historia*.

120 Koldo San Sebastian says that Matilde was seventeen when she arrived in Elko in 1908: *Basques in the United States*, 95.

120 Her daughters also stated that she arrived in Elko in 1908: Elko Jaietan, 52nd Urte Program Guide, 33.

121 According to Constantina Bengoechea at the Winnemucca Hotel . . . there were times when beds were rented not for the night but for eight hours: personal communication, 1990.

124 *"Home away from home for Basque immigrants"*: Conversation with Scotty Ygoa.

127 *"But they are broke"*: Conversation with Scotty Ygoa.

Chapter 11: Elko Euzkaldunak Basque Club

130 *"From the Pyrenees has come a hardy race of people, Basques"*: Chris H. Sheering, *Elko Daily Free Press*, June 29, 1968, 4.

132 Carol Hovey . . . writes that when her great-grandfather "Palo Alto" met someone, . . . *"Hello, you sonofabitch, my friend! Stop and have a drink with me"*: "Pedro and Bernardo Altube," 59.

137 In the year 1968, there was also a change in the festival's date. . . . To make extra money. . . . All these activities paid off . . . in the words of Liz Moiola, *"The club has been good ever since"*: Liz Moiola, interview by Gretchen Skivington, NNM.

137 A couple of years later the club became a corporation, and the bylaws were approved in January of 1971: *Euzkorria* no. 2.

139 Winnemucca-born Bob Echeverria . . . says that NABO helped the Basques overcome their regional differences: personal communication, 2019.

Chapter 13: Early Festivals—Catching the Wind

151 Of course, the Basque sheepherders in America had already played a role . . . Elko Basques were on Madrid's radar: Iker Saitua, *Basque Immigrants*, 215, 247.

Chapter 15: Festivals on Steroids

163 On May 28, 1980, ABC Sports, Inc. representative Eleanor Riger: conversation with Lopategui.

165 According to him, *"In 1976 we bought 2,000 lbs. of chorizos. . . . Many Basques showed up from Europe, and some 3,000 people attended the festival"*: Bob Echeverria, personal communication, 2019.

Chapter 17: Euskal Etxea—The Clubhouse

183 Echeverria shared that they raised $40,000 with Betiko memberships: personal communication, July 8, 2019.

184 Circa 2015, more landscaping and tree planting were done: Bob Echeverria, personal communication, 1991.

Chapter 18: Food and Service Businesses

189 Eventually, the Jaureguis did retire. . . . Pete liked beans and makailu. . . . He had a big barn. . . . Pete was one of the earliest Basques naturalized in Elko: Matilde Jauregui, interview by Begoña Pecharroman, 1998, NNM.

194 *"We had our own gasoline pump, two Cadillacs. . . . They spoke Basque . . . when they did not want us to know"*: Lina Bilbao Blohm, interview by Gretchen Skivington, NNM.

194 Soon after moving to Winnemucca, Bilbao and his partners bought the Stockmen's. . . . By 1974, Dan had passed the business to his son Dan Jr. . . . [who] was elected Elko City councilman in 1981. . . . he was the first . . . with a gaming license elected to public office: Lina Bilbao Blohm, interview by Gretchen Skivington, June 13, 2016, NNM.

199 Albert Garamendi Jr. owned the Silver State Trucking business . . . which he then sold to Pedro Olabarria. The third owners . . . were the Urriola Bros. . . . Garamendi and Olabarria hauled mostly livestock: Valerie Olabarria Rodgers, personal communication, 2016.

Chapter 19: Construction, Manufacturing, and Mining

207–208 Bilbao held the Lost Mine antimony claims since the 1940s: *Elko Daily Free Press*, July 22, 1977.

209–210 *"I started in 1970 as a grease monkey in the cabin next to the operator. . . . I operated several shovels, and one was the Demag H285. . . . Later I operated a Hitachi 5500 shovel. . . . Shovels ran 24 hours. . . . The shovel operator works 12-hour shifts. . . . That's 45,000 tons per shift"*: Joe L. Mallea, personal communication, March 2020.

Epilogue—"Gaur Eta Bihar" (Today and Tomorrow)

232 On the club's property there was more control of the event: Zugazaga, personal communication, 2018.

237 *"It was no big deal being Basque when I was young"*: NNM newspapers.

238 He was a proud American. . . . When pressed, he would say, *"Basque values are American values, patriotism, hard work, honor"*: NNM-FM.

243 John Goicoechea, who grew up in a sheep-owning family, says that his mother, Mariana, *"would save everything"*: John Goicoechea, personal interview, ca. 2020.

243 *"you could walk anywhere [in town]. I used to walk down Bridge Street to Winnemucca Mountain with my dog and my .22 rifle. Today I would be arrested"*: Bob Echeverria, personal communication, 2019.

Selected Bibliography

Altuna, Jesus. *Selected Writings of Jose Miguel de Barandiaran: Basque Prehistory and Ethnography*. Center for Basque Studies, 2009.

Alzola, Arsen V. "History of the JP Country." *Owyhee Outpost: A Publication of Owyhee Historical Society*, no. 16 (1989): 3–20.

Arrizabalaga, Marie-Pierre. "A Statistical Study of Basque Immigration into California, Nevada, Idaho and Wyoming Between 1900 and 1910." Master's thesis, University of Nevada, Reno, September 1986.

Camus Etchecopar, Argitxu. "History [of NABO]." Basque Government's Urazandi Project.

Cavalli-Sforza, Luigi Luca. *Genes, People, and Languages*. University of California Press, 2000.

Douglass, William A., and Jon Bilbao. *Amerikanuak: Basques in the New World*. University of Nevada Press, 1975.

Echeverria, Jeronima. *Home Away from Home: A History of Basque Boardinghouses.* University of Nevada Press, 1999.

Elliott, Russell R. *History of Nevada*. University of Nebraska Press, 1973.

Erskine, Grace van Dalfsen. "Tom Eager, Sheepman." *Northeastern Nevada Historical Society Quarterly* 3 (1983): 99–109.

Etchamendy, Mattin. *Ezterentzubi: Urruneko Mendebalean Artzain*. Maiatz, 2012.

Etulain, Richard, and Jeronima Echeverria, eds. *Portraits of Basques in the New World*. University of Nevada Press, 1999.

"Euskadi, Making Progress in Sustainable Human Development." *Euskal Etxeak*. Basque Government-General Secretariat for Foreign Action 80 (2007): 10–15; Lehendakaritza, prensa [www.lehen-prensa@ej-gv.es], April 4, 2008.

Euzkorria. Elko Euzkaldunak Club Newsletter. Nevada, 1971–1972.

Garate, Donald T. *Juan Bautista de Anza: Basque Explorer in the New World, 1693–1740*. University of Nevada Press, 2003.

Holbert (Skivington), Gretchen. "Elko's Overland Hotel." *Northeastern Nevada Historical Society Quarterly* 5, no. 3 (Winter 1975): 13–20.

Hovey, Carol W. "'Pedro and Bernardo Altube': Basque Brothers of California and Nevada." In *Portraits of Basques in the New World*, edited by Richard Etulain and Jeronima Echeverria, 57–79. University of Nevada Press, 1999.

Juaristi, Vince. *Back to Bizkaia: A Basque-American Memoir.* University of Nevada Press, 2011.

———. *Basque Firsts: People Who Changed the World.* University of Nevada Press, 2016.

Lacarra, José M. *Historia política del Reino de Navarra desde sus orígenes hasta su incorporación a Castilla.* Vol. 3. Caja de Ahorros de Navarra, 1973.

Laughlin, Mike. "Basque Ranching Culture in the Great Basin." *Northeastern Nevada Historical Society Quarterly* 3, no. 4 (2010): 38–45. https://www.cowboyshowcase.com/basque-ranching.html.

Legarza, Shawna. *No Grass.* BookSurge Publishing, 2009.

Mallea-Olaetxe, J. *Speaking Through the Aspens: Basque Tree Carvings in California and Nevada.* University of Nevada Press, 2000.

———. *The Power of Nothing: The Life and Adventures of Ignacio "Idaho" Urrutia.* Idaho Grocery, Inc., 2000.

———, comp., ed., and trans. *Shooting from the Lip: Bertsolariak Ipar Amerikan. Improvised Basque-Verse Singing.* North American Basque Organizations, 2003.

Martin, Gregory. *Mountain City.* North Point Press, 2000.

Patterson, Edna, Louise Ulph, and Victor Goodwin. *Nevada's Northeastern Frontier.* Western Printing and Publishing, 1969.

Petersen, Janet P., and Cyd McMullen. "From Gupuzkoa [*sic*] to the Independence Valley: The Altube Family and the Spanish Ranch, 1872–1918." *Northeastern Nevada Historical Society Quarterly* 2 (2022): 2–14.

Reich, David. *Genes, People, and Languages.* University of California Press, 2000.

———. *Who We Are and How We Got Here: Ancient DNA and the New Science of the Human Past.* Pantheon Books, 2018.

Robles, Vito Alessio. *Francisco de Urdiñola y El Norte de la Nueva España.* Biblioteca Porrúa, S.A., 1981.

Saitua, Iker. *Basque Immigrants and Nevada's Sheep Industry: Geopolitics and the Making of an Agricultural Workforce, 1880–1954.* University of Nevada Press, 2019.

Sallaberry, Joe. *I Achieved the American Dream: A Basque Man's Autobiography.* Self-published, n.d.

San Sebastian, Koldo. *Basques in the United States.* Vol. 1, *Araba, Bizkaia, Gipuzkoa.* Center for Basque Studies, 2016.

Shedd, Margaret. *A Silence in Bilbao.* Doubleday, 1974.

Silen, Sol. *La historia de los Vascongados en el oeste de los Estados Unidos.* Translated by Manuel J. De Galvan. Las Novedades, Inc., 1917. https://basquemuseum.eus/research/la-historia-de-los-vascongados-en-el-oste/.

Skivington, Gretchen. *Echevarria.* Center for Basque Studies, 2017.

Toll, David W. "Basques in the Limelight." *Chevron US* (Summer 1969): 2–5.

Urriola Smith, Mary. "Memories of Jack Creek, 1925–1935." *Northeastern Nevada Historical Society Quarterly* 2 (1990): 30–44.

Urza, Carmelo. *Solitude: Art and Symbolism in the National Basque Monument.* University of Nevada Press, 1993.

Vennemann, Theo. *Europa Vasconica, Europa Semitica.* Walter de Gruyter, 2003.

Wells, Spencer. *The Journey of Man: A Genetic Odyssey.* Princeton University Press, 2002.

Wines, Claudia. *Hidden History of Elko County.* History Press, 2017.

Index

Page numbers in italics indicate illustrations.

About the Authors

JOXE K. MALLEA-OLAETXE arrived in the United States from the Basque Country in the mid-1960s. He earned his PhD from the University of Nevada, Reno, in 1988. Mallea-Olaetxe is the author of *Speaking Through the Aspens: Basque Tree Carvings in California and Nevada*; *The Power of Nothing: The Life and Adventures of Ignacio "Idaho" Urrutia*; *Shooting from the Lip: Bertsolariak Ipar Amerikan, Improvised Basque Verse-Singing*; *The Basques of Reno and the Northeastern Sierra*; *Pedro Juan Etxamendy: Californiako Bertsolari eta Musikari* (edited). He taught history and language classes at both UNR and Truckee Meadows Community College.

JESS LOPATEGUI immigrated to Elko in 1957 and herded sheep from 1958 to 1965. He served as president of the Basque Club and, with his wife, Denise, and father-in-law, Frank Arregui, was co-owner of the Elko Blacksmith Shop. After his retirement in 2006, he became more involved in researching the history of the Basques in Elko County.